POPE PIUS XII LIB., ST. JOSEPH COLLEGE
3 2528 01329 4154

S0-ANW-592

PROFESSIONAL RESPONSIBILITIES IN PROTECTING CHILDREN

Sexual Medicine, Volume 9

HAROLD I. LIEF, M.D., SERIES EDITOR

VOLUMES IN THE SERIES

Lief and Hoch: **International Research in Sexology, 1984**
Selected Papers from the Fifth World Congress

Seagraves and Haeberle: **Emerging Dimensions of Sexology, 1984**
Selected Papers from the Sixth World Congress

Burgess and Hartman: **Sexual Exploitation of Patients by Health Professionals, 1986**

Ross: **Psychovenereology, 1986**

Pope and Bouhoutsos: **Sexual Intimacy between Therapists and Patients, 1986**

Persky: **Psychoendocrinology of Human Sexual Behavior, 1987**

Schuster: **Alcohol and Sexuality, 1988**

Stotland: **Social Change and Women's Reproductive Health Care, 1988**

Maney and Wells: **Professional Responsibilities in Protecting Children, 1988**

PROFESSIONAL RESPONSIBILITIES IN PROTECTING CHILDREN

A Public Health Approach to Child Sexual Abuse

Edited by
Ann Maney
and
Susan Wells

PRAEGER

New York
Westport, Connecticut
London

Library of Congress Cataloging-in-Publication Data

Professional responsibilities in protecting children.
(Sexual medicine; v. 9)
Grew out of a symposium held Nov. 22–23, 1985, co-sponsored by the National Legal Resource Center for Child Advocacy and Protection of the American Bar Association and the Antisocial and Violent Behavior Branch of the National Institute of Mental Health.
Includes bibliographies and index.
1. Child molesting—United States—Prevention—Congresses. 2. Public health personnel—Professional ethics—United States—Congresses. 3. Social workers—Professional ethics—United States—Congresses. 4. Child care workers—Professional ethics—United States—Congresses. I. Maney, Ann C. II. Wells, Susan (Susan J.). III. National Legal Resource Center for Child Advocacy and Protection (U.S.) IV. National Institute of Mental Health (U.S.) Antisocial and Violent Behavior Branch. V. Series. [DNLM: 1. Child Abuse, Sexual—congresses. 2. Child Abuse, Sexual—United States—legislation—congresses. 3. Ethics, Professional—congresses. 4. Professional-Patient Relations—congresses. W1 SE99F v.9 / WS 320 P964 1985]
HQ72.U53P76 1988 362.7′044 87-32798
ISBN 0-275-92966-3 (alk. paper)

Library of Congress Catalog Card Number: 87-32798
ISBN: 0-275-92966-3

First published in 1988

Praeger Publishers, One Madison Avenue, New York, NY 10010
A division of Greenwood Press, Inc.

Printed in the United States of America

The paper used in this book complies with the Permanent Paper Standard issued by the National Information Standards Organization (Z39.48-1984).

10 9 8 7 6 5 4 3 2 1

For
Evelyn, Jatan, and Lakia

Contents

Foreword

Child sexual abuse is a topic that arouses strong feelings. It has captured the attention of the media, especially the visual media; the public has been exposed to a number of films, television documentaries, and dramas highlighting the harmful consequences of child sexual abuse. Health professionals, childcare workers, teachers, and clergymen, who have a stake in preventing such abuse (as well as other forms of maltreatment) or in treating or otherwise caring for its victims and their families, and lawyers involved in criminal or civil procedures resulting from allegations of child sexual abuse, have a very special interest in this topic. These are the people who will find this book a very valuable addition to their libraries.

The statistics of child sexual abuse are frightening: more than 100,000 cases per year are now officially reported. Public health statistics are usually presented as incidence figures, as the frequency per 100,000 per year. For example, the suicide rate in the United States is approximately 12 per 100,000 per year. Extrapolating from the estimates of child sexual abuse, one comes up with approximately 159 officially reported cases per year per 100,000 children. Though the incidence of reported child sexual abuse is rising rapidly each year, many more times that number go unreported. The reasons for the failure to report are discussed in great detail in a number of chapters.

Part I, which deals with the issues in the failure to report child sexual abuse, is very useful for physicians and mental health professionals. There are difficulties in making this judgment, and professionals often have conflicting feelings about when to report to the proper authorities or agencies; these issues are dealt with forthrightly. Underreporting of white affluent families does occur; the authors scrutinize this among other social and cultural factors in the reporting process. A key issue is the need through careful outcome studies "to demonstrate the benefits of reporting and the intervention it precipitates in contrast to intervention not accompanied by reporting. Part and parcel of this is a demonstration of the iatrogenic conseuences of intervention undertaken in the absence of official reporting to child protective services."

Part II contains several illustrative case histories in which professionals—a pediatrician in one case, a priest in another—committed multiple sex abuse against children. The ways in which these cases were handled or mishandled by responsible authorities and organizations are painfully enlightening.

An important aspect of prevention is the regulation of the profession. This is comprehensively described in an introductory chapter in terms of statutory regulation, namely licensure, certification, and registration, non-statutory regulations, such as membership in a professional organization, hospital privileges, or graduation from an approved training facility. An entire section of the volume deals with legal sanctions for professional misconduct, such as failure to report or molestation, including civil damage suits, disciplinary proceedings, and even criminal prosecution against professionals who are themselves the victimizers. Aspects of societal response, including the obligations of professional organizations, possible legislation, and changes in the enforcement of regulations are reviewed. Finally, summary chapters on the decision to report suspected abuse and or professional misconduct complete the volume.

The authors of the chapters in this book are advocates. Sometimes their anger and even their outrage can be felt between their measured lines. We need this. Still, statements sometimes occur which may appear extreme to the reader. One author claims that only 5 percent of children's reports of sexual abuse are falsified. Yet one reads the following in the Harvard Medical School Mental Health Newsletter (vol. 4, no. 5, November 1987, p. 4): "Heightened public and professional concern has led to over-reporting of suspected child sexual abuse. According to the American Humane Association, 60% of such reports are unsubstantiated." Obviously, we need much more research. Even if we accept the 60 percent finding—and I suggest on the basis of a discussion in the introduction that this may be as misleading as the 5 percent mentioned above—a *substantiated* figure of 40 percent is mind-boggling and frightening. This book deals specifically with professional misconduct in abuse or in the failure to deal appropriately with abuse and poses a challenge to all of us who are entrusted with the care and protection of children.

As the editor of the Sexual Medicine Series, I welcome this ninth volume. I would like to call the attention of readers to two other volumes in the series that concern professional sexual exploitation of patients, clients, and others: *Sexual Intimacy between Therapists and Patients*, by Kenneth S. Pope and Jacqueline C. Bouhoutsos, and *Sexual Exploitation of Patients by Health Professionals*, edited by Ann W. Burgess and Carol R. Hartman.

Harold I. Lief, M.D.

Preface

This volume grew out of a symposium on professional ethics and child abuse that was cosponsored by the National Legal Resource Center for Child Advocacy and Protection of the American Bar Association (ABA) and the Antisocial and Violent Behavior Branch of the National Institute of Mental Health (NIMH). The impetus for the symposium originated with Dr. Ann Maney, then head of the NIMH National Center for the Prevention and Control of Rape, in response to growing community concerns about protecting children from sexual abuse by the very professionals who are entrusted with their care. Dr. Eli Newberger already had raised this issue in a provocative address at the Third National Conference on Sexual Victimization of Children, with particular emphasis on the response of professional organizations to allegations of child sexual abuse involving their members. Many were responding to sexual abuse in childcare settings with similar professional concerns.

In cooperation with Howard Davidson, director of the ABA's National Legal Resource Center for Child Advocacy and Protection, a symposium was conceived to address professional responsibilities in protecting children from maltreatment. The symposium focused on problems and potential solutions for two regulatory issues: recourse available in responding to child sexual abuse by professionals and remedies for the failure of professionals to comply with child abuse reporting statutes. Dr. Susan Wells, then a consultant with the ABA, undertook major responsibility for organizing the symposium, conducting a survey of professional licensing boards, and developing program proceedings.

The symposium, convened November 22–23, 1985, brought people from many different professional fields together for a discussion of the ethical, legal, and practical dilemmas that arise when professionals either subject children to abuse or do not protect them from the maltreatment of others.

Representatives of professional organizations and licensing boards in nursing, medicine, psychiatry, pediatrics, social work, law, childcare, early childhood education, education, and psychology attended. The papers presented at the symposium provided a basis for discussion, analysis, and further action at the legislative, organizational, and practice levels. They are presented as chapters in this volume to enable a greater number of people to consider the issues and determine the types of actions that are required to ensure the protection of children in the professional community.

The volume chapters are placed in the context of the range of models for professional regulation available within U.S. society as well as in the context of the U.S. experience with reporting legislation as a particular regulatory strategy for the prevention and control of child sexual abuse. In the first two sections of the volume, the issues underlying problems of professional regulation in child abuse are explored first. In Part I, ethical/moral, political, and cultural factors are identified as obstacles to reporting of child abuse or neglect by a professional. Case studies of professionals who have abused a child sexually make it clear in Part II that similar factors are at work in the failure to apply sanctions to abusers who are from the ranks of the professions. Part III then examines in depth the legal remedies available to those who have been sexually abused by a professional or whose abuse was known or suspected by a professional who failed to make an official report. Part IV proposes other kinds of remedies for extralegal issues that underlie failures in professional regulation. These include redefinition through the development of new structures bridging the gap between other professionals and child protective services through system change and the implementation of collective responsibility and remedy by professional associations. The contents of this publication should not be construed as official policy of the American Bar Association, the National Institute of Mental Health, or any other agency of the federal government.

Ann Maney, Ph.D., and Susan J. Wells, Ph.D.

Acknowledgments

As with any effort of this size, many people were instrumental in the accomplishment of the series of tasks that led to this publication. First and foremost, we thank the chapter authors for their generous contribution of time and effort to this project. Their work led to a fruitful symposium and an even more valuable publication. Special thanks are due to those who prepared original papers in response to specific requests. Second, the symposium discussants added immeasurably, raising pertinent questions during the symposium and highlighting issues for further consideration.

In addition, the staff of the National Legal Resource Center has been critical in the smooth operation of the project. Most notably, Howard Davidson, Robert Horowitz, and the interns who worked on this project have contributed their time, effort, and support to the symposium and publication of the proceedings. The interns included Stacy Jordan, Marilyn Agner, Beth Wanger, and Cindy Barnes.

Finally, it is with pleasure that we acknowledge Joan Benefiel for her role in preparing the manuscript and Lori Miller, of the NIMH Office of Policy Analysis and Coordination, for her assistance in the editing process.

PROFESSIONAL RESPONSIBILITIES IN PROTECTING CHILDREN

Introduction

1

Professional Involvement in Public Health Strategies for the Prevention and Control of Child Sexual Abuse

Ann Maney

The term "child sexual abuse" refers, at a minimum, to heterosexual or homosexual penile intrusion of a body cavity—oral, anal, or genital—of a person under 18 years of age. The term usually includes, as well, the promotion or permission of illicit sexual acts or the production of pornography, molestation with genital contact, and other unspecified or unclassified forms of physical contact (Burgdorf, 1980). The professional literature yields varying estimates of the social and psychological effects of such experiences in childhood. Some researchers have documented short-term effects in the form of depression, guilt, learning difficulties, sexual promiscuity, runaway behavior, somatic complaints, physical complaints, dramatic behavior changes, and hysterical seizures. Others, however, have not uncovered ill effects. Adult women who were sexually abused as children report a variety of effects, including drug abuse, sexual dysfunction, negative self-image, depression, interpersonal difficulties, and revictimization, yet a number of studies of adult men and women report mixed effects (Conte, 1982). These observed trauma have been conceptualized in terms of four underlying psychological dimensions: traumatic sexualization, betrayal, powerlessness, and stigmatization (Finkelhor and Browne, 1985), which are undergoing testing as researchers begin to employ standardized psychological assessment instruments (for example, OJJDP, 1984). Nonetheless, it is already clear that a potential for serious psychological harm in both the short and the long term exists as a result of child sexual abuse.

Due in part to undisclosed cases, as well as to problems in research design and methodology, the true incidence of child sexual abuse in this country is unknown. This form of child abuse has been included, however, in the massive public mobilization for identification of child maltreatment that has taken place nationally since the early 1970s through the efforts of welfare, medical, and legal communities. The major policy formulations have included the Child Abuse Prevention and Treatment Act of 1974 (P.L. 93-247); the 1975 Federal Standards on the Prevention, Identification, and Treatment of Child Abuse and Neglect; the Model Child Protection Act issued by the National Center on Child Abuse and Neglect; and the Model Child Abuse Reporting Law developed by the Juvenile Justice Standards Project of the Institute for Judicial Demonstration. Currently, all states and territories have reporting laws. A comprehensive review of these statutes has been conducted by the Clearinghouse on Child Abuse and Neglect:

> These reporting laws name those individuals, classes of professionals, or institutions mandated to report, provide penalties for failure to meet that mandate, indicate who is permitted to report, provide immunity from legal liability for reporters, describe the conditions and age limits of children subject to identification, define in detail the types of maltreatment to be reported, explain how reports are to be filed and the information to be contained therein, and name the agency with which the reports are to be filed. (Younes, 1984, p. 10)

STATE REPORTING LAWS

The content of state reporting provisions has been highly variable, however, as has the range of broader reforms in which they have been embedded (Younes, 1984, Ch. II). Although the majority of states and territories simply indicate that abuse and/or neglect are to be reported, for instance, only 37 explicitly include sexual abuse in their definitions of maltreatment, only 20 include sexual exploitation, and only a few give special emphasis to sexual abuse or sexual exploitation in the course of specifying "other" forms of maltreatment to be reported. Most states limit the perpetrators covered by reporting laws, with most of these including only persons responsible for the child's welfare or supervision, or family and family familiars. In addition, a majority of the welfare codes in states and territories set forth provisions for thorough and impartial investigations of allegations of maltreatment in state-operated institutions or facilities, provisions that a few states have extended to group or other foster homes and community daycare facilities. A majority of states either specify or imply that reports must be accusatory, in that the name or other information concerning the suspected abuser is required, though the majority remain silent on the acceptability of anonymous reports. In 1984 some 100,000 incidents of suspected child sexual abuse are believed to have been reported to mandated agencies throughout the nation as a result of such laws, approximately 1.59 for every 1000 children in the population (AHA, 1986).[1] This estimate is almost triple the 1980 statistic and more than 16 times the 1976 figure. Child sexual abuse is, in fact, the most rapidly increasing form of maltreatment in the state-mandated case identification systems, but it is a small portion (13 percent) of the 1,727,000 incidents of suspected child maltreatment believed to have been officially screened in U.S. communities during 1984.[2]

The explicit legislative intent behind state reporting laws is usually child protection. (A few states focus on family preservation or on prevention, but only Utah and New Hampshire include an explicit concern about the sexual exploitation of children.) The procedures specified for bringing about this child protection, which appear in welfare codes as well as in reporting legislation, contain many common themes. Typically the state legal frameworks for response to reports of child maltreatment establish a bifurcated system in which the role of law enforcement or court agencies increases with the seriousness of the situation uncovered in the course of investigation. However, the role of social services is assumed throughout, from receipt of the report to the sheltering of a child removed from his or her home in the interest of protection. No jurisdiction designates only a law enforcement agency to receive reports, and a majority permit both law enforcement agencies and social service agencies to do so, sometimes with provisions for cross-notification or restricting the role of law enforcement to emergency conditions. State welfare codes, if not reporting laws, always specify the actions required of the responsible agency upon receiving a report, more often than not specify a time frame for investigation, and almost always specify a designation of the agency to conduct the investigation. The identity of the investigating agency is variable, but it is typically a mix of child protective service and law enforcement or court activity, with legal activity usually restricted to criminal or special cases, such as those involving sexual abuse, severe physical abuse, or fatalities.

Where an emergency situation requires that a child be removed from parental custody, precise procedures are specified that vary considerably across states. However, virtually all provide for emergency removal of a child without a court order, and all authorize the police, at least, to act in such “immediate danger” situations. Half also authorize physicians to hospitalize a child without parental approval, and almost half permit child protective services or other social service personnel to take children into protective custody. Most set time limits within which court action must begin after such emergency removal (AHA, 1986, Chs. I and III). It is clear, altogether, that the reporter in the typically mandated state system is setting off a process that can lead to serious, and seriously intrusive, protective actions involving law enforcement and medical as well as social service personnel. It also is clear that child sexual abuse reports are among those most likely to set off this serious chain of consequences.

STATE COURT AND PENAL CODES

It is not surprising, then, that judicial intervention may be required for one of two purposes: to protect the child's right to a safe, secure, and healthy environment or to determine the guilt or innocence of an adult accused of a crime against a child. Where protection is the issue, the juvenile court is employed; where accusation of crime is the issue, a criminal court is employed.[3] State court and penal codes provide the framework for both in child abuse and neglect actions (AHA, 1986, Ch. IV).

All states have juvenile court-based child protection systems. More than half of these juvenile courts are separate from or independent of the trial-level courts. While all states empower juvenile courts to protect maltreated children and all subsume abuse and neglect as dependency under the *parens patria* responsibilities of the state, the majority explicitly refer to abuse and neglect, and a few extend their authority to the possibility of termination of parental rights. Although very few states include commercial sexual exploitation or child pornography in naming particular forms of abuse within the purview of the juvenile court, half do explicitly mention sexual assault. The authority for hearing maltreatment actions may extend in limited ways to adults, but the majority of states do not grant juvenile courts jurisdiction over adults who contribute to dependency, perpetrate abuse or neglect, or operate under court order; most states do not permit juvenile courts to use criminal sanctions, nor do they confer criminal jurisdiction on juvenile courts for any purpose. The authority of juvenile courts in hearing maltreatment actions is largely confined to orders directed to the care, custody, or control of a child. The fact that the majority of states do not require the juvenile court to conduct postdispositional reviews underlines the extent to which their role can in fact be more legitimating/facilitating than protective per se.

All states do have penal sanctions against crimes committed by adults against children, although child abuse and neglect are adjudicated less often in criminal courts than in juvenile courts. Even so, slightly more than half the states explicitly provide penalties for sexual crimes committed against a child by a parent or family member, such as sexual abuse, sexual battery, or sexual exploitation.[4] However, few have statutory rape and/or sexual-contact-with-a-minor laws that would provide penalties for sexual offenses committed by stepparents, paramours of the child's parent, or professionals, and few have expanded definitions of possible perpetrators of abuse and neglect to include persons who occupy a position of special trust (and thus encompass professionals). Until civil remedies for child maltreatment came on the scene, the range of sanctions for child sexual abuse that had evolved nationally was largely limited to relatively infrequent trial of intrafamilial offenses in criminal courts as felonies.

PROFESSIONAL INVOLVEMENT IN REPORTING

The trend in recent state reporting legislation has been to broaden classes of reporters (AHA, 1986, Ch. II). While all 50 states early required physicians to report, now all have extended mandated reporting by specification or implication to include other medical personnel, teachers, daycare personnel, social workers, and mental health professionals. A majority of the states/territories include law enforcement personnel, and a few have gone so far as to apply civil or criminal sanctions for noncompliance to any group in ongoing contact with children. Almost all jurisdictions, in fact, have attempted to enforce their reporting mandates by defining noncompliance as a misdemeanor at least. All jurisdictions extend immunity from liability, civil or criminal, to reporters in the making of a report, a majority in the taking of photos or X-rays or otherwise gathering evidence without parental permission, or in participating in judicial proceedings; typically state laws waive confidentiality for physicians/therapists and spouses. Immunity from liability in reporting, however, is almost always limited by a "good faith" requirement that ultimately could require judicial interpretation. Nonetheless, professionals made half the reports of suspected maltreatment received nationally in 1984 (AHA), a proportion that was slightly higher among 1982 reports of suspected *sexual* abuse (55 percent; Russell and Trainor, 1986), but that has fluctuated only slightly between 1976 and 1984. What this means is that professionals have contributed substantially to the dramatic increase that has been taking place in absolute numbers of suspected maltreatment reports in general, and suspected sexual abuse reports in particular, though the change in their reporting behavior has not been substantially different from what has taken place among the public at large.

Despite these extensive changes, the failure of many professionals to comply with legal requirements for reporting has become increasingly obvious. A 1980 study sponsored by the National Center on Child Abuse and Neglect found that, nationally,[5] the majority of professionally identified, intrafamily maltreatment cases was being dealt with apart from legally mandated child protective service systems (Burgdorf, 1980). While this was less true of professionally identified child sexual assault cases, almost half (46 percent) of these were unknown in child protective services but active with other investigatory agencies (23 percent) or other major agencies (23 percent). Supplementary analyses of the original sample (Finkelhor and Hotaling, 1983) indicate that it was sexual maltreatment cases originally identified by the criminal justice system or by the schools that were most likely to be unknown to child protective services but known to other investigatory agencies, such as the police, courts, corrections, or public health, or to other major service agencies, such as schools and hospitals. These agencies were prominent in the identification of teenage victims, a majority of whom had experienced more serious forms of sexual assault, including penile intrusion. Cases identified by medical or mental health personnel were about as likely to be unknown to child protective services as to be known.

In contrast, virtually all of the small number of cases originally identified by social service personnel were known to child protective services. Although these findings can be explained in part by the variation from state to state in agencies mandated to receive or act on reports, as well as by the bifurcation that develops with seriousness, Burgdorf (1980) has suggested that unresolved or disputed questions of definition and responsibility also could be at work. Children in other investigation systems may be "officially known" as alleged victims of crime or disease and meet the study criteria for abuse or neglect without having been defined as abused or neglected or receiving assistance for abuse or neglect. Children receiving services in other major agencies may remain unreported to any specialized investigation agency out of professional ignorance, rivalry, distrust, or apprehension.

Perhaps we shouldn't be startled by these facts. As long ago as 1971, Silver, Dublin, and Lourie documented considerable resistance to reporting from mandated and mental health professionals in one community. The opposition of individual physicians and educators was apparent throughout the 1970s (Sussman and Cohen, 1975; Holmes, 1977). Either doubt about reporting legislation as a strategy in case finding or doubt about the capacity of service agencies to meet the resulting increase in demand (Brown, 1974) seemed to be reinforcing concerns about the threat to legal protections surrounding the client-professional relationship (Poller, 1975; Goldney, 1972; Ramsey and Lawler, 1974). The controversies continue into the present, bolstered by new data on the class and racial biases operative in medical reporting (for instance, Hampton and Newberger, 1985), the questions that the social work community itself is raising about the suitability of mandated reporting when the resources to provide services are declining (Faller, 1985), and growing concern about the secondary trauma that can result to children who become involved in the court process or extended foster care (Runyan, 1982; Berliner and Stevens, 1980). Now, however, liability issues are becoming translated into rising insurance costs (for instance, "APA Malpractice . . . ," 1983),[6] and the legal debate over how best to balance the rights and needs of children embodied in mandated reporting against the rights and needs of service professionals is expanding to include the right of parents to the least possible intrusion by the state into their family lives (Goldstein, Freud, and Solnit, 1979; Besharov, 1985).

PROFESSIONAL MISCONDUCT

An even more heated issue than that of professional noncompliance with reporting requirements is that of the professional who is a perpetrator of child maltreatment. Although this is essentially a criminal matter, a few states have expanded definitions of possible perpetrators of abuse or neglect to include persons who occupy a position of special trust and, thus, an adult who stands in a professional relationship to the child/family. As a result, the American Humane Association's data base of official reports yields a little information on this point; national criminal justice statistics are not adequate to the question (National Institute of Justice Clearinghouse, telephone communication, March 1987).

The American Humane Association statistics indicate that 9 percent of the official 1984 suspected maltreatment reports involved a perpetrator other than a parent or relative, 26 percent of the suspected sexual maltreatment. Many of these were boyfriends or girlfriends of the child's parent and a very few were employees of residential institutions, but little is known about the remainder.[7] Official reports do not permit the identification of child maltreatment that takes place within the families of professionals.

On the other hand, the sexual exploitation of clients by professionals has been an area of growing concern since the early 1970s. Sexual exploitation by counselors and therapists, for example, has received considerable attention (see Plaut and Foster, 1986). A series of surveys and small studies have elicited reports of erotic contact with clients from therapists in the traditional professions of psychology and psychiatry that range from 5 to 17 percent for male therapists and 1 to 3 percent for females. There also is increasing evidence that therapists are aware of the problem within their professions, most of it unreported to any official body. Psychologists have gone so far as to review suspensions and revocations by state boards, and both psychologists and psychiatrists have reviewed ethical complaints to their national associations for sexual misconduct. Recently singled-out reports of cases reaching the appellate courts have involved physicians, chiropractors, dentists, and optometrists as well as psychologists. Although little of this attention includes, much less focuses on, sexual exploitation of child or adolescent clients by professionals (Sanderson, 1985), the resulting climate has been favorable for related activities by these professional associations, such as the development of educational materials. Indeed, the recent outbreak of highly publicized scandals surrounding sexual maltreatment of children in daycare, and highly publicized litigation concerning educators and clergy who have exploited children in their trust, are magnifying the issue in the more traditional professions as well.

It will become apparent in subsequent chapters that issues involving the apprehension and rehabilitation of professionals who sexually maltreat children are just beginning to be treated collectively by various professional groups. This is a matter of considerable concern, given the statistics on child molesters in the one community treatment program, including nonincestuous subjects, that has undergone systematic study of outcomes utilizing physiological measures of sexual responsiveness. Though the range was considerable, the average nonincestuous perpetrator reported 138 "touching" victims over his lifetime, with some exploited more than once if the average self-count of 226 incidents is valid (Abel, 1985a). It is significant that the rate of arrest among such pedophiles[8] is low, and that the rate of rearrest among the formerly incarcerated is also low, although we do not yet know whether the latter reflects a similar absence of apprehension or the absence of continued offenses (M. Weinrott, personal communication, March 24, 1987). It is significant that findings are available from only the one community treatment study employing a proximally acceptable scientific methodology for measuring sexual responses. Despite optimistic clinical reports from programs, such as that for pedophiles who are professionals that is available in Minneapolis, (Satterfield, 1985), the Abel treatment study (1985b) reports that it is extremely difficult to enlist pedophiles in treatment voluntarily, extremely difficult to keep them in treatment or to find them when they drop out, and extremely difficult to validate the self-reported, one-year treatment success of the minority who remain in treatment.

On the other hand, 33 weeks of satiation and desensitization treatments specifically designed to eliminate the offender's attraction to children were reported to be highly effective with those who stayed the course. Reductions took place in (self-reported) frequency of crimes and number of victims, interest in children, *and phallometrically measured sexual responses to children*. Significant increases took place in sexual knowledge, the appropriateness of attitudes toward child molestation, assertiveness skills, and social skills. Furthermore, treatment had the differential effect of decreasing child molestation without decreasing sexual interests/behavior toward adults. These changes become even more impressive in that those from the original study group who volunteered for treatment had a much higher frequency of child molestation and poorer control over their urges to molest than those refusing treatment.

Other data from this study indicate that the characteristics of prior molestations can be predicted from psychophysiologic measurements. To paraphrase liberally, the stimuli presented during psychophysiologic assessment describe "tactile sexual behaviors" with girls, boys, adult females, or adult males. Only sexual response to pedophile cues, either heterosexual or homosexual, were positively correlated with multiple episodes. However, only response to the homosexual pedophile cues, with descriptions of high violence against the child, was associated with a history of violence during molestations. While predicting child molestation and the use of physical force post treatment from psychophysiological responses could not be done for several methodological reasons, original personality profiles were effective in predicting posttreatment recidivism. The predictors included attraction to male children, attraction to children outside the home, and duration of interest in children. (Factors not predicting recidivism included the lifetime number of molestations completed, frequency of molestation acts immediately pre treatment, attraction to female children, and involvement in incestuous child molestation.) Eighty-nine percent of all recidivism involved the molestation of boys, and molestations involving victim touching (as opposed to voyeurism, exhibitionism, and such) were perpetrated predominantly against boys. Since the class structure of the study population approximated that of the New York City male population generally, and therefore included professionals and semiprofessionals, this methodological pioneering study could provide a starting point for developmental work aimed at future strategies for decision making regarding suspected professional pedophilia or for state and federal statutory reform.

THE REGULATION OF PROFESSIONAL MISCONDUCT

Professional administrators and professional disciplinary bodies are beginning to be required by statute to incorporate into the procedures and sanctions that ordinarily control professional practice—or at least to consider—remedies for professional noncompliance with reporting or investigation requirements, as well as strategies for preventing maltreatment by professionals, or for facilitating successful prosecution should such maltreatment occur. This is, in part, the outgrowth of an interaction between statutory law and case law that already has broadened the right of the child to protection from abuse, progressively adding to the seriousness of the penalties for violation of these rights by individuals and organizations, and transferring the legal, if not the actual, prerogative for decision making to child protection specialists from the professional originally in contact with the child. It is also, in part, the outgrowth of deliberate efforts at system reform. The details of these trends should become apparent in the chapters that follow. It also should become apparent that professional associations have been active participants in their evolution.

Given the extent to which child protection overrides other value issues in statutory and case law bearing on mandated reporting, and given the trend toward imposing collective as well as individual accountability, the data that the American Bar Association (ABA) gathered from state licensing boards of medicine, law, and social work, combined with the case studies in professional regulation of misconduct, are troubling. As in earlier studies of other professions, a minuscule number of disciplinary cases can be identified, and the sanctions employed are mild, largely educational in nature. This disparity does not bode well for the effectiveness of professional sanctions alone, as professional regulatory bodies now operate. A careful distinction is made in the later description of the National Education Association (NEA) response to child maltreatment, between congruent, collective interests of child and professional, evident in educational and legislative campaigns, and potentially conflictual individual interests. The NEA's apparently idiosyncratic procedure seeks reconciliation of individual conflicts of interest in the legal arena—in the interest of its member, but where the child's interest also will be represented—before it is moved into the largely peer-based arena of professional regulation. The value disparity between law and practice further suggests that some norms in the professions might well support or at least countenance the nonreporting behavior found in the National Incidence Survey. Subsequent chapters deal in detail with cultural, ethical, and political issues underlying the failure of professionals to report child abuse, and suggest remedies. Similar value conflicts emerge as personal experiences with the regulation of professional misconduct are examined.

Statutory provisions are already attempting to remedy underlying issues in the failure to report. The most broadly established is an essentially educational approach to cultural biases in the labeling of abuse (Younes, 1984, Ch. III, Sec. D). Reporting legislation in almost half of the states and territories makes provision for programs designed to improve identification and reporting, as well as to generally improve treatment and prevention efforts. More than half of these specifically target mandated reporters rather than relying on reaching them through more diffuse public awareness efforts, and one specifically includes programs directed at child sexual abuse. A substantial minority also provide for special training for child protective service personnel, with some targeting the state social service departments responsible for such training programs and others directly targeting employees or volunteers (social service/law enforcement) who must have such training. A few states are funding these efforts, along with other identification, prevention, or treatment efforts, by establishing funds out of surcharges on various state documents, while an even larger number have established trust funds for general efforts to deal with child abuse or neglect. Understandably, the development of standardized technology to support training for mandated reporters or investigators has progressed more slowly, with only one tested curriculum currently available (Stein and Rzepnicki, 1984).

There are statutory provisions that attempt to remedy underlying ethical and political issues by incorporating other community agencies and professionals, public and private, into child protective decision making. The Clearinghouse review indicates, for instance, that the reporting statutes of a majority of states contain expressions of legislative concern that medical and legal services be provided in addition to social services, usually in the context of delineating the roles and functions of members of the child protection team (Younes, 1984, Ch. III, Secs. E–F). (However, analysts find little similarity in team conceptualization across states.) Most states also make general legislative statements to child protection agencies urging coordinated state agency efforts. Some explicitly include or make independent provision for cooperation with specific agencies: the police in reporting, investigation assistance, protective custody actions, or information sharing; district attorneys or prosecutors for information sharing; other agencies for parent locator services, daycare licensing, adoption or foster care placement, or employee record checks in childcare institutions and group homes. Subsequent chapters detail further possibilities for such an expansion of boundaries, but they also make clear suggestions for rebalancing the distribution of professional authority either within an expanded system or across system boundaries. However, it is a presentation about a relatively unprofessionalized occupation, daycare, that most systematically outlines the effective reform of mechanisms for professional regulation in accomplishing an effective expansion of system boundaries.

LEGISLATION AS A CASE-FINDING STRATEGY

Given the dramatic increase that has been taking place in official reporting of suspected sexual maltreatment, the doubts that have been articulated about legislation as a case-finding strategy require attention at this point. The answers are less than clear-cut. This is largely because the available national data are neither as reliable nor as directly to the point as one would wish. This is not surprising, given the diversity of the legal frameworks, reporting systems, service orientations, and funding patterns involved. The evaluations currently in process through the National Center on Child Abuse and Neglect (NCCAN) may well correct the worst of such problems. In the meantime, past data permit approximate answers to the basic questions: (1) Are most incidents of child sexual maltreatment now officially reported? (2) Does reporting in fact result in case identification? (3) Do the benefits to the child from case identification outweigh the psychic and social costs all the way round?

Reporting Saturation

While the answer to the question of whether most incidents of child maltreatment are now officially reported seems to be "no," a solid assessment of how far we are from reporting saturation is unavailable nationally despite the early work by NCCAN on this question. However, various estimates of official sexual abuse reporting rates can be tentatively compared with Barth and Schleske's (1985) derivations of incidence from published (local) prevalence studies (for instance, Finkelhor, 1979 and 1984; Russell, 1983), given the conservative assumption that an incident occurs with equal likelihood in any of a child's years under 18 and in the course of only one year. The results suggest that for every official, substantiated report of sexual maltreatment (involving physical contact) in the 1979–80 NIS data, 14–52 incidents were unreported; for every substantiated report of sexual maltreatment (involving physical contact) that was active with a major investigation agency other than child protective services (CPS), 8–31 incidents were unreported. More recent epidemiological surveys in communities with larger minority populations yield prevalence estimates for retrospectively reported child sexual maltreatment consistently lower than Russell's, thereby suggesting more reliability at the lower portion of these ranges, although definitional issues complicate comparisons (Blazer, 1987; Karno, 1987; Kilpatrick, 1984).

An alternative strategy in accomplishing such estimates involves the examination of reporting increases that take place when comprehensive treatment programs are made available. Barth and Schleske (1985) present California data on the effect of Giaretto's comprehensive, intrafamily sexual abuse treatment program and its subsequent replication in 29 counties. "Under this program, the [incestuous] offender is subject to criminal prosecution, but has the option to become involved in a comprehensive therapy program for the family aimed at rehabilitating the marriage and family situation" (p. 287). A comparison of Santa Clara County, which had been running the program for seven years, with Sacramento County, which had developed no special therapeutic services by 1977, yielded an almost double per capita (not per child) sexual abuse reporting incidence rate (Kroth, 1979). Barthe and Schleske's own analysis of per capita incidence of reporting in California counties that replicated the comprehensive sexual abuse treatment protocol between 1972 and 1978, relative to matched counties without comprehensive treatment protocols,[9] documents a reporting increase in response to comprehensive services over and above the general increase in child sexual maltreatment reporting that was taking place in California between 1972 and 1980.

Closer examination reveals that in 1975, state legislation established a training and demonstration center for the prevention of sexual abuse of children statewide that resulted in four years of general public and professional information campaigns in addition to fostering improvements within the criminal justice system and efforts to facilitate emulation or adaptation of the model comprehensive treatment program. Thus, calculations of per child reporting rates show low initial incidence but an increase by a factor of six as community awareness was heightened and the existing response system improved. The increase accompanying the additional availability of comprehensive treatment programs for a minimum of two years was more than double that general increase.[10] Although the incidence measures are not completely comparable,[11] the change in the rate of California counties experiencing the largest range of improvements (×14) was in the low-to-middle range of national estimates of unreported incidents derived from prevalence studies. Despite the high and currently growing incidence rate of sexual maltreatment reporting nationally, (1.6 per 1000 children in 1984), the inference is that saturation has not yet been reached, and such a goal will dramatically impact on the volume of investigation activity, though that impact can be reduced considerably by incorporating investigators who are not CPS personnel into the official process.

Case Identification

The question of how many of the incidents of child sexual maltreatment being reported nationally are actually valid cases in need of services is difficult to answer. Although the American Humane Association (AHA) has published "substantiation" data over the years, the caveats about variation in definition across states have become so numerous that only state-level data are now calculated, and even at that level interpretation can be difficult (AHA, 1986, p. 7). The AHA has conducted a survey that indicates that 26 percent of the states do *not* have written policies on substantiating cases, and that among states that do, half practice the policies inconsistently. Other data cited by the AHA suggest that as reporting outstrips staff and resources, some states increase telephone screening and restrict investigations to more serious reports or those involving children under 12. Complementary data suggest that even when cases are investigated, caseworkers in high-volume systems have tended to retreat to substantiating those for which services are available or those they judge to be serious. Apparently this problem has been compounded by a decline in federal funding for protective services and backup family services without compensatory increases in local funding (De Panfilis, 1983). Even in the earlier National Incidence Survey (NIS), however, almost half of the maltreatment reports to child protective services were "unsubstantiated" on the grounds that the maltreatment was not serious enough, that the evidence was not strong enough to take into court, or that the worker had been unable to conduct an investigation because the child couldn't be found, or whatever—judgments implying an uncertainty inconsistent with a finding of invalidity outside a courtroom setting. The considerable research now under way that bears on this variability in decision making further documents the current difficulty in using substantiation as a validity criterion.

The NIS took another step in the interest of case validity that is revelant. It not only limited the total child protective service sample to substantiated cases but also dropped substantiated cases that did not involve physical contact (53 percent). This subset among *sexual* maltreatment cases might be expected to involve siblings at unusual risk for molestation as well as offenses in which protracted harassment or escalating deviance is at issue. (Some of these might have been directed into the emotional abuse category.) Although the limitation was an appropriate research strategy for securing construct validity and was consistent with a legal standard for establishing abuse that requires the presence of serious harm, there is considerable question about such an underinclusive approach in practice. Clearly, the one fairly successful piece of risk prediction research now in progress concerning physical abuse is of major importance, even urgency (Milner, 1986). Although Finkelhor (1979) has done some work on risk assessment for sexual maltreatment employing demographic data, specialized, tested, prediction instruments for use in sexual maltreatment investigations have not yet been developed.[12]

The AHA has now substituted service as an operational indicator of the utility of reporting. Its 1984 data, from states where the finding of maltreatment and the decision to provide services are made only as a result of investigation, indicate that reported cases of sexual maltreatment are among the most likely to receive protective services: 89 percent (AHA, 1986, Table 12). Sexual maltreatment data from 1980–1982 (Russel and Trainor, 1984, Table V-2) indicate a lower rate of service response when data are included from systems that do not investigate every report: 72 percent. Thus, for every report of sexual maltreatment received by child protective services and closed, three-nine receive some services, with the indications being that resources for services are more likely to be available, at least on a priority basis, in systems where resources for investigation also are available.

The 1976–1982 national estimates by Russell and Trainor (1984, Figure V-2) indicate that typically the service involves at least one or two sessions of casework counseling (53 percent) and very little by way of crisis services alone (3 percent). Sexual maltreatment cases, in fact, are more likely than other forms of maltreatment to receive long-term, supportive services—such as daycare, homemaker, or, especially, mental health services (24%),[13]—court action associated with the child's removal to foster care (26 percent), or court action unassociated with foster care (14 percent). The odds that these services will be brought to bear generally are even greater when the report is made by a professional, particularly a law enforcement or medical professional. However, not all are served, and the rendering of service does not guarantee its effectiveness; there is grounding in national statistics for the concerns articulated by other community professionals, though progress has been considerable.

Costs and Benefits

The social psychological costs and benefits of case identification for sexually maltreated children nationally are virtually impossible to assess from existing data. Several indirectly or partially related studies are informative but inadequate to the question. Ongoing research grants address the point, but their findings are as yet unavailable and will be of limited generalizability (for example, Herrenkohl; Kinard; Runyan).

Russell and Trainor (1984) have assembled most of the indirectly related data. On the negative side, they quote Birch's 1983 finding that the size of the average CPS case load has increased beyond the standard for good practice in 28 states, presumably reducing the likelihood of effectiveness. They also suggest that the heavier-than-usual reliance on foster care in suspected sexual abuse cases nationally flies in the face of findings from service improvement projects that removal of the child from the family should be a last resort—a departure from earlier thinking that removal of the child was the first action to take place in intrafamily sexual maltreatment cases (Kendrick, 1984). On the positive side, they note that the Adoption Assistance and Child Welfare Act of 1980 (P.L. 96-272) seems to have reduced the use of foster care between 1976 and 1982 in all categories of maltreatment, including sexual maltreatment, thereby avoiding the secondary trauma of separation from supportive family relationships where those are available. They might well have cited the general reductions of length of stay in foster care that have accompanied that legislation.

The concerns that have been voiced regarding the secondary trauma associated with the legal processing of a case might equally well have been noted (see Berliner and Stevens, 1980 or Goodman, 1984). The statutory review conducted by the NCCAN Clearinghouse reports that most states have made statutory provision for the issues that arise when the victimized child becomes a witness in criminal or civil cases arising from the maltreatment, as well as for evidence admissible in juvenile court proceedings. While these provisions are usually intended for juvenile courts, some—particularly those concerning sexual abuse—are applicable to criminal proceedings as well. As a result, evidentiary standards in criminal cases are eased, and particular problems surrounding the child witness in criminal proceedings are removed. For instance, the age of the child ordinarily might disqualify his/her competence or the ordinary course of testifying might induce trauma from facing the accused, recounting the crime, or undergoing cross-examination.

Some of the innovative laws designed to overcome these problems are particularly relevant in cases of child sexual abuse: hearsay exceptions are made to permit admission of statements by the child outside court, as in videotapes of the child in therapy sessions; determination of the child's reliability or competency is left to the courts or children are defined competent to testify; permission is given to televise the testimony into the courtroom; sanctions against the child who is found in contempt or refuses to testify are limited; the need for corroboration of a child's testimony is eliminated in response to the prosecution problem in secretive intrafamily cases; and limitations are placed on the number of pretrial interviews that can be conducted with a child for law enforcement or discovery purposes. A 1985 evaluation of these statutory reforms found only two to be unambiguously useful and effective: (1) abolishing special competency requirements for children "by establishing a presumption that every witness is competent and leaving the determination of credibility to the trier of fact;" and (2) hearsay exceptions that admit particular out-of-court statements of child sexual assault victims (Whitcomb, 1985, p. 7). Otherwise the study reports that the introduction of modern technology to alleviate the stress of testifying and provisions for closing courtrooms are seldom used, because of judicial and practical concerns. However, a series of procedural innovations that do not require statutory reform are recommended to prosecutors and judges, who must cope with unresolved issues in the determination of credibility as reflected in estimates of invalid initial allegations (1–20 percent) and subsequent contradictions/retractions (13–50 percent).

What is badly needed are child outcome data that tell us to what extent the interventions provided by child protection agents, or by any other investigation system, accomplish the primary intent of most state reporting legislation—protection—and meet the professional expectation that the harm caused by the maltreatment will be alleviated without inflicting secondary trauma. In sexual maltreatment, venereal disease data would be very much to the point (see Wyatt, in progress; Hicks, in progress), as would pregnancy/abortion and AIDS data. With the particular relevance of psychological and social harm to the legal standard for intervention in this form of maltreatment, data on child and family functioning (including strengths) would be to the point (Berkeley Associates, 1983). With the sensitivity of the sexual assault treatment community generally to "the second assault" of the helping and legal systems, systematic work on the differential, objective, and subjective nature of the paths through those systems is surely appropriate. Evaluation guides are available in the NCCAN evaluations of their abuse treatment demonstrations, as well as in NCCAN evaluations of their system improvement projects. More sophisticated technologies for the assessment of harm and future risk are now under development in special studies. Nonetheless, available outcome data do not present a reliable and systematic picture of what happens when a sexually maltreated child becomes known to the official reporting system. Even more, they fail to instruct us on the reverberations of the victimization and official processes for other family members, and little but anecdote is available on the repercussions of false accusation. Criticisms by professionals who fail to make official reports or the controversy being generated by advocates for a narrowing of the legal standard for intervention can hardly be resolved rationally without this picture of costs and benefits.

NOTES

1. Virtually all of these official reports reflect domestic child abuse or extrafamilial abuse to which a parent/caretaker substantially contributed. Very few involve public or private institutional settings.

2. Based on a convenience sample of 16 states with 41 percent of the U.S. child population in the 50 states, the District of Columbia, Puerto Rico, the U.S. Virgin Islands, Guam, and the Marianas. Serious questions have been raised about the representativeness and reliability of this data base, but it remains an excellent resource for those interested in the role and response of the CPS system (Hotaling, 1986).

3. A major controversy in the treatment of family sexual abuse revolves around the use of criminal proceedings as a therapeutic tool for keeping the perpetrator out of the home and/or in therapy thereby avoiding the removal of the child (Rogers, 1982).

4. A large number of states define sexual exploitation in the form of permitting/encouraging "one's child to engage in illicit sexual acts or to be involved in the production of pornography" as felonious. The majority of states also specify penalties for those who profit financially by producing or distributing child pornography.

5. The national representativeness of this sample has come under attack for underrepresentation of very large urban counties, with an associated underrepresentation of minority populations; some undersampling of schools and hospitals in the two large counties in the sample; the omission of daycare centers, women's shelters, and nonpublic schools from "other major agencies" considered in all counties; analytic limitations associated with the small number of counties and states actually sampled; and the generally deficient quality control. It is, however, the most representative of the available studies and unusual in its use of standard operational definitions.

6. By 1985 the Board of Trustees of the American Psychiatric Association (APA) dropped coverage for unethical sexual behavior from its almost 10,000-member malpractice insurance plan. The new plan provided for the defense in court of insured physicians who deny the allegations but does not pay for judgments against psychiatrists. Although the board members saw the move as a deterrent, charges of "undue familiarity" made up 17 percent of the malpractice claims filed under the former plan, and premium quotes from insurance companies were 25 percent higher when they included such coverage. The APA's Committee on Women took a strong stand in favor of retaining insurance coverage to compensate victims for their distress.

7. A disproportionate number of male sexual assault victims were abused by "other" perpetrators.

8. DSM III restricts the definition of pedophilia to those who molest children under age 14. Victims up to 17 years of age are included in these Abel statistics.

9. Nontreatment counties could have referrals to criminal justice sources or to individual mental health counselors. Treatment counties had an established, separate, therapeutic protocol involving professionals trained to deal with sexual abuse cases, but no checks were made on how consistently, comprehensively, or effectively the protocols were used.

10. Counties without a comprehensive treatment program shifted from an estimated 2.2 child sexual maltreatment reports (presumably of all kinds and including unsubstantiated) per 1000 children in 1972 to 11.5 in 1980; counties with the comprehensive treatment program shifted from an estimated 1.0 reports per 1000 children in 1972 to 14.3 per 1000 children in 1980.

11. And therefore accepting the assumption that the substantiation rate for reports involving physical contact does not differ from that for reports not involving physical contact—a conservative assumption.

12. Russell and Trainor (1984) report that three states are now employing decision-making guides in screening reports, but no information is provided on developmental testing or effectiveness in practice.

13. The provision of mental health services, in sexual abuse cases only, declined between 1976 and 1982.

REFERENCES

Abel, G. (1985a). *The evaluation of child molesters*. Report # R01 MH 33678. Rockville, Md.: National Institute of Mental Health.

Abel, G. (1985b). *The treatment of child molesters*. Report # R01 MH 36347. Rockville, Md.: National Institute of Mental Health.

American Humane Association. (1986). *Highlights of official child neglect and abuse reporting, 1984*. Denver: American Humane Association.

APA malpractice claim types constant, but frequency, costs have doubled. (1983, November 4). *Psychiatric News*, p. 3.

Barth, R. P. & Schleske, D. (1985). Comprehensive sexual abuse treatment programs and reports of sexual abuse. *Children and Youth Services Review, 7*, 285–92.

Berkeley Planning Associates. (1983, November). Evaluation of the clinical demonstrations of the treatment of child abuse and neglect. Berkeley, CA: Berkeley Planning Associates. Executive summary of Final Report on NCCAN Contract # (HEW) 105-78-1108.

Berliner, L. & Stevens, D. (1980). Advocating for sexually abused children in the criminal justice system. In *Sexual abuse of children: Selected readings*. DHHS Publication # (OHDS) 78-30161 (Ch. X). Washington, D.C.: U.S. Government Printing Office.

Besharov, D. J. (1985). Doing something about child abuse: The need to narrow the grounds for state intervention. *Harvard Journal of Law and Public Policy, 8*, 539–89.

Blazer, D. G. (1987). *Epidemiologic catchment area—Duke University*. Report # U01 MH 35386. Rockville, Md.: National Institute of Mental Health.

Brown, R. H. (1974). Child abuse: Attempts to solve the problem by reporting laws. *Women Lawyers Journal, 60*, 78.

Burgdorf, K. (1980). *Recognition and reporting of child maltreatment: Findings from the national study of the incidence and severity of child abuse and neglect*. Rockville, Md: Westat, Inc.

Conte, J. R. (1982). Sexual abuse of children: Enduring issues for social work. *Journal of Social Work and Human Sexuality, 1*, 1–20.

DePanfilis, D. (1983). Findings and implications: Survey of the status of child protective services—1983. Denver: American Humane Association. Unpublished report.

Faller, K. C. (1985). Is the child victim of sexual abuse telling the truth? *Child Abuse and Neglect: The International Journal, 1*, 473–81.

Finkelhor, D. (1979). *Sexually victimized children*. New York: Free Press.

______. (1984). *Child sexual abuse: New theory and research*. New York: Free Press.

Finkelhor, D. & Browne, A. (1985). The traumatic impact of child sexual abuse: A conceptualization. *American Journal of Orthopsychiatry, 55*, 530–41.

Finkelhor, D. & Hotaling, G. T. (1983). *Sexual abuse in the national incidence study of child abuse and neglect*. Report # 90-CAB 40101. Washington, D.C.: National Center on Child Abuse and Neglect.

Goldney, R. D. (1972). Abusing parents: Legal and therapeutic aspects. *Medical Journal of Australia, 2*, 596–600.

Goldstein, J., Freud, A. & Solnit, A. J. (1979). *Before the best interests of the child*. New York: Free Press.

Goodman, G. S. (ed.). (1984). The child witness. *Journal of Social Issues, 40*, 1–157.

Hampton, R. L. & Newberger, E. H. (1985). Child abuse incidence and reporting by hospitals: The significance of severity, class and race. *American Journal of Public Health, 75*, 56–60.

Herrenkohl, R. (In progress). *Development of social competence in abused children*. NIMH research grant # R01 MH 41109. Rockville, Md.: National Institute of Mental Health.

Hicks, D. (In progress). *Ethnicity and impact of rape*. NIMH research grant # R01 MH 40837. Rockville, Md.: National Institute of Mental Health.

Holmes, M. (1977). *Child abuse and neglect programs: Practice and theory*. DHEW Publication # (ADM-78-344). Washington, D.C.: U.S. Government Printing Office.

Hotaling, G. T. (1986). *National data systems on child abuse and neglect and the non-accidental death of juveniles: An evaluation*. Washington, D.C.: National Institute of Justice. A draft report for the Office of Juvenile Justice and Delinquency Prevention.

Karno, M. S. (1987). *Epidemiologic catchment area—L.A. Hispanics and Anglos*. Report # U01 MH 35865. Rockville, Md.: National Institute of Mental Health.

Kendrick, M. (1984). What we've learned from community responses to intrafamily child sexual abuse. In *Perspectives on child maltreatment in the mid-80s*. DHHS Publication # (OHDS) 84-30338. Washington, D.C.: U.S. Government Printing Office.

Kilpatrick, D. (1984). *Assessing victims of rape: Methodological issues*. Report # R01 MH 38052. Rockville, Md.: National Institute of Mental Health.

Kinard, E. M. (In progress). *Competence, social support, and adjustment in children*. NIMH research grant # R01 MH 42739. Rockville, Md.: National Institute of Mental Health.

Kroth, J. A. (1979). *Child sexual abuse: Analysis of a family therapy approach*. Springfield, Il.: Charles C. Thomas.

Milner, J. (In progress). *Prediction and explanation of child abuse.* NIMH research grant # R01 MH 34616. Rockville Md.: National Institute of Mental Health.

Office of Juvenile Justice and Delinquency Prevention. (1984). *Sexually exploited children: Service and demonstration project.* Report #80-JN-AX-0001 S-2. Washington, D.C.: Office of Juvenile Justice and Delinquency Prevention.

Plaut, S. M. & Foster, B. H. (1986). Roles of the health professional in cases involving sexual exploitation of patients. In A. W. Burgess (ed.), *Sexual exploitation of patients by health professionals.* New York: Praeger.

Polier, J. W. (1975). Professional abuse of children: Responsibility for the delivery of services. *American Journal of Orthopsychiatry, 45*, 357–62.

Ramsey, J. A. & Lawler, B. J. (1974). The battered child syndrome. *Pepperdine Law Review, 1*, 372–81.

Rogers, C. (1982). Child sexual abuse and the courts: Preliminary findings. *Journal of Social Work and Human Sexuality, 1*, 145–54.

Runyan, D. (1982). Determinants of foster care placement for the maltreated child. *Child Abuse and Neglect: The International Journal, 6*, 343–50.

Runyan, D. (In progress). *The impact of courts on the sexually abused child.* Grant # 85-IJ-CX-0066. Washington, D.C.: Office of Juvenile Justice and Delinquency Prevention.

Russell, A. B. & Trainor, C. M. (1984). *Trends in child abuse and neglect: A national perspective.* Denver: American Humane Association.

Russell, D. E. H. (1983). The incidence and prevalence of intrafamily and extrafamily sexual abuse of female children. *Child Abuse and Neglect: The International Journal, 7*, 133–46.

Sanderson, B. E. (1985). *Taskforce on sexual exploitation by counselors and therapists.* Report to the Minnesota Legislature from the Minnesota Department of Corrections. St. Paul, Mn.

Satterfield, S. (1985, November). *A treatment group for professionals who are pediophiles.* Paper presented at the ABA-NIMH Symposium on Professional Ethics and Child Abuse, Washington, D.C.

Silver, L. C., Dublin, C. & Lourie, R. (1971). Agency action and interaction in cases of child abuse. *Social Casework, 52*, 164–71.

Stein, T. J. & Rzepnicki, T. L. (1984). *Decisionmaking in child welfare services.* Boston: Kluwer-Nijhoff.

Sussman, A. & Cohen, S. J. (1975). *Reporting child abuse and neglect: Guidelines for legislation.* Cambridge, Ma.: Ballinger.

Wald, M. S. (1980). Thinking about public policy toward abuse and neglect of children: A review of *Before the best interests of the child. Michigan Law Review, 78*, 645–93.

Whitcomb, D. (1985, November). *Prosecution of child sexual abuse: Innovations in practice.* Rockville, Md.: National Institute of Justice Research in Brief.

Wyatt, G. (In progress). *Factors affecting the sexual experiences of Afro-American women.* NIMH research grant # R01 MH 33603. Rockville, Md.: National Institute of Mental Health.

Younes, L. A. (1984). *State child abuse and neglect statutes: A comparative analysis, 1984.* Washington, D.C.: National Center on Child Abuse and Neglect.

2

The Range of Models for Professional Regulation: A Review

Mark R. Ginsberg and Elaine A. Anderson

The regulation of the professions by state government has become both prevalent and controversial. Historically, the concept of professional regulation existed as early as 2080 BC within the Babylonian Code of Hammurabi. It has been traced to the era of Roger II of Sicily in AD 1140 and has been linked to medical practice laws and edicts that existed during the times of the ancient Egyptians, ancient Greeks, and the Roman Empire. More recently, the first health-related licensure statutes in North America, which governed the practice of medicine, were enacted by the colonies of Virginia in 1639, Massachusetts in 1649, and New York in 1665 (Gross, 1984).

Traditionally, the professional regulatory laws allow a state to use its police power to establish minimum standards for entry into a profession or area of practice. Although in effect a legal monopoly, a regulatory program that is designed to protect the safety and welfare of the citizenry has been upheld by the U.S. Supreme Court. As early as 1889, Justice Field wrote a historic Supreme Court opinion that upheld this state right:

> It is undoubtedly the right of every citizen of the United States to follow any lawful calling, business or profession he may choose subject only to such restrictions as are imposed upon all persons of like age, sex and condition. . . . All may be pursued as sources of livelihood, some requiring years of study and great learning for their successful prosecution. . . . The right to continue their prosecution is often of great value to the possessors, and cannot be arbitrarily taken from them . . . [b]ut there is no arbitrary deprivation of such right where its exercise is not permitted because of a failure to comply with conditions imposed by the State for the protection of society. The power of the State to provide for the general welfare of its people authorizes it to prescribe all such regulations as in its judgment will secure or tend to secure them against the consequences of ignorance and incapacity as well as of deception and fraud. (*Dent* v. *State of West Virginia*, 1889, pp. 121–122)

Today, nearly all of the major professions, most notably the health professions, are regulated by statutes in some or all of the states. For example, health professions—medicine, nursing, psychology, podiatry, and optometry—are regulated in all states, and a growing number of states have enacted regulatory statutes for social workers, marriage and family therapists, and mental health counselors. The purpose of this chapter is to provide both a brief overview of the models of statutory regulation for the health professions and to discuss the merits of several nonstatutory alternatives to state-mandated regulation.

WHY REGULATE?

A license or certificate, offered by a state and earned by an individual meeting specific criteria, provides an important statement to the public about the individual's qualifications. Such a credential informs inquirers who do not know the regulated individual that this person has met or exceeded a set of minimum standards that the state has promulgated. This function of professional regulation addresses the principal reason why the setting of such standards exists: to protect the public. The inference of this argument is that regulation protects consumers from inadequately trained practitioners. In addition, consumers seeking the services of a practitioner will be assured that the practitioner has met established standards and criteria. For example, when consumers seek the services of a physician, they are assured that the physician they choose actually has been trained as a physician, or at least has met the state's criteria for licensure. It should be noted, however, that critics of licensure laws have cited the uncertainty of the relationship among an individual's training, the acquisition of a license, and professional competence (Hogan, 1979). That is, although a competence-based system of assessment would be preferable to a credential criterion review system, regulatory agencies generally do not have the resources, either human or fiscal, to develop and manage such a system. Nonetheless, a credential-based regulatory system does provide important guidance to the public.

Several other concepts have been identified by Fretz and Mills (1980) as compelling rationales for the enactment of regulatory programs across the health professions. These include that, inherently, regulatory programs prompt practitioners to become more competent and better distributed, and that they facilitate the upgrading of professional practice through the development of improved practice standards. For example, the American Psychological Association has developed standards for providers of psychological services, and other recognized national professional associations, such as the American Association for Marriage and Family Therapy, the American

Psychiatric Association, and the American Nurses Association, also have developed statements related to proper, ethical practice.

These arguments support the view that professional regulatory laws merit the support of state legislators responsible for their shaping and passage. Aside from the issue of "why regulate," another controversial issue is "how to regulate"—what form a regulatory program should take. In the next section of this chapter, several statutory and nonstatutory forms of professional regulation will be discussed.

HOW TO REGULATE

There exists an array of models for occupational and professional licensure by state statute or through nonstatutory mechanisms. Generally, the enactment of statutory regulation takes one of three forms: licensure, certification, or registration. Forms of nonstatutory regulation include the accreditation of academic departments and/or experiential training institutes by a professional association, the designation by a professional association or other such organization that an individual has met an established set of standards, and the review of an individual's credentials by a service delivery facility, such as the privilege review mechanism of hospitals.

Statutory Regulation

The most restrictive form of regulation is a true licensure law, also commonly referred to as a practice act. Practice acts specify both the educational and the experiential criteria that are prerequisites to licensure, including in most cases the requirement that candidates for licensure successfully pass an examination, and also define the scope of practice in which licensees are legally permitted to engage. For example, medical practice acts prohibit unlicensed individuals both from using the title "physician" and from practicing medicine, as defined by the licensure statute. Generally, a board of individuals who are professional peers to the licensees oversee the licensure process, with administrative and legal support provided by the state. The board is granted the authority by the state to license individuals such that unlicensed persons are prohibited from using the professional title protected by the statute and from engaging in the scope of practice defined by the statute.

The second general form of a statutory regulatory program is certification, also known as title protection. Title protection statutes are similar to licensure or practice acts in that they specify a professional title that noncertificated individuals are prohibited from using. However, they differ from licensure laws in that a certification act does not also specify a scope of practice. Gross (1984) suggests that certification acts are permissive in that they do not restrain practice but only restrain the use of a specific title. For example, statutes certifying marital and family therapists identify criteria that must be met by individuals who wish to use the title "certified marital and family therapist" (or some permutation of this title) but do not define the practice of marital and family therapy. Thus, in this example, the title "certified marital and family therapist" would be protected such that the use of the title, rather than the title and area of practice, is restricted to certificated individuals. Like a practice act, certification statutes generally are implemented by a board of peers, with administrative and legal support provided by the state. Certificated persons must show evidence that they meet established educational and experiential standards and, generally, must pass an examination to determine minimum knowledge and competence to enter the profession. These acts, although quite prevalent among health professionals, afford the public less protection than the more stringent licensure statutes.

The third form of regulation authorized by state statute is registration. Registration is the least restrictive form of statutory regulation. Generally, registration consists of a state-generated list of individuals who actively practice a given profession or specialty area. Registration programs can be either voluntary or mandatory. They usually do not require documentation of credentials or the passage of entry examinations. In most cases, regulatory boards of peers are not involved with the registration process, which is administered by the state (Gross, 1984). There are few registration programs in the health care area, but this regulatory system does exist for other areas of practice.

These forms of statutory regulation—licensure, certification, and registration—are authorized upon the enactment of a state statute. Statutory regulation provides the public with more than a state-administered program of assuring minimal training and the inference of competence for regulated individuals. It also provides the public with a legal means of redress should a grievance occur. That is, regulated professionals who violate professional ethics, are convicted of a felony or other legal infraction, or are in other ways practicing inappropriately are subject to discipline and sanctions by the state regulatory authorities. For example, an individual found guilty of malpractice could have his/her license suspended or revoked. Thus, the state, through available sanctions, can act to restrain professionals from practice and/or discipline those who have violated the public trust. The control over professional practice that the threat of sanction provides is an important element of statutory regulation in the public interest.

In addition, also in the public interest, statute-based regulatory programs generally provide regulated individuals and their patients/clients with the legal protection of confidentiality, privileged communication, and an array of other statute-based and consumer-directed legal protections. Further, state-regulated professionals generally are subject to other state-promulgated mandates, such as the requirements of child abuse reporting statutes, guardianship, and custody determinations. Certainly, the enactment of state statutes regulating the health professions is preferable to nonstatute-based regulatory mechanisms.

Nonstatutory Regulation

The three most widely recognized forms of nonstatutory regulations are the accreditation of academic departments and training institutes, the development of professional designation programs as a component of recognized professional associations, and the privilege determination mechanism used by institutions such as hospitals.

A large number of accreditation programs for academic programs and training institutes exist. At the core of this activity are the U.S. Department of Education and the Council on Post-Secondary Accreditation, which sanction the most widely recognized and accepted accreditation programs. Social work, psychology, and marital and family therapy provide examples. The Council on Social Work Education, the American Psychological Association, and the American Association for Marriage and Family Therapy each accredit graduate training programs in academic institutions as well as nonacademic-based postgraduate internship and other such training programs. These programs, and others like them, establish reliable and valid criteria for curricula and other components of professional training. Academic departments and institutions that meet established objective criteria become accredited. The value of accreditation is twofold. First, the accredited program benefits because it is recognized and validated as having met a critical set of standards. Secondly, the students and graduates of accrediting programs generally are viewed as having met a defined set of educational and experiential requirements that frequently serve as entry requirements for a profession or area of practice.

The second form of nonstatutory regulation is the designation, by a recognized professional association or related organization, that an individual has met a set of established criteria. In contrast with accreditation for academic training programs, designation focuses on those individual credentials which frequently serve as entry requirements for a profession or area of practice. Generally these programs, such as the program designating clinical membership in the American Association for Marriage and Family Therapy, mirror statute-based licensure and certification programs. Many such programs, like regulatory statutes, are based exclusively on a credential and experience review, without the evaluation of critical or simulated practice. These programs rarely include an objective examination. Also, association-based programs do not have the range of sanctions available that statute-based programs have. For example, while a statute-based program can, in many cases, both recall the license or certificate and file civil or criminal charges against a regulated individual, an association-based regulatory program only can recall the credential and dismiss the individual from membership in the association. In addition, the investigative authority of associations is limited. Other legal protections and responsibilities, earlier discussed, usually are not extended to such regulated persons.

The third form of nonstatute-based regulation is the privilege mechanism instituted by facilities such as hospitals. Generally, such regulatory programs include a review of an applicant's credentials by a committee of peers. The applicant's credentials are viewed objectively against a defined set of criteria, much like licensure or certification programs. However, in most cases, this form of regulation is facility-specific and, in some facilities, may supplement the earlier identified forms of statutory or nonstatutory regulation. Such is the case with the hospital-based clinical privilege mechanism required of hospitals by the Joint Commission on Accreditation of Hospitals (JCAH). Regulatory-like programs, such as the JCAH, are influential in that they set operational standards for facilities such as hospitals. These criteria also are used by payers for identification of facilities that deliver reimbursable services. Thus, when organizations such as the JCAH specify criteria regarding an individual's credentials, these criteria become a de facto regulatory program. For example, in the case of providers, JCAH typically defines an acceptable mechanism, usually referencing either state law or the facility's bylaws or both, for determining practice standards.

In addition to these three most prevalent models of self-regulation, Gross (1984) points out other important nonstatutory, regulatory-like mechanisms: the ethics and other professional standard-setting programs of professional associations; continuing education requirements of statutes, associations, and facilities; and the function of professional peer review committees. These mechanisms represent but a subset of a larger universe of regulatory forms developed by states, professional associations, service delivery institutions, and public interest groups.

SUMMARY

Both statute-based and nonstatutory regulatory programs function in the public interest to identify appropriately trained and credentialed professionals. Generally these programs function well, although they have been criticized as more of a protection for a profession than for the public (Hogan, 1979). Nonetheless, state professional regulatory programs help the public to identify providers while specifying a mechanism for policing the services of professionals. That is, regulatory programs define standards of practice and ethical principles that professionals must abide by. These standards are critical because they regulate practice and provide a mechanism for the public to identify qualified practitioners.

It is critical to emphasize that the central purpose of professional regulation is the protection of the public. In order to meet this important public interest goal, professional regulatory programs provide an administrative mechanism to implement a succinct and carefully developed set of educational and experiential criteria for entrance into a profession. Both statute-based and nonstatute-based regulatory programs function in the public interest by identifying trained and credentialed practitioners and specifying mechanisms for policing the practices of regulated professions. For example, standards for practice and ethical codes are adopted, and regulated practitioners must abide by these and other such codes. In addition, boards of peers oversee most regulatory programs and, by inference, stand at the interface between the consumer and the provider. Thus, safeguards are instituted that protect the rights and interests of the general public.

Professional regulatory programs function best when boards that oversee them are well trained to evaluate the credentials of applicants, and state agency personnel who administer the programs also are well trained and supervised. Regulatory agencies must maximize their ability to investigate complaints, carefully and properly conduct disciplinary proceedings, and adjudicate cases with the fair determination of appropriate judgments and sanctions. In addition, we should advocate that an understanding of regulatory mechanisms, ethics, and standards of practice should be integrated into academic programs that are preparatory for professional practice.

The professions support strong regulatory programs, preferably statute-based. Professional regulatory programs that specify carefully conceived entry-level requirements, are well administered and properly resourced, and adjudicate complaints fairly are welcomed by both the professions and the public. Such programs are important mechanisms to assure that professional practice is provided by well-trained and competent individuals. The goal of both professionals and regulators is to make the regulatory process even more effective for the public interest in the years ahead.

REFERENCES

Dent v. *State of Virginia* (1889), 129 U.S.114.

Fretz, B. R. and Mills, D. H. (1980). *Licensing and certification of psychologists and counselors.* San Francisco: Jossey-Bass.

Gross, S. J. (1984). *Of foxes and henhouses: Licensing and the health professions.* Westport, Ct.: Quorum Books.

Hogan, D. B. (1979). *The regulation of the psychotherapies: A handbook for state licensing laws*, 4 vols. Cambridge, Ma.: Ballinger.

Part I

Issues in Professional Failure to Report Child Maltreatment

3

Cultural Obstacles to the Labeling of Abuse by Professionals

Sharon D. Herzberger

Each year a substantial number of cases of parent-to-child violence never become labeled as child abuse and are not reported to child protective services (Hampton & Newberger, 1985; James, Womack & Strauss, 1978; Swoboda, Elwork, Sales & Levine, 1978). Kim (1985) surveyed physicians in two metropolitan areas and found that less than half of suspected cases of child abuse were reported, and that almost 70 percent of the physician sample had never reported any suspected cases. Finkelhor's (1984) sample of Boston professionals from various disciplines revealed that approximately 36 percent failed to report sexual abuse cases, with mental health and criminal justice professionals failing to report suspected cases most often.

There are a variety of reasons why cases of abuse are not reported. A failure to report an incident of abuse may be willful, with the potential reporter cognizant of the strong probability of substantiating a label of abuse but reluctant to confront the family and to meet the legal obligations to report. The nonreport also may be due to a lack of awareness of the possibility that an abusive incident occurred.[1] And, finally, the nonreport may result from a process of weighing the facts, considering ambiguous and unambiguous information, using one's "intuition," and rendering a judgment that the incident should not be labeled abuse.

While many researchers have studied the failure to report cases of abuse, few have attempted to isolate the exact point in the process at which a decision is made (whether consciously or not) that leads to a nonreport. The professional's judgment that an act of parental violence is "serious" does not necessarily lead to a judgment that "abuse" has occurred. Furthermore, the professional who labels a case as suspected abuse may not proceed with a report to a child protection team. Thus, we can think of a report to child protective services as the culmination of a series of decisions that resulted in a label being applied and in which the professional decided for one reason or another to comply with the law and file a report.

Given that the factors influencing the various decisions are likely to be diverse, each step in the process should be investigated fully and independently. This chapter will concentrate upon the first stages of the decision-making process: the factors affecting professional judgments that an act of parent-to-child violence is serious and should be regarded as suspected abuse.

PROBLEMS OF DEFINITION

One of the problems in expecting universal compliance with the reporting laws is that the definition of abuse is not precise and the application of the definition is left to individual practitioners. Sincerely and strongly held differences of opinion exist both within and across the professions about what constitutes physical, emotional, and sexual abuse and neglect. Gelles (1977), for example, found that overfeeding was regarded by 33 percent of the social workers he sampled as abuse, while only 20 percent of the physicians felt the same. Lack of emotional and intellectual stimulation was regarded as abuse by 34 percent of the physicians but, interestingly, by only 26 percent of the principals surveyed. Giovannoni and Becerra (1979), in their landmark study of defining abuse, found that social workers and police officers were in general agreement (73 percent of the time) about the severity of certain acts and that both sets of professionals tended to see a given act as more serious than did physicians and, especially, lawyers.

The probability of labeling a given act as abuse also varies by the type of abuse under consideration. Instances of sexual abuse, particularly those involving intercourse between a parent and child, seem to provoke stronger feelings and less ambivalence among potential reporters. In Gelles' survey of professionals (1977), over 95 percent labeled sexual activity between parent and child as abuse. Giovannoni and Becerra (1979) found that sexual intercourse between parent and child was rated 8.15 on a scale of 9 in seriousness, and a parental suggestion that parent and child engage in sex warranted a 6.85. Repeated genital manipulation and mutual masturbation also resulted in serious ratings (6.97 and 7.60, respectively). More ambivalence exists about the child viewing or knowing about sexual behavior of parents, behavior that does not directly involve the child. The divorced parent who informs her child that she works as a prostitute earned only a 3.79, and the divorced mother who has intercourse regularly with her boyfriend merited a 2.63. Among the professional groups studied by Giovannoni and Becerra, only police officers tended to see parental sexual behavior not involving the child as relatively serious.

In contrast with the almost uniform concern about parent-child sexual activity, professionals show much more apathy over emotional or neglectful forms of maltreatment. With the exception of locking up a child since birth (8.31), Giovannoni and Becerra (1979) found lenience about emotional rejection. Constantly screaming at one's child and calling him or her names earned a 4.59; ignoring one's child most of the time merited only a 4.67. Thus, acts that produce no immediate physical consequences are not seen as serious. This result may be due to the difficulty of identifying the proximate cause of a child's emotional disturbance or the absence of any immediate life-threatening danger. When we consider the long-term consequences, however, it would be wise to identify emotionally abusive acts and to train social service workers for appropriate interventions.

AMBIGUITY OF EVIDENCE

In many instances, potential reporters would label a given act as abuse if they could be certain that it was inflicted purposefully or negligently on the child by the parent and that it was not due to an accident. While the general principle of comparing the parent's or child's account of the event with the available evidence may reduce the ambiguity on some occasions, on many occasions ambiguity will remain. An example is provided by Morris, Johnson, and Clasen (1985). They showed a group of physicians a picture of a young boy whose mother claimed that he had fallen off a tricycle and hit his head. While some physicians promptly decided to report the incident (for instance, "The last time I saw a child like this with a story like this, he ended up dead"), others were unsure (for instance, "No bruising on forehead—this looks suspicious . . . ") and still others did not suspect abuse (for instance, "If this were one of my patients, and they came in with that story, I'd probably believe them"; Morris et al., 1985, p. 195). Even protective service workers, whose job it is to substantiate or refute suspicious cases referred by reporters, find it difficult to render a decision. Nagi (1977) found that 56 percent of protective service workers agreed with the statement "It is difficult to say what is and what is not child maltreatment."

A special problem occurs when the child retracts an account that originally substantiated the abuse label. Attias and Goodwin (1984) studied the effects of a retraction in incest cases and found that more than half of the psychiatrists sampled and about a third of the professionals from other disciplines (psychologists, pediatricians, and family counselors) would not refer a case to child protective services following the child's retraction. The psychiatrist's interpretation of the retraction followed from their greater tendency to believe, relative to other professionals, that children's allegations of incestuous activities are often fantasies. In fact, evidence (Chang, Oglesby, Wallace, Goldstein & Hexter, 1976) suggests that fewer than 5 percent of children's reports of sexual abuse are falsified. Following the child's retraction, about 50 percent of the professionals (75 percent of the physicians) recommended a physical examination and all professionals recommended a psychological evaluation of the child. The fact that many professionals neglected to urge the collection of more physical evidence and would instead opt for a psychological evaluation of the suspected victim is astounding and reveals an ignorance of the dynamics of the family situation that may coerce a child into a retraction.

Lack of certainty about the circumstances surrounding an incident dissuades many potential reporters (Saulsbury & Campbell, 1985), particularly when they are aware that a high proportion of reports are not substantiated by child protection teams (Groeneveld & Giovannoni, 1982). When uncertainty about a case is combined with a belief that some cases are best handled privately (James et al., 1978; Saulsbury & Campbell, 1985; Swoboda et al., 1978), it is not surprising that many professionals fail to label a given act as abuse.

EXTRALEGAL FACTORS

Thus far, I have discussed factors that stem from the act itself: the account offered, physical or emotional evidence, and the potential reporter's own definitions of abuse. In recent years, much research has focused on extraneous and perhaps extralegal factors that influence whether the label of abuse is applied. This research has shown that abuse is a socially defined phenomenon, with certain types of cases more likely to be labeled as abuse than others. While sexual intercourse between parent and child and the infliction of severe physical injuries by the parent may produce fairly uniform labeling, more moderate cases may elicit variation in interpretation of the facts and caution in applying the label. Hence, these cases may afford more opportunity for extralegal factors, such as those discussed below, to affect judgments.

Gender of Parent

Acts committed by mothers against children tend to be viewed less severely by professionals than acts committed by fathers (Finkelhor, 1984; Hampton & Newberger, 1985). Hampton and Newberger found that abuse by mothers also was less likely to be reported by hospital personnel. Martin (1983) found that although similar proportions of mothers and fathers were referred to the court by social workers, a disproportionate number of cases involving fathers were processed by the criminal justice system. Other research suggests that reduced reporting may be due at least partially to a lessened tendency to label an act as abusive, rather than solely to an unwillingness to file reports about or to punish mothers. For example, Finkelhor (1984) found that sexual abuse perpetrated by mothers was seen as less serious than sexual abuse perpetrated by fathers. Furthermore, emotional and physical maltreatment are judged by laypeople as less serious when mothers are involved (Herzberger & Tennen, 1985a).

Exceptions to this general trend exist, however. Garrett and Rossi (1978) found no differences in the judgments of laypeople attributable to the gender of the parent. Furthermore, Gil (noted in Leishman, 1983) randomly collected 15 reports of malnutrition filed by social workers, police, and medical personnel, and found that in all cases, regardless of the fact that both parents lived at home, the mother was named as the perpetrator in the report. If further evidence replicates this finding, it may be that women are held more accountable for neglect since feeding the child may be regarded as more the mother's role.

Gender of Child

Finkelhor (1984) found that the most severe judgments of sexual abuse resulted from cases that involved the father and daughter or other male relative and girl. However, Garrett and Rossi (1978) and Martin (1983) failed to find such differences. Thus, more research is needed to isolate the circumstances in which the child's gender affects the decision to label.

Race/Ethnicity and Socioeconomic Status

Race and socioeconomic status profoundly affect the judgments of professionals in cases of abuse. Hampton and Newberger (1985) note that hospital personnel underreported cases involving high-income perpetrators and those who were white. O'Toole, Turbett, and Nalepka (1983) found that 70 percent of their sample of physicians labeled an injury as child abuse when the parent was described as being from a lower socioeconomic background, whereas only 51 percent so labeled when the parent was described as being from a higher socioeconomic background. In contrast, nurses did not use socioeconomic status or race as a determinant of abuse.

Some professionals explicitly use race, ethnic status, and social class as cues to abuse (O'Toole et al., 1983). One doctor noted, for example, "I always look at race first. That's an important indicator" (O'Toole et al., 1983). Professionals may be correct, sometimes, in using these indicators as a means of deciding whether abuse has occurred. Abuse does appear to be more prevalent among lower socioeconomic groups (Garbarino, 1977), and among black and Hispanic families, who disproportionately comprise those groups (Simons, Downs, Hurster & Archer, 1966)—even when reporting bias is considered. However, when these factors are permitted consciously or unconsciously to affect the labeling process, the professional runs a substantial risk, documented by Hampton and Newberger (1985), of underestimating the incidence of abuse among white families and the middle and upper classes, and overestimating the incidence among minority families and the lower classes. Thus, the evidence must be weighed carefully in each case, without reference to race or socioeconomic status.

Some argue that professionals should purposefully consider the family's race and ethnic status when deciding whether to label a case as abuse, in order to ensure that ethnocentric interpretations of parental behavior are avoided (Gray & Cosgrove 1985). Samoan-Americans, for example, are represented in abuse statistics in Hawaii more than eight times what would be predicted, given their population. Yet, the practices of spanking teenagers until they are bruised or beating children to a point just short of requiring medical help are commonly accepted by the minority culture, by the children, and by Samoan-American caseworkers. Similarly, among the Blackfeet Indians, laxity in rearing children that in other cultures might be termed neglect is considered normal and appropriate by members of the tribe and by caseworkers of the same background. Circumcision, so prevalent in the United States among varied populations, is an example of an unnecessary medical procedure that some would label abuse (Wallerstein, 1980), but that others would argue is normal and completely acceptable. Some professionals undoubtedly disagree with Gray and Cosgrove (1985) and urge that the primary consideration in the labeling process should be the harm or potential harm to the child – not whether the child or even the caseworkers accept the rationale behind the practice.

In general, results of these studies support the contention of O'Toole et al (1983) that it is easier to apply the label when the abuser is "socially distant from the labeler and powerless" (p. 359).

Ages of Perpetrator and Victim

While it is generally believed that younger children are at risk of abuse more frequently than older children (Parke & Collmer, 1975), little research has addressed the extent to which age affects judgments about the occurrence of abuse. One possibility is that professionals and others are more protective toward young victims and are thus more likely to label incidents that involve young children as abuse. Hampton and Newberger's (1985) study provides a partial examination of this question. Controlling for severity of the incident, they examined the degree to which age of victim affected the rate of referral by hospital personnel. Children below age five comprised the majority of the sample (55 percent of the cases), thus supporting the notion that younger children are more at risk. Yet, younger children were no more likely than those aged 6 through 12 to be reported to authorities. Cases that involved teenagers were substantially less likely to be reported, however. Somewhat conflicting evidence comes from a study by Groeneveld and Giovannoni (1982). They studied the factors that led child protective workers to substantiate reported cases of abuse and the factors that affected case disposition following substantiation. For neglect cases, but not for other forms of abuse, cases involving older children were more likely to be referred to the legal system for further examination, and older children were more likely than younger children to be removed from the home following substantiation of the abuse. However, these results may not pertain to differential judgments about the severity of abuse incidents; they may stem more from caseworkers' beliefs about beneficial interventions with children of different ages.

Finkelhor (1984) studied lay attitudes toward sexual abuse and found that the public judged most severely cases that involved victims in middle childhood. Younger children were viewed as naive and probably untainted by the abuse, whereas teenagers were viewed as close to the "age of consent" and perhaps more capable of resisting the activity. The age of the perpetrator also affected judgments. Perpetrators over the age of 25 were judged most harshly, and teen perpetrators were judged more harshly than child perpetrators. This finding is consistent with the thought of some professionals that the age differential between adult and child is critical in defining the crime as sexual abuse (see Finkelhor, 1984).

As is evident from these few studies, age may be a factor that affects judgments of abuse cases. The pattern of the effect and the rationale are unclear, however, which suggests a fruitful area of investigation.

Child's Provocation

Finkelhor (1984) found that when the child collaborated with the adult, even by passively accepting sexually abusive behavior, professional judgments of the adult were less harsh, a finding that has been replicated with laypeople (Herzberger & Tennen, 1982). Given the inequity in power between the parent and child, and the child's emotional and intellectual immaturity, one would think that the child's provocation or compliance with a given deed should not legitimately affect one's judgment. Yet, state law sometimes supports the use of such information. California's criminal statutes, for example, permit incarceration of an individual who "willfully causes or permits any child to suffer . . . unjustifiable physical pain or mental suffering" (California Penal Code, Sec. 273A). While the meaning of the term "unjustifiable" is uncertain, it may serve to excuse parental abuse when the child's behavior is deemed provocative.

Characteristics of the Potential Reporter

As noted previously, the occupation of the potential reporter affects judgments of abuse (Attias & Goodwin, 1984; Giovannoni & Becerra, 1979). The gender of the reporter also weighs in the decision. Attias and Goodwin (1984) found that male professionals were more likely than female professionals to overestimate the number of children who would falsely accuse a relative of sexual abuse, were more likely to underestimate the occurrence of incest, and were less likely to refer a case to child protective services following a child's retraction of an accusation. Studies with laypeople almost uniformly show that females are less tolerant of physical, sexual, and emotional abuse of children than males (Finkelhor & Redfield, 1984; Garrett & Rossi, 1978; Herzberger & Tennen, 1985a; Shrum & Halgin, 1984). Giovannoni and Becerra (1979), however, claim that professional orientations can override gender differences, and they support their claim by noting that social workers (mainly female) and police officers (mainly male) judge acts similarly.

We know that abused children tend to carry into adulthood a notion that parental maltreatment is deserved (Kempe & Kempe, 1978) or at least is not as serious as nonabused adults believe (Herzberger & Tennen, 1985b). It is also true that professionals, like other well-educated people, view abusive acts as less serious than do laypeople in general (Giovannoni & Becerra, 1979). This may be due to the social or economic distance of professionals from many of the abusive families or to an attempt to cope with the volume of serious cases of abuse handled on a regular basis (Wolock, 1982). Furthermore, professionals who are tolerant of physical discipline view a wider range of physical and emotional punishments as nonabusive (Morris et al., 1985). However, therapists who have been abused reverse this trend; they are likely to view abusive treatment of children as more serious than do their nonabused counterparts (Howe, Herzberger, and Tennen, In press).

CONCLUDING REMARKS

In many recent books and articles on the process of defining child abuse, one sees a call to halt further exploration of this topic. Researchers and practitioners alike frequently state that "enough is enough"—let us stop debating what constitutes child abuse and get on with the business of treating and preventing the maltreatment of children. In my view, however, discussion of the definition of abuse has finally gotten to the heart of the matter by focusing on the elaborate social process behind the act of labeling. Now we can begin to address issues of bias and can train professionals to be more cautious in their application of labels in some circumstances and to be less cautious in others. Understanding the process of labeling may result in the accurate identification of children whose families need help and in the reduction of false labeling that can be so harmful to the child and his/her family.

In 1976 Wald revealed his suspicions about the ability of professionals to make decisions independent of their own biases. He asked the legal and social service communities to develop scientifically based guidelines to aid professionals in their judgments of abuse. His plea is beginning to see fruition. Interestingly, Wald's suspicions about professional judgment processes can be generalized to the judgments of laypeople as well. Both laypeople and professionals appear to be subject to the same biases and judgmental efforts. This suggests that the problems are inherent in the human judgment process and can be further understood by studying the wealth of psychological literature on such topics as how we form impressions of one another and how we categorize and stereotype individuals (for instance, Fiske & Taylor, 1983; Hastorf & Isen, 1981). For example, research has consistently shown that people spontaneously categorize others on the basis of salient characteristics such as gender, race, and socioeconomic status (Fiske & Taylor, 1983). We also readily divide individuals into two distinct groups, "like me" and "unlike me," on the basis of these and other characteristics (Tajfel & Turner, 1979). People who are judged to be like us are viewed more favorably, in general, than people who are judged to be unlike us (Wilder & Thompson, 1980). People in other groups also are judged to be more homogeneous in attitudes and behavior than are people in our own group (Park & Rothbart, 1982). Herein lie the roots of stereotyping and of the development of prejudicial attitudes.

Unfortunately, these biases in cognitive processing are difficult to remedy, even when substantial contact between the groups exists (for instance, Linville, 1982). Findings that professionals and laypeople make similar errors in judgment of abuse cases reinforces this notion and suggests that neither the current training of professionals nor on-the-job experience serves to remedy the problem. Therefore, means must be derived to counter the prevailing judgment system. One possibility is to provide professionals with simulation tasks in which abuse cases are presented that vary the characteristics of the involved parties and the parental acts. The professional could be asked to read the cases and to decide which should be labeled abuse and which should be referred to child protective services. The factors that affect each person's set of judgments could be identified and each respondent's judgments could be compared with those of other respondents. Through repeated work on the simulator, professionals would be able to identify their own biases and to alleviate them.

The errors in the human judgment process noted above are universal and unmotivated. Some of the biased judgments of professionals, however, are likely to be consciously motivated, such as those stemming from prejudice.

Therefore, it is essential that methods be devised for identifying this subset of judgments and for working with biased professionals to eliminate this problem. Biased professionals perhaps could be identified by comparing the proportions of their referrals that involve certain types of cases with the proportions of such referrals by professionals in general. For example, if a given physician at a hospital reports more cases of abuse that involve fathers or lower socioeconomic people than do other physicians, stereotypes or prejudice should be viewed as a possible cause of the differential reporting.

Attention to professional errors in judgment is particularly important because such errors are relatively less correctable. Child protective workers are more likely to substantiate a label of abuse when the case is referred by a professional than when it is referred by a layperson (Groeneveld & Giovannoni, 1982). Although the increased substantiation rate may be due to the professional's clearer notion of the child protection team's working definition of abuse or to better evidence collected by the professional, it is also possible that labels applied by professionals are more credible because of the professional aura of the reporter. If the latter is true, then biases on the part of professionals may not be easily detected and may be more likely than lay errors to lead to harm.

NOTE

1. Giovannoni and Becerra (1979) note that some professionals may not label a given act as abuse because of the "psychic strain" produced by identifying with the victim or the perpetrator. Furthermore, Elmer (1960) believes that some professionals who fear their own violent impulses repress thoughts about the possibility of another person's aggression.

REFERENCES

Attias, R. & Goodwin, J. (1984, September). Knowledge and management strategies in incest cases: A survey of physicians, psychologists and family counselors. Paper presented at the Fifth International Congress on Child Abuse and Neglect, Montreal, Canada.

Chang, A., Oglesby, A., Wallace, H., Goldstein, H. & Hexter, A. (1976). Child abuse and neglect: Physicians' knowledge, attitudes and experiences. *American Journal of Public Health, 66,* 1199–1201.

Elmer, E. (1960). Abused young children seen in hospitals. *Social Work, 5*, 98–102.

Finkelhor, D. (1984). *Child sexual abuse*. New York: Free Press.

Finkelhor, D. & Redfield, D. (1984). How the public defines abuse. In D. Finkelhor (ed.), *Child sexual abuse*. New York: Free Press.

Fiske, S. T. & Taylor, S. E. (1983). *Social cognition*. Reading, MA.: Addison-Wesley.

Garbarino, J. (1977). The human ecology of child maltreatment: A conceptual model for research. *Journal of Marriage and the Family, 39*, 721–35.

Garrett, K. A. & Rossi, P. H. (1978). Judging the seriousness of child abuse. *Medical Anthropology, 2*, P. 3.

Gelles, R. J. (1977). Problems in defining and labeling child abuse. Paper presented to the Study Group on Problems in the Prediction of Child Abuse and Neglect, Wilmington, DE.

Giovannoni, J. M. & Becerra, R. M. (1979). *Defining child abuse*. New York: Free Press.

Gray, E. & Cosgrove, J. (1985). Ethnocentric perception of childrearing practices in protective services. *Child Abuse and Neglect, 9*, 389–396.

Groeneveld, L. P. & Giovannoni, J. M. (1982). Disposition of child abuse and neglect cases. *Social Work Research and Abstracts, 18*, 9–15.

Hampton, R. L. & Newberger, E. (1985). Child abuse incidence and reporting by hospitals: Significance of severity, class and race. *American Journal of Public Health, 75*, 56–60.

Hastorf, A. & Isen, A. (eds.). (1981). *Cognitive social psychology*. New York: Elsevier-North Holland.

Herzberger, S. D. & Tennen, H. (1982). The social definition of abuse. Paper presented at the American Psychological Association Convention, Washington, DC.

Herzberger, S. D. & Tennen, H. (1985a). "Snips and snails and puppy dog tails": Gender of agent, recipient, and observer as determinants of perceptions of discipline. *Sex Roles, 12*, 853–865.

Herzberger, S. D. & Tennen, H. (1985b). The effect of self-relevance on judgments of moderate and severe disciplinary encounters. *Journal of Marriage and the Family, 47*, 311–318.

Howe, A., Herzberger, S., & Tennen, H. (In press). The influence of personal history of abuse and gender on clinicians' judgments of children. *Journal of Family Violence*.

James, J., Womack, W. M. & Strauss, F. (1978). Physician reporting of sexual abuse of children. *Journal of the American Medical Association, 240*, 1145–46.

Kempe, R. S. & Kempe, C. H. (1978). *Child abuse*. Cambridge, MA: Harvard University Press.

Kim, D. S. (1985). Most doctors don't tell. *Justice for Children, 1*, 16–17.

Leishman, K. (1983). Child abuse: The extent of the harm. *Atlantic Monthly*, November, 22–32.

Linville, P. W. (1982). The complexity-extremity effect and age-based stereotyping. *Journal of Personality and Social Psychology, 42*, 183–211.

Martin, J. (1983). *Gender-related behaviors of children in abusive situations*. Saratoga, CA: R & E Publishers.

Morris, J. L., Johnson, C. F., & Clasen, M. (1985). To report or not to report: Physicians' attitudes toward discipline and child abuse. *American Journal of Diseases of Children, 139*, 194–97.

Nagi, S. Z. (1977). *Child maltreatment in the United States*. New York: Columbia University Press.

O'Toole, R., Turbett, P., & Nalepka, C. (1983). Theories, professional knowledge, and diagnosis of child abuse. In D. Finkelhor, R. J. Gelles, G. T. Hotaling, & M. A. Straus (eds.), *The dark side of families: Current family violence research*. Beverly Hills, CA: Sage.

Park, B. & Rothbart, M. (1982). Perception of out-group homogeneity and levels of social categorization: Memory for the subordinate attributes of in-group and out-group members. *Journal of Personality and Social Psychology, 42*, 1050–68.

Parke, R. & Collmer, C. W. (1975). *Child abuse: An interdisciplinary analysis.* Chicago: University of Chicago Press.

Saulsbury, F. T. & Campbell, R. E. (1985). Evaluation of child abuse reporting by physicians. *American Journal of Diseases of Children, 139*, 393–95.

Shrum, R. A. & Halgin, R. P. (1984, August). Gender differences in definitions of the sexual victimization of children. Paper presented at the Second International Conference of Family Violence Researchers, University of New Hampshire, Durham, N.H.

Simons, B., Downs, D. R., Hurster, M. M. & Archer, M. (1966). Child abuse: Epidemiologic study of medically reported cases. *New York State Journal of Medicine, 66*, 2783–88.

Swoboda, J. S., Elwork, A., Sales, B. D. & Levine, D. (1978). Knowledge of and compliance with privileged communication and child abuse reporting laws. *Professional Psychology, 9*, 448–57.

Tajfel, J. & Turner, J. (1979). An integrative theory of intergroup conflict. In W. G. Austin & S. S. Worchel (eds.), *The social psychology of intergroup relations.* Monterey, CA: Brooks/Cole.

Wald, M. D. (1976). Legal policies affecting children: A lawyer's request for aid. *Child Development, 47*, 1–5.

Wallerstein, E. (1980). *Circumcision: An American health fallacy.* New York: Springer.

Wilder, D. A. & Thompson, J. E. (1980). Intergroup contact with independent manipulations of in-group and out-group interaction. *Journal of Personality and Social Psychology, 13*, 589–603.

Wolock, I. (1982). Community characteristics and staff judgments in child abuse and neglect cases. *Social Work Research and Abstracts, 18*, 9–15.

4

Ethical Obstacles to Professional Reporting of Child Maltreatment

James Garbarino

Depending upon one's point of view, reporting a suspected case of child maltreatment may be interpreted as an ethically elegant act, as a violation of confidentiality, as the meeting of a legal responsibility, as an act of physical courage, as a threat to one's livelihood, as an act of naive faith, or even as an act of folly. Our task is to sort out how these various interpretations reflect the actions of professionals faced with instances of child maltreatment.

We begin with what appear to be the facts of the matter when it comes to reporting by professionals. Every study conducted to date validates the widespread observation that professionals do not report all—and in some cases, most—of the cases of child maltreatment with which they come in contact. To start with, we turn to the federally funded National Incidence Study (NIS).

THE EXTENT AND NATURE OF NONREPORTING

The NIS attempted to discover the degree to which professionals were aware of cases of child maltreatment but did not report them to their local child protective services (CPS) agency (Burgdorf, 1981). Working in some 26 counties during 1979–1980, the NIS matched the records of the official CPS agency with the result of a survey of professionals from the community—investigatory agencies (such as probation and law enforcement) and social services (schools, hospitals, mental health agencies). Overall, the results indicated that only about one-third of the cases known to professionals were known to (that is, reported to) CPS. Using an estimation procedure to extrapolate from the sample of counties in the study, the NIS projected that of the some 652,000 cases identified by professionals across the United States, only about 212,400 were in CPS agency records.

In the NIS, the likelihood of cases known to a community's professionals being reported to protective services varied as a function of characteristics such as the age of the child (cases involving young children were reported more often than cases involving adolescents), type of agency (hospitals were more likely to report than were schools), and type of maltreatment (at 56 percent, sexual abuse was more likely to be reported than other forms of abuse and neglect).

Hampton and Newberger (1985) conducted further analysis of the NIS data to explore the operation of hospitals as reporters of child maltreatment—primarily abuse. They found underreporting of white, higher-income, older parents involved in emotional abuse and neglect, particularly of adolescents. In their small-scale study of 307 Virginia physicians' reporting practices, Saulsbury and Campbell (1985) report congruent results with respect to type of maltreatment (emotional maltreatment was underreported). They also found that 38 percent of the physicians justified nonreporting on the grounds of "reluctance to report before one is certain of the diagnosis," and 30 percent did so on the basis "that the physician believed he could work with the family to solve the problem without outside intervention."

However flawed they may have been by problems in representativeness of the cooperating agencies and correspondence of the maltreatment definitions to public and professional conceptions, the NIS findings did demonstrate the magnitude of the "reporting gap." In so doing, they were consistent with earlier efforts to estimate the difference between reported and "true" incidence of child maltreatment (see Nagi, 1977). Interestingly, however, when the NIS's substantive findings with respect to the demographic and socioeconomic correlates of child maltreatment were compared with the findings of the American Humane Association's National Study of Child Abuse and Neglect Reporting (which relies entirely upon reports to CPS agencies), the net result was a very similar picture of who is involved in abuse and neglect (Schene, 1982).

The probable validity of the NIS findings with respect to the existence of a reporting gap as it applies to professionals is bolstered by a number of small-scale surveys of professionals and their child abuse reporting patterns (often involving projected response to hypothetical cases presented by the investigator). The magnitude of the reporting gap varies from study to study, however, with most being smaller than that indicated in the NIS.

In 1967 Silver, Barton, and Dublin reported that more than 20 percent of the physicians they surveyed said they would not report cases of suspected physical child abuse that came to their attention. More recently, James and his colleagues (1978) found that 62 percent of a sample of pediatricians and family physicians said they would decline to report a case of sexual abuse brought to their attention unless the family supported making such a report.

In a study of 18 psychiatrists and 83 psychologists, pediatricians, and family counselors, Attias and Goodwin (1984) found that "more than half the psychiatrists" but "less than a third" of the other clinicians said they would not report a family to CPS in the case of an 11-year-old girl who "describes graphically to her school counselor fellatio and cunnilingus with her natural father, ongoing for more than 2 years," if the child later retracted the allegation. The authors link this in part to widespread misunderstanding of the likelihood that such retractions, rather than the original allegations, are false.

INFLUENCES ON REPORTING BEHAVIOR

Muehleman and Kimmons (1981) found that 81 percent of the psychologists they studied said they would report the hypothetical physical child abuse case presented by the investigators. This represented an increase from an earlier study by Swoboda, Elwork, Sales, and Levine (1978) in which 87 percent said they *would not* report the same hypothetical case. In a much more developed form of the same procedure, Williams, Osborne, and Rappaport (1985) used a four-point scale (4=certainly would report; 1=certainly would not report) and randomly offered four different hypothetical cases to a range of professionals (varying combinations of type of abuse—psychological or physical—and privileged versus nonprivileged communication).

Overall, most of the professionals indicated likelihood of reporting (an average score of 2.95 on the four-point scale), with the case of physical abuse in the nonprivileged communication condition being most likely to be reported (average score 3.68). Among the professional groups studied, school nurses and ministers were most likely to report (average scores of 3.35 and 3.32, respectively), and psychologists were least likely to report (an average score of 2.42). Teachers (2.90), psychiatrists (2.87), and physicians (2.85) stood in between these extremes.

Interestingly, on a separate test of knowledge about reporting statutes, ministers scored highest and nurses lowest, suggesting that knowledge of reporting obligations under the law was not the decisive factor in differentiating among the professional groups. Whether or not the case involved privileged communication (information given in the context of therapy) made a significant difference in likelihood of reporting. As the investigators point out, this is particularly interesting in light of the fact that the child abuse reporting statute in the state in which the study was conducted "specifically excludes privilege (excepting attorney-client relationship)."

We must note here, as we do in all social problems containing a "moral" dimension, that the distance between the hypothetical and socially desirable "should" and the actual day-to-day "do" can be quite large. Chang, Oglesby, Wallace, Goldstein, and Hexter (1976) reported the results of a survey of

1367 physicians in which more than 90 percent said they agreed with the statement "Physicians in your community should report cases." More than half (61 percent) said "Physicians in their community usually report cases." About 30 percent said they had actually seen cases of abuse in the preceding year (1973), but only about one-third of these cases were "referred to a community agency." This suggests that an even smaller number were actually reported to CPS.

Using the NIS as a basis for comparison, it seems safe to say that reporting has improved since the 1960s and 1970s. Nonetheless, a recent study of professionals' reporting of sexual abuse cases tells us the issue is still quite live. Using a self-selected sample of professionals with special interest in and/or responsibility for sexual abuse cases in New England, Finkelhor (1984) found that 64 percent said they reported such cases to protective services when faced with them. The range across professional groups was from 48 percent (mental health professional) to 76 percent (school personnel). Who you are (at least institutionally) seems to affect what you do about reporting.

What else do we know about influences on reporting? A report by Morris, Johnson, and Clasen (1985) involved a study of how physicians' attitudes toward discipline affected reporting. The 58 Ohio physicians in the study indicated a significant differentiation between parental action they classified as "inappropriate" and action they would report. For example, while 98 percent identified "bruising with a belt" as inappropriate discipline, only 48 percent said they would report it to protective services as child abuse. In general, the higher the physicians' tolerance for physical punishment, the less likely they were to report abuse (using a common set of ten hypothetical cases as the standard for comparison). "Personal experience with the family through previous visits" was an important factor in deciding whether to report abuse for 57 percent of the physicians participating in the study, only 30 percent of whom had in fact reported more than one case of suspected abuse in the preceding year.

These results come from physicians who agreed to participate in the survey, of course. Given that they represented a little less than half (43 percent) of the physicians originally contacted, we can expect that their responses reflect a "better-than-average" awareness of and commitment to the issue of child maltreatment. This is true of most (virtually all) of the surveys of professionals, which usually have a participation rate of approximately 50 percent.

CURRENT ISSUES

What can we learn from this review? Several conclusions emerge. Three are worth highlighting here. First, the reporting gap is an empirical fact of life in the social issue that is child maltreatment. The NIS is being replicated in 1986. Every expectation is that its results will mirror the findings from 1979–1980, that is, that a major proportion of the professionally identified child maltreatment "case load" is being dealt with apart from the legally mandated CPS system. Has the reporting gap changed? Results of the NIS replication should shed some light on this issue. Due principally to the dramatic increase in identified cases of sexual abuse, the total number of child maltreatment cases reported to CPS units has increased significantly in the period since the first NIS. The most recent data from the American Humane Association's National Study of Child Abuse Reporting suggest a reduction in the rate of increase, however (NCPCA, 1985).

Is reporting catching up with case identification? This is an empirical question capable of being answered in the NIS replication. However, Alfaro's 1985 survey of 243 professionals mandated by New York State law to report suggests that the problem remains significant (and may even be growing as frustration with the ability of overburdened CPS agencies grows). In his survey of 131 school personnel, 62 hospital personnel, and 50 law enforcement personnel, Alfaro found that "the most important impediment to reporting is a combination of fear of reprisal against the child and doubts about the efficacy of child protective services." Forty percent of the school personnel and 8 percent of the police acknowledged instances of nonreporting. Alfaro found that "Professional judgment, not the state reporting law, is the most decisive factor in reporting. Only 19 percent indicated the law was the most important factor in the decision to make a report" (1985, p.1).

Second, moving beyond the "narrow" issue of professional reporting, we find the "broader" issue of professional case identification. Child maltreatment is intrinsically a social problem. That is, it exists not as some objective entity but as the result of an ongoing social process of negotiation between community standards—values, beliefs, ethical principles, conceptions of the rights of children, concepts of human nature, and folk wisdom—and professional expertise—research findings, theoretical deductions, and clinical insight (Garbarino and Gilliam, 1980; Garbarino, Guttmann, and Seeley, 1986). Thus, the very existence of child maltreatment as a category of human experience is not fixed.

The definition of child maltreatment changes, and perhaps even grows and develops, as professional knowledge increases and community standards change. For example, acts that were once considered "accidental injuries" (such as deaths of infants in automobile accidents while riding on the laps of their parents) may become definitionally transformed as knowledge increases (and these deaths come to be defined as "preventable accidents"). As the knowledge-values negotiation proceeds, these same events may eventually be seen as culpable acts of maltreatment (when, as is now happening, deaths of infants riding unprotected in automobiles come to be defined as "neglect").

A similar history is evident with respect to the use of violence against children—which once was generally accepted as "positive discipline," but came to be seen first as "corporal punishment" and more recently as "physical assault," enroute to being defined as "physical abuse." This implies that the "fact" of the matter is that a gap in reporting can exist only in response to a gap between case conceptualization/identification and legally mandated response.

PROTECTIVE INTERVENTION AND REPORTING BEHAVIOR

The period since the late 1960s has seen a dramatic improvement in case identification. As Alfaro's evidence (1985) suggests, however, the practitioner implications of this change are not clear-cut. We must differentiate between a professional response that stymies further therapeutic and protective action (for instance, by suppressing case identification with its implied moral imperative to intervene) and a response that facilitates such intervention (be it with or without the legal mantle of CPS involvement). At least, we must make this differentiation conceptually. In legal matter of fact, of course, there is usually no such distinction.

Legal realities do not always correspond to social and psychological realities, however. Even a cursory look at the process and outcomes of litigation and criminal prosecution will demonstrate this. If we are permitted to approach this question empirically, however, we must acknowledge the authenticity of the question of whether CPS involvement results in more and better intervention for children. The concerns raised by students of this issue must give us pause. In its extreme form this concern underlies Goldstein, Freud, and Solnit's (1979) objection to protective intervention at all except in the most dire circumstances.

In the arena of sexual abuse, particularly, voices are raised to hypothesize (and in some cases even to assert) that involving the CPS machinery (particularly if it invokes a law enforcement response) produces unnecessary negative consequences that outweigh any benefits (and thus constitutes "iatrogenesis"). Certainly the respondents to Alfaro's survey (1985) believe this to be the case. Most respondents cited "quality of CPS intervention" as a concern that dissuaded them from meeting their legal mandate to report child maltreatment. Newberger (1985) has been outspoken in articulating the view that when official intervention is iatrogenic (as it tends to be, in his opinion, when criminal prosecution is involved), professional intervention will be pushed outside the law.

We must recognize that different solutions are required to deal with nonreporting that stems from negative motivations (from a self-interested refusal to get involved or a tolerance for maltreatment) versus that which stems from a positive belief that the best interest of the child is served by intervention outside the context of reports to CPS agencies. Nonreporting of the first type can and should be dealt with by education, training, and legal sanctions. But such nonreporting appears to be only part, and probably the smaller part, of the current "problem."

Having reviewed the issues, we can assume that narrowing the reporting gap does not depend principally upon further training of professionals with respect t[illegible] legal obligations. Neither does it depend upon simple exhortation. [illegible] impact of showcase prosecutions [illegible] upon more active implem[illegible] ther, the answer seems t[illegible]

The [illegible] sponse by protective se[illegible] agencies. Existing eviden[illegible], of course, is an experi[illegible] ed improvement in the qu[illegible] g decrease in well-intent[illegible]

Eve[illegible] ional link between quali[illegible] would be a valuable contr[illegible] ng conducted could prov[illegible] nt with the hypothesis t[illegible] nce to reporting (Alfaro [illegible]

A [illegible] y lies in a quality of response [illegible] ce reporting by being responsive to the reporter's need for [illegible] up, and participation in the process that reporting initiates (Alfaro, 1985). Second, it must significantly reduce iatrogenesis, go to great lengths to explain the "inevitability" of such effects where they do occur, and demonstrate good faith efforts to prevent such effects (Newberger, 1985). Third, it must assemble a convincing data set to demonstrate the benefits of reporting and the intervention it precipitates in contrast with intervention not accompanied by reporting (Goodwin and Geil, 1982). Part and parcel of this is a demonstration of the iatrogenic consequences of intervention undertaken in the absence of reporting to protective services.

This is a tall order, to be sure, as is evident in Goodwin and Geil's (1982) effort to make the case with respect to sexual abuse. Their report offers five reasons for reporting: to decrease morbidity, to generate accurate information about incidence, to destigmatize the process of being reported, to provide help to otherwise unserved families, and to increase influence with CPS agencies. Demonstrating the validity of these hypotheses will prove difficult and will require both empirical study and changes in policies, practices, and resource allocation. A tall order, yes, but it is the only course of action likely to reduce significantly the reporting problem as it affects well-intentioned professionals.

REFERENCES

Alfaro, J. (1985, November). Impediments to mandated reporting of suspected child abuse and neglect in New York City. Paper presented to the Seventh National Conference on Child Abuse and Neglect, Chicago, Il.

Attias, R. & Goodwin, J. (1984, September). Knowledge and management strategies in incest cases: A survey of physicians, psychologists and family counselors. Paper presented to the Fifth International Congress on Child Abuse and Neglect, Montreal, Canada.

Burgdorf, K. (1981). *Results of the National Incidence Study*. Washington, D.C.: National Center on Child Abuse and Neglect.

Chang, A., Oglesby, A., Wallace, H., Goldstein, H. & Hexter, A. (1976). Child abuse and neglect: Physicians' knowledge, attitudes and experiences. *American Journal of Public Health, 66*, 1199–1201.

Finkelhor, D. (1984). *Child sexual abuse*. New York: Free Press.

Garbarino, J. & Gilliam, G. (1980). *Understanding abusive families*. Lexington, Ma.: Lexington Books.

Garbarino, J., Guttmann, E., & Seeley, J. (1986). *The psychologically battered child*. San Francisco: Jossey-Bass.

Goldstein, J., Freud, A., & Solnit, A. (1979). *Before the best interests of the child*. New York: Free Press.

Goodwin, J. & Geil, C. (1982). Why physicians should report child abuse: The example of sexual abuse. In J. Goodwin (ed.), *Sexual abuse: Incest victims and their families*. Boston: Wright/PSG.

Hampton, R. & Newberger, E. (1985). Child abuse incidence and reporting by hospitals: Significance of severity, class and race. *American Journal of Public Health, 75*, 56–60.

James, J., Womack, W. M. & Strauss, F. (1978). Physician reporting of sexual abuse of children. *Journal of the American Medical Association, 240*, 1145–46.

Morris, J., Johnson, C. & Clasen, M. (1985). To report or not to report: Physicians' attitudes toward discipline and child abuse. *American Journal of Diseases of Children, 139*, 194–97.

Muehleman, T. & Kimmons, C. (1981). Psychologists' views on child abuse reporting, confidentiality, life, and the law: An exploratory study. *Professional Psychology, 12*, 631–38.

Nagi, S. (1977). *Child maltreatment in the United States: A challenge to social institutions*. New York: Columbia University Press.

National Committee for the Prevention of Child Abuse (1985). Results of the state survey of reported cases of child abuse and neglect. Unpublished report.

Newberger, E. (1985, November). *Prosecution is not the best response to ending child abuse*. Presentation to the Seventh National Conference on Child Abuse and Neglect, Chicago, Il.

Saulsbury, F. & Campbell, R. (1985). Evaluation of child abuse reporting by physicians. *American Journal of Diseases of Children, 139*, 393–95.

Schene, P. (1982). *National study of child abuse and neglect reporting*. Denver: American Humane Association.

Silver, L., Barton, W. & Dublin, C. (1967). Child abuse laws: Are they enough? *Journal of the American Medical Association, 199*, 65–68.

Swoboda, J., Elwork, A., Sales, B. & Levine, D. (1978). Knowledge of and compliance with privileged communication and child abuse reporting laws. *Professional Psychology, 9*, 448–57.

Williams, H., Osborne, Y. & Rappaport, N. (1985). Child abuse reporting laws: Professionals' knowledge and compliance. Unpublished manuscript, Louisiana State University.

5

Political Obstacles to Reporting in Residential Childcare Settings

Nolan Rindfleisch

There have traditionally been several strategies for preventing and remedying maltreatment in residential institutions: law enforcement, licensing, deinstitutionalization, quality assurance, and oversight by elected officials. Efforts to introduce protective services into the institutional situation have been given impetus since 1976 by the National Center on Child Abuse and Neglect. In two separate projects funded by the National Center on Child Abuse and Neglect to study protective service in childcare institutions (Rindfleisch, 1984; Shafer, 1985) three studies examined the factors that influence reporting of institutional abuse and neglect. This chapter summarizes the findings of those three studies and discusses some remedies for nonreporting.

In residential institutions, there appear to be three types of barriers to reporting. The first type stems from the conflicts that grow out of the differing perspectives of residents, on the one hand, and the professionals who are responsible for the care and treatment of residents, on the other.

The second type of barrier to reporting stems from a general absence of consensus regarding just what acts and omissions require protective intervention.

The third type of barrier to reporting, what we are calling willingness to take protective action, is organizational in nature. For while there is widespread agreement among administrators of children's residential facilities

Note: The research upon which this article is based was sponsored through Grant no. CA-801-02-03, the National Center on Child Abuse and Neglect, Administration for Children, Youth and Families, O.H.D.S., D.H.H.S. The opinions and conclusions expressed are those of the author, who wishes to acknowledge the contributions made by Joel Rabb, Ph.D., Jerry Bean, Ph.D., and Robert Foulk, Ph.D. in the conduct of the research upon which this article is based.

that program monitoring, professional rapport with the residents, and an "open door" policy are sufficient to assure the safety and security of residents, reporting of maltreatment has been negligible.

INTEREST GROUP PERSPECTIVES

The assertion by professionals that only they can regulate themselves and the increasing recognition of children's rights represent two, often diametrically opposed, perspectives on safeguarding residents' health and welfare. The insistence by professional groups on maintaining absolute control of their own work may be understood by reference to Hughes's (1958) analysis of what he terms "mistakes at work." He observes that the more often a procedure is performed, the greater is the risk of making a mistake. Clearly, some mistakes are more fateful than others. To deal with the possibility of risks of mistakes, members of professions need some rationale to carry them through. It is expected that those who share the same risks will compose a collective rationale that they whistle to one another and that will build up collective defenses against the lay world. These rationales and defenses, according to Hughes, tend to spread the risk of fateful mistakes psychologically.

What constitutes a mistake in any occupation is very difficult to determine. Most occupations argue that a group of peers is the only group that has a right to say when a mistake has occurred. The colleague group feels that it alone understands the contingencies involved when mistakes occur, and that it should be given the sole right to say when a mistake has been made. This attitude may be extended to complete silence concerning mistakes of a member of the colleague group, because the very discussion before a larger audience may imply the right of the layperson to make a judgment; and it is the right to make the judgment that is most jealously guarded. If matters have gone to such a point, Hughes continues, that mistakes and failures are not discussed within the colleague group, public discussion may be doubly feared.

Advocates remind us, on the other hand, that for American colonists the ultimate explanation of every political controversy was the disposition of power (Glasser, 1978). Power was defined as dominion—the dominion of some people over others, the human control of human life, ultimately force and compulsion. The essential characteristic of power was its endlessly propulsive tendency to expand itself beyond legitimate boundaries. Power was dangerous; liberty was the concern of the governed. Further, the colonists held that those who exercise power should not be entrusted or expected to protect liberty. After 1960, this analysis was more often applied to the service situation; it was found that citizens living under the jurisdiction of service professionals were without rights. Throughout this awakening to clients' rights, professionals have typically defended their own discretion and opposed the rights of their clients.

When applied to children's residential facilities, this analysis has produced several new features, such as the formalization of residents' rights, rights enforcement machinery, a reduction in professional discretion, and an adversarial process between residents and their service professionals.

The response of the children's institutional field to the children's rights movement was summed up by Mayer et al. (1978):

> It is unjustifiable to discredit the whole field on the basis of some negative experiences. . . . The emphasis should not be on the curtailment of the decision-making power of the staff in group care facilities, but on the development of a staff who can make socially fair and psychologically correct decisions about children. This can be fostered by the establishment of legal rights, codes, evaluation committees and review committees within the group setting. But the main job has to be done by staff of the group care facilities.
>
> The child welfare field has in fact been the oldest advocate of children's rights and does not need to be defensive about this new development. It can make itself the spearhead of the "movement" and in peer review it can give leadership in guaranteeing the rights and meeting the needs of children (p. 263).

But, as a practical matter, others argue that the very norms that define practice as professional contribute to the negligible level of reporting of maltreatment of institutional residents. Thomas (1980), for example, argues that residential placements and maltreatment have been justified by the intent of the professional community to manage harmful events on their own. Justification of professional behavior by intent is reflected in the following claims:

1. The doctrine of "in loco parentis" is invoked by administrators of institutions. Since the facility is operating in place of parents, it has the rights of parents when it comes to judging itself culpable of abuse or neglect.
2. The concept of "in the child's best interest" is invoked to justify actions of staff as having been done for the child's own good.
3. "Best professional judgment" is based on the presumed special knowledge of staff members as they perform the work of the facility, such as in therapeutic intervention or in the use of punishment and work.
4. The "argument of limited resources" is invoked to reduce the degree of administrative culpability for the occurrence of maltreatment in residential facilities.

However, with increases in the rights of children in recent years, especially where these have been specified in public law, a widening has resulted in the range of staff behaviors that are definable as maltreatment.

DYNAMICS OF JUDGMENTS OF SEVERITY

To what extent is there consensus, among those involved in residential care, regarding just what acts and omissions are more or less serious? Community studies of perceived severity of maltreatment would lead one to expect variation in such judgments—variation associated with the role of the observer, the observed consequence, and the circumstances in which the abuse occurs (Giovannoni and Becerra, 1979). Rabb and Rindfleisch (1985) explored these hypotheses in a study of 630 persons having direct connection to residential group care. The respondents included administrators, board members, care providers, foster parents, child welfare workers, and residents.

Judgments of severity were elicited on 24 vignettes developed from actual cases reported to other institutional abuse and neglect projects. Each of eight categories of institutional maltreatment, derived from Draft Federal Standards for Abuse and Neglect Prevention, other institutional projects, and the Giovannoni and Becerra classification of abuse and neglect in families, was represented by three different vignettes believed to reflect high, medium, and low levels of severity. The domains sampled were physical maltreatment, sexual maltreatment, failure to provide, failure to supervise, emotional maltreatment, questionable moral behavior, harmful restraint/control, and "setting up." Independent variables were varied systematically across the 24 vignettes to determine the effect on judgments of site (institutional or family), consequences of maltreatment, impairment of the "offending" adult, and the level of difficulty presented by the child depicted. Three sets of findings are to the point here.

A high degree of consensus emerged in this heterogeneous set of respondents concerning the general seriousness of the events judged, but the assessment of harm to a child does not translate directly into an equivalent judgment of abuse or neglect. All of the events but one had average scores under 4.5 on a 9-point scale of harm, with 1 being the most severe. The average score for abuse/neglect was substantially higher than the score for harm on every event. This would suggest that it is easier to agree that harm has been done than it is to agree that an act is abusive.

Ratings of seriousness did not seem to be influenced by the type of event under consideration, as predefined by sampling domains. Of the 24 vignettes judged, the following were found to be the most harmful:

1. Double dose of medication to control behavior
2. Adult has sex with a youth
3. Adult smokes pot with a youth
4. Adult administers humiliating punishment for bed-wetting
5. Adult strokes youth's thigh in a suggestive manner.

The five events judged to be least serious among the 24 submitted for judging were

20. Adult ignores child's complaint of an earache
21. Youth roughly subdued; grabbed by hair, forced to wall
22. Youth locked in quiet room and left for an hour
23. Youths left to fight it out
24. Outing canceled for fighting.

To a substantial degree the standard employed by respondents in judging institutional events was similar to the standard employed in judging intrafamilial events. However, in 9 of the 24 events submitted to respondents, significant differences in severity occurred when the caregiver was depicted as a parent compared with when the caretaker was depicted as a residential facility employee. A narrower range of acceptable behavior was defined for staff members than for parents in cases of failing to give seizure medication, pushing a resident into a fall downstairs, lying to a resident, ignoring a resident's earache, and letting youths fight it out. A wider range of acceptable behavior was defined for staff members than for parents in cases that involved ignoring a child, calling a child names, or locking a child in a quiet room for an hour. Although these seven items do not disproportionately reflect any one type of situation as defined out of the literature on institutional/family standards, all but one of those eliciting a narrower range of acceptable behavior for institutional staff seem to imply potential for serious physical consequences to the resident, while those eliciting a wider range of acceptable behavior for institutional staff seem to imply a negative emotional effect.

The presence of a negative consequence in a vignette did, in fact, systematically influence judgments of respondents. *Assessments of harm changed in half of the events when the respondent was aware of a consequence to the child resulting from an adult's behavior.* Assessments of abuse and neglect, on the other hand, were influenced by an awareness of consequence in only a third of the events. Again, the assessment of harm did not translate directly into an equivalent judgment of abuse or neglect, and the items on which change occurred did not disproportionately reflect any one type of situation as defined out of the literature on institutional/family standards.

In contrast, judgments of most of the events did not appear to have been strongly influenced by the circumstances under which the staff behavior portrayed in the vignette took place. When multiple correlations were obtained for the association between judgments of seriousness and the four circumstances of site and consequence, only five events produced significant R's.

ORGANIZATIONAL FACTORS IN REPORTING

It can be seen that the judgment of severity is not a straightforward process, though there is a substantial consensus regarding what adult behaviors are more or less serious. If statutes were specifically related to residential group care and if operational definitions were developed so that there was less uncertainty about what to report, there would continue to be reason to believe that reporting would not increase. Having recognized a sufficiently serious event, what additional factors need to be present to increase the likelihood that protective action will occur?

In an effort to determine what factors influenced the willingness to report, the author (Rindfleisch, 1984) presented study respondents with one of eight descriptions of residential facility staff behavior and asked what action they would be likely to take to deal with the situation depicted. The eight vignettes were selected from the severity study reported above. One event for each type of maltreatment was included, with restraint/control represented by two vignettes. In addition, measures of several other sets of factors were obtained from 600 respondents in 6 states. Administrative/treatment staff, childcare staff, residents, and child protection staff were represented in the sample. The six sets of factors measured were

1. Position of staff member depicted in a vignette
2. Eleven characteristics of staff and resident depicted in the vignettes
3. Assessment of the severity of the event
4. Respondent's commitment to the well-being of residents
5. Organization support for reporting
6. Role/position of the respondent.

A multiple correlation of .673 ($p=0.000$) was obtained when these several sets of factors were entered into the analysis in a hierarchical fashion. About 45 percent of the variance in willingness to take protective action was explained.

The type of maltreatment was influential in its effect on the willingness to report. However, the direction of the influence of some of the types of maltreatment was not expected. Physical and sexual events led to an increased level of willingness to report. Other types of maltreatment—such as restraint/control, moral, emotional, and failure to provide—led to lowered levels of willingness to report.

When a social worker or a childcare worker were depicted in an event, rather than the supervisor, more willingness to report was in evidence. Higher levels of assessed severity of the events depicted in the vignettes led to increased willingness to take protective action. The 11 variables that characterized the situation of each event influenced willingness to report to a degree similar to assessed severity.

However, the effects of these factors were modest when they were compared with the effects of the four items that tapped the respondents' commitment to report adverse events even if reporting threatened the agency's funding, or were to result in anger from one's peers or the loss of one's job. Finally, being a resident increased the willingness of the respondents to report. Being a direct care worker, an administrator, or a public child welfare worker led to lower levels of willingness to report.

The major findings of this study were that among the seven types of events depicted, only sexual and physical events led to increased willingness to report. Besides the severity of the event, being a resident and being committed to resident well-being regardless of threats to oneself or to one's agency, were associated with increased willingness to report.

APPLICATION OF RESULTS

Following this research, a statewide demonstration and test of the effectiveness of alternative approaches to detecting and reporting possible maltreatment in licensed public and private children's residential facilities was undertaken in Ohio with sponsorship by the National Center on Child Abuse and Neglect (Shafer, 1985). The case-finding methods tested were advocate within the line of authority, complaint box accessible to staff and residents, advocate outside the line of authority, and a hot line accessible to residents and staff. These mechanisms were accepted as feasible by the cooperating residential facilities.

The two approaches that generated the most investigations were the hot line and the advocate outside the line of authority. They tended to confirm research results cited above indicating that residents would be more likely to report and that an independent internal advocacy mechanism would lead to a higher willingness to report. The use of the hot line as a case-finding mechanism was not well received by child protective agencies. The internal advocate outside the line of authority was accepted by both residential facilities and child protective agencies.

SUMMARY AND CONCLUSION

Overall, respondents are unlikely to define as serious events that rank at the less severe end of a measured continuum, events in which there are lower expectations held of childcare workers than of parents and events in which contingencies significantly influenced the judgment. The major findings of the Willingness to Report Study were that among the seven types of events depicted, only sexual and physical events led to an increase in the willingness to report. Besides the severity of the event, being a resident and being committed to resident well-being, regardless of threats to oneself or to one's agency, were associated with increased willingness to report.

A strategy for developing an efficient and fair resident protection system requires that several steps be taken. Such a strategy should include passage of state abuse and neglect statutes that specifically refer to the residential group care situation, development of consensus regarding operational definitions of what is reportable at the state and local level, maintenance of a case-finding structure within the facilities that is as independent of administration as feasible, and use of specialized independent investigation units at multicounty or state levels. Clearly these steps would constitute the basis of a new relationship of accountability between administrator/professionals and lay audiences.

It is our view, based on our experience, that reporting behavior is also influenced by the degree to which residential facilities maintain an active role with the independent investigative agency in case finding, investigation, and corrective action, and further by the extent to which this process is managed so as to minimize the threat to direct care staff from sanctions, such as terminations, directed at them as the persons assumed to be solely responsible for the problem.

REFERENCES

Giovannoni, J., & Becerra, R. (1979). *Defining child abuse*. New York: Free Press.

Glasser, I. (1978). Prisoners of benevolence: Power versus liberty in the welfare state. In W. Gaylin, I. Glasser, S. Marcus and D. Rothman (eds.), *Doing good: The limits of benevolence* (pp. 97–168). New York: Pantheon Books.

Hughes, E. (1958). *Men and their work* (pp. 88–101). New York: Free Press.

Mayer, M. F., Richman, L. H., & Balcerzak, E. (1978). *Group care of children* (2nd ed.). New York: Child Welfare League of America.

Rabb, J., & Rindfleisch, N. (1985). A study to define and assess severity of institutional abuse and neglect. *Child Abuse and Neglect, 9*, 285–94.

Rindfleisch, N. (1984). A study of the willingness to report in identification, management and prevention of child abuse and neglect in residential facilities. Final report submitted to the National Center on Child Abuse and Neglect, Administration for Children, Youth and Families, Office of Human Development Services, Department of Health and Human Services.

Shafer, J. (1985). Protection of children in institutional care project. Final report submitted to the National Center on Child Abuse and Neglect, Administration for Children, Youth and Families, Office of Human Development Services, Department of Health and Human Services.

Thomas, G. (1980). A contemporary definition of institutional child abuse and neglect. Paper presented at the Regional Conference on Institutional Abuse and Neglect, sponsored by the Region VII Child Abuse and Neglect Resource Center, Institute of Child Behavior and Development, University of Iowa, Oakdale, Iowa.

Part II

Issues in the Regulation of Professional Misconduct: Sexual Abuse as a Case in Point

6

When the Pediatrician is a Pedophile: Is There a Moral Defect in the Practice of Professional Regulation?

Carolyn Moore Newberger and Eli H. Newberger

As recently as the late 1970s, child sexual abuse was considered extremely rare. Recent retrospective surveys, however, suggest that from 3 to 6 percent of males and from 12 to 38 percent of females are sexually victimized during their childhoods (Finkelhor, 1979; Russell, 1983). Although there is variation from study to study in estimates of incidence, the magnitude of the problem is clear. During the past few years, cases of child sexual abuse have involved daycare centers, prominent families, and respected institutions (Trainor, 1984).

Little is known about adults who commit sexual acts with children. Available data suggest that about 95 percent of the sexual abuse of girls and about 85 percent of the abuse of boys is committed by men, most of whom are known to the child. The offenders come from all ethnic and income groups and may be community leaders who exploit their positions of prestige to gain access to children. They are more likely than the general population to be outwardly religious and especially to be rigid about sexual mores (Finkelhor, 1984).

Most child sexual abusers appear normal to the rest of the world, and their deviancy is frequently not recognized by their wives, friends, or colleagues. They may be homosexual, heterosexual, or bisexual; they may have sexual relations with adults as well as children or only with children. Some individuals prefer sustained relations with one child, while others favor brief sexual encounters with many. They may rape infants or "initiate" adolescents. Some sexual abusers operate "sex rings" in which groups of children

---

This chapter is reproduced from *Sexual Exploitation of Patients by Health Professionals*, edited by A. W. Burgess and C. R. Hartman. New York: Praeger Publishers, 1986.

become involved with one or more adults, usually through some neighborhood or recreational activity (Finkelhor, 1984; Burgess et al., 1984).

Pedophiles, individuals whose sexual preference is for children, may select professional contexts in which access to children is assured. Within the medical profession, pediatrics offers such access. The pediatrician, usually a beloved and trusted member of the community, has intimate and often private contact with children's bodies. When the pediatrician is a pedophile, the interests and needs of many parties are compromised: the children's needs to be free of abuse and exploitation and to trust adult caregivers, the medical profession's needs to maintain its standards for care and its status within the community, and the community's needs to maintain social order and to trust those on whom it relies for the care of children.

Such multiple needs and interests are reflected in our society's confusion over what to do about the sexual abuse of children. This confusion reflects a fundamental set of moral conflicts: (1) the conflict between personal and institutional needs and the assumption of responsibility for others, and (2) the conflict between responding with standard rules of justice and responding with individualized prescriptions for care. In this chapter, we present a case that illustrates these central moral conflicts and discuss how we might resolve them in ways that achieve an enlightened moral response.

WHOSE INTERESTS ARE SERVED? THE CASE OF THE PEDIATRICIAN PEDOPHILE

When we are confronted with sexual abuse, especially abuse by a powerful professional, all too often every interest but the child's seems to take priority. This appears to be true in the case of a pediatrician we call Dr. Smith.

Dr. Smith was the subject of a disciplinary proceeding before a state board of registration in medicine. The pediatrician is a respected, prestigious, and powerful member of the community. He is married and an active member of a local church.

During the routine physical examination of a 14-year-old boy, Dr. Smith removed the child's undershorts while the boy lay on the examining table, and began stroking his genitals and asking questions about injury to the penis, sperm color, and problems with ejaculation. After masturbating the child to ejaculation, the doctor hugged the boy, saying "I'm a pretty cute guy," and then kissed him on the neck. By this time, the child had become very nervous and confused. He was subjected to several more hugs before leaving the examination room. After the boy and his mother left the doctor's office he told her what had happened.

Shortly after, the boy's family called the police. Although an initial contact was made, the police inquiry apparently then stopped. No criminal charges were filed and there was never any public disclosure of the incident. Rather, the matter was addressed six months later in a closed hearing of the state board of registration in medicine. The board retained a private attorney to conduct its own investigation and to serve as the prosecutor in a closed meeting in which the complainant, other witnesses, and the doctor would appear.

During the closed inquiry, the doctor claimed that boys often had ejaculations during physical examinations and revealed the names of two other boys. His records showed a private shorthand for the events and lavish descriptions of the boys' bodies. He also said that he served often and without compensation as a lecturer on teenage sexuality, that he worked as both a school and a camp physician, and that his examinations of boys' genitals often lasted more than five minutes. He steadfastly maintained that there was no harm in what he did.

The doctor's license was suspended for 30 days and he was placed on probation for 10 years, during which time he was to seek psychiatric help until discharged by the psychiatrist. Dr. Smith was instructed to have a third person present during the examinations of his patients throughout the probation period. Responsibility for arranging for that third person was left with the doctor.

The parents of Dr. Smith's patients were not notified of the hearing or its findings, and public communication was limited to a small notice in the local newspaper. The self-monitoring and limited public communication, especially in light of the doctor's failure to acknowledge any wrongdoing, made the effectiveness of controls over Dr. Smith's practice questionable. Dr. Smith discontinued psychiatric treatment following an evaluation period.

In the meantime, two other cases of past abuse were revealed. The victims were boys who had approached Dr. Smith with problems after a sex education class during which he invited children concerned about sexuality to consult with him. One boy had worries about homosexuality; the other was worried about venereal disease and about whether he had impregnated his girlfriend. These disclosures prompted a reopening of Dr. Smith's case by the state board of registration.

The deliberations of the second hearing, 18 months after the initial disclosure, resulted in Dr. Smith's permanently losing his license to practice medicine. Dr. Smith again refused to admit wrongdoing. During at least part of this time, he had continuing opportunity to molest his young patients.

Dr. Smith demonstrates some of the classic characteristics of pedophilia (Lanning 1984):

- The perpetrators are male.
- They select a particular age and gender of victim.

- They choose professions (medicine) and specialities (adolescent pediatrics) that provide legitimate reasons for sustained (and in the doctor's case, intimate) contact with the children they prefer.
- The perpetrators keep a personal record that permits prompt retrieval of material about their victims.
- They protect themselves.

Several aspects of this case are particularly interesting. First, after being contacted by the parents of the child who first reported the abuse, police contacted the boy's school before even contacting the doctor. The school secretary was asked to check the boy's records, and she found four minor disciplinary infractions. No mention is made in the police records of whether this was done with the permission of the child or his family. The implicit statement in the police action is that the child's behavior in school will have something to do with how the police will respond to the accusation. This means that the victim, rather than the act, is the first line of investigation, at least when the accused is a powerful member of the professional community.

Second, according to Dr. Smith's testimony, he was informed by the state and national offices of the American Academy of Pediatrics and by the American Medical Association that there are no guidelines for dealing with this offense. In light of new estimates of the prevalence of the sexual abuse of children, of the likelihood that the abuser is known and trusted, and of the probability that pedophiles choose positions where they have access to the victims, these organizations have an obligation to establish clearly articulated values and procedures.

Third, following a brief period, the discreet police inquiry stopped. There were no criminal charges or public disclosures. The doctor continued his practice while the board of registration in medicine conducted an investigation that resulted in a closed hearing six months later. These procedures served to protect the physician and his profession, but failed to protect the public.

A final highlight of this case is that Dr. Smith's conduct was found by the board to be improper, inappropriate, and unprofessional. This is tantamount to saying he was a "bad boy" and does no justice to the seriousness of the charges and to the effects of the abuse on the victims. Because there was no public disclosure, Dr. Smith could take a month-long vacation and thus camouflage the suspension. He arranged for his own chaperoning. When the case was reopened after the two previous patients came forward, he stated on deposition that he did not believe that he needed treatment, that what he had done was not wrong, and that his actions had no effects on the children.

A MORAL ANALYSIS OF THE CASE OF DR. SMITH

The issue of morality is not an issue simply for the sexual victimizer, but also for the systems and individuals that respond to the victimization. How do we articulate a framework for moral choice to guide public and private behavior, especially when the interests of powerful adults threaten to obscure the rights and needs of children?

When we examine professional practice and policy in relation to child sexual abuse, moral tensions and conflicts between self-interest and responsibility, and between justice and care, are present. Some of the confusion and conflict surrounding the sexual victimization of children centers on the extent to which we feel we should take public responsibility and, when we do, whether a morality of justice or a morality of care is the appropriate response.

The Conflict Between Self-Interest and Responsibility

The conflict between self-interest and responsibility is generated in this case in at least three ways:

1. Dr. Smith's sexual desires for his patients versus his responsibility to these children as a pediatrician
2. The inferred need on the part of the police to stay in favor with the powerful medical community versus their responsibility to investigate openly a case considered a crime by community standards
3. The desire of the medical community to protect its reputation by secrecy versus its responsibility to the public to protect children from sexual exploitation and to allow parents an informed choice about whether they want their children to be treated by a man who molested other children in his care.

Clearly, each of these was resolved on the side of self-interest.

The first step in applying moral choice is interpersonal awareness, being aware of the effects of actions on others. Dr. Smith appears unable to make that first step, insisting that what he is doing is not wrong and does not affect his patients. That he acted out his own needs, rather than his patients', is clear. Less clear is how self-interest and responsibility are defined by his professional peers, who suspended his license to practice for a brief period but did not take steps to ensure that additional children would not be victimized. Is it self-interested not to inform people that their pediatrician is a pedophile? Does it protect the image of the profession that has the task of judging him? Or does it protect people from the knowledge that caregivers might be capable of hurting them, knowledge that might cause harm if people then fail to seek medical care?

The Conflict Between a Morality of Justice and a Morality of Care

The justice versus care dilemma in child sexual victimization might be articulated as follows: How can we maintain social order and justice while at the same time responding to individual needs for healing and care?

As a society, we are confused about whether to treat adult sex with children as a crime to be punished or as a symptom of pathology to be cured. This confusion has led to a continuing conflict, some people arguing for universal criminalization of child sexual abuse and other people advocating a more family- and treatment-oriented approach.

The conflict between a morality of justice and a morality of care is evident in two aspects of this case:

1. On the part of the police, the conflict was whether to treat this case as any case of sexual molestation would be treated (to apply a standard of equal justice with the consequent exposure of a member of the medical community), or whether to respond to the needs of the medical community by turning the case over to its own governing body.
2. On the part of the board of registration, the conflict was whether to treat this case as a violation of medical conduct, which requires loss of the privileges of the profession, or to approach it as a case of a sick physician who needs to be cured.

The issue of justice or care in relation to the victims appears not to have been considered.

Resolving the Moral Conflicts of Sex with Children

For everyone who must respond to the sexual victimization of children (families of victims, clinical providers, protective workers, members of the criminal justice and judicial systems, and architects of social policy), there is a need to recognize the moral conflicts the victimization presents. Can we face the problem when it conflicts with our own needs and interests? Can we provide justice and not neglect individual needs for healing and care?

Three orientations toward persons and problems can be viewed as characterizing how individuals and institutions have responded to sex with children. We suggest that these orientations define a developmental progression of response to child sexual victimization.

1. An egocentric orientation: The problems of child sexual victimization are avoided, denied, or responded to out of individual need. In the case of Dr. Smith the response was in terms of protecting a powerful profession and a colleague rather than the children.

2. A conventional orientation: Criminal or clinical rules and procedures bind and constrain action on child sexual victimization. Individual differences are not understood or acknowledged. For example, a conventional interpretation of sexual victimization as a criminal act leads to the universal prescription of prosecution and punishment. A conventional interpretation of sexual victimization as psychopathology leads to a universal prescription of psychotherapy. Although responsibility for responding to sex with children is assumed, response tends to be rigid and ideological. In this case, psychotherapy was ordered without considering the doctor's motivation to change. His steadfast belief in the normalcy of his behavior and his consequent failure to follow through with treatment means that unless other options can be considered and applied, children with whom he has contact will continue to be at risk.
3. An individualized orientation: Evaluation of each situation in terms of its own particular needs and realities guides a response that considers the needs of the child for emotional support and protection, the offender's need for corrective intervention, and our institutions' needs to do their jobs. A variety of options are available to be applied in the service of both justice and care.

TOWARD RESPONSIBILITY IN THE CASE OF DR. SMITH

Can we define a response to Dr. Smith's victimization of his patients that will protect children from further abuse and will permit intervention to be both fair and individualized? As a first step, we identify goals of intervention for the four primary constituencies in this case: the community, the medical profession, the victims, and Dr. Smith.

The Constituency	Goals
Community	• To maintain laws that deter others and provide equitable redress for crimes
	• To apply the law without favoritism
	• To protect its population from harm
Medical profession	• To uphold the ethical imperative to do no harm
	• To maintain public trust and confidence
Victims (past and future)	• To have an opportunity to recover from the abuse, and to know the abuse was not their fault
	• To be protected from sexual exploitation
Dr. Smith	• To be removed from situations where he can sexually abuse others
	• To be rehabilitated so as to assure that he assumes responsibility for his acts and will not sexually abuse others

The task of the responding institutions is to identify flexible and realistic options that would satisfy as fully as possible all these goals. Our preference is for a system of interdisciplinary practice, with members from the mental health, law enforcement, legal, and medical communities, to evaluate such cases. The protection of children must be the primary concern, with the protection of the needs of offenders and institutions secondary.

In our opinion, justice was not served by the doctor's treatment as a special case, and the care of children was violated by the failure to inform parents of the risk of child sexual abuse by Dr. Smith. In addition, the goal of rehabilitation was not served by the prescription of mental health treatment in the face of Dr. Smith's denial of a need for change. In this case, criminal action may have been warranted in order to impress upon Dr. Smith the seriousness of his behavior. Strong external controls may be necessary, at least initially, in the face of minimal internal acknowledgment.

Although the ultimate removal of Dr. Smith's license to practice medicine may be a removal from opportunities to abuse children sexually, this action may protect the medical profession more than it protects children from Dr. Smith. He will no longer have access to children as a pediatrician, but it does not prevent access to children in other ways. The power of sexual desires and preferences in pedophiles is extremely strong, and pedophiles often form rings and networks that enable them to have contact with children. In this context, Dr. Smith is a pedophile first and a pediatrician second. He should be treated not as an errant pediatrician, but as a pedophile who remains a threat to children.

REFERENCES

Burgess, A., Hartman, C., McCausland, M., & Powers, P. (1984). Impact of child pornography and sex rings on child victims and their families. In A. Burgess (ed.), *Child Pornography and Sex Rings* (pp. 111–126). Lexington, MA.: Lexington Books.

Finkelhor, D. (1979). *Sexually Victimized Children*. New York: Free Press.

Finkelhor, D. (1984). *Child Sexual Abuse: New Theory and Research*. New York: Free Press.

Lanning, K. (1984). Child pornography and sex rings. Paper presented at the annual meeting of the American Orthopsychiatric Association, Toronto.

Russell, D. (1983). The incidence and prevalence of intrafamilial and extrafamilial sexual abuse of female children. *Child Abuse and Neglect, 7*, 133–46.

Trainor, C. (1984). Sexual maltreatment in the United States: A seven-year perspective. Paper presented at the Fifth International Congress on Child Abuse and Neglect, Montreal.

7

The Politics of Child Sexual Abuse by Professionals: Mental Health Policy, Practice, and Research

Ann W. Burgess, Susan J. Kelley, and Carol R. Hartman

This chapter is about professionals who sexually abuse children. Although there have been many conferences, hearings, and books on the topic of sexual assault, this chapter is about a type of situation that is often difficult to believe—a situation in which a person uses his or her work or professional role to gain sexual access to children.

Sexual victimization in which one person exerts force over another person—legally defined as rape—has been well documented in terms of crime statistics, national surveys, motivational intent of the rapist, and trauma response of the victim. Rape research has aided in refuting the sexual myth that women enjoy rape, has served to increase our understanding of human sexuality, and has provided arguments against the use of psychiatric examination of the victim in sex offense cases.

Sexual victimization, however, in which one person exerts sexual dominance over a person of unequal power or status, has been less adequately addressed in the clinical literature and deals primarily with family member sexual assault (incest) and the child sex industry (sexual abuse). These situations involve child-adult sexual activity—parameters of exploitative behavior that are proscribed by federal and state statutes. This type of abuse involving professionals and multiple children is the focus of our discussion. The implications of such behavior for mental health policy, practice, and research will be examined.

With the current highly publicized accounts of child sexual abuse and our knowledge of the dynamics of adult offending behavior (access, entrapment, sex, silence, and repeat), it should be no surprise that in some cases professionals are identified as the adult offenders. That such abuse occurs within a trusted relationship and is repeated with multiple children is quite compatible with our understanding of the type of adult-child sexual behavior labeled incest.

Sexual abuse occurring in trusted relationships outside the family and involving multiple children has been termed a sex ring (Burgess, Groth, and McCausland, 1981). This type of behavior is defined by the number of adults involved and by their use of the children. A solo ring consists of one adult who is sexually involved with small groups of children. There is no sexual transfer of the children or of child erotica/pornography to other adults. A syndicated ring includes several adults who form a well-structured organization for the recruitment of children, the production of pornography, the delivery of direct sexual services, and the establishment of an extensive network of customers. In a transitional ring there may be more than one adult with several children, and the organizational aspect of the syndicated ring is missing. The transitional ring may be moving toward the organizational status of the syndicated ring; for example, photographs of the children may be sold.

Entrance into a sex ring introduces children to an elaborate socialization process that not only binds them to the ring but also locks them into patterns of learned behaviors. The maintenance of children in the ring is through a distortion of a belief system that convinces the child that activities are "normal" and strongly discourages any challenges to the behavior. This explains, in part, why children do not reveal their involvement to parents and authorities ("I was scared not to do what he said.") and why it is so difficult to leave ("All the kids were doing it."). The leader uses a peer network that forces a pattern of adaptation that perpetuates sexually aggressive and potentially sadistic behaviors.

In the organized rings the sexual abuse of the children by the adult is compounded by the adult's supporting the children's exploitation of each other. The adult acts benevolently and pits the group members against one another, encourages them to act out, and vicariously enjoys the peer sadism. There is a definite hierarchy within the group, and the older, stronger children in the ring harass and abuse the smaller, weaker, and more vulnerable ones.

The adult offenders gain access to the children through a trusted relationship. In our study of 55 sex rings (Burgess, 1984), the offenders were in some manner entrusted to watch or care for the young children. This privilege of trust came from the parents as well as extended family and community institutions, for example, school bus drivers or sports coaches who were part of the school system. The range of trusted caretakers extended to the most privileged professionals, those to whom intimate life issues are exposed for help and care. Three of the ringleaders were physicians—one a child psychiatrist, another a family practitioner, and one a pathologist.

Statements from the children and adolescents clearly revealed that involvement with sex rings and pornography had an impact on their lives. Although the exploiter builds in certain social rewards for the child's participation in the activities, there is a psychological price paid for the attention, money, drugs, and alcohol holding the child hostage to the ring. We found that a child's or adolescent's involvement in a sex ring represented much more than a sexual triumph for the adult. Money and heightened emotional arousal are obtained through the unchallenged position of power held and easily sustained by the adult at the expense of the young person (Burgess et al., 1984).

The following example of a solo sex ring involving a student professional illustrates the problems and issues that arise in such cases.

THE CASE OF MICHAEL

Michael, a nine-year-old black boy, was brought by his mother to the pediatric walk-in clinic of a large urban hospital with a three-day history of headache and abdominal pain. Further history revealed peer withdrawal, irritable behavior with his siblings, disruptive behavior in school, and sleeping and eating problems. Physical examination was negative. When told these results, the mother then related that Michael had mentioned a "homosexual experience" at summer camp. This disclosure embarrassed and frightened Michael, and he refused to talk about the experience. Michael was referred for crisis intervention to a nurse victim counselor who, using drawings in her sessions with Michael, and meeting individually with the mother, obtained the following information.

The summer camp was operated by a nonprofit agency for children from lower socioeconomic backgrounds, the same agency that employed the mother as a homemaker. Thus, the mother was familiar with the sponsoring agency and felt comfortable sending her son for his first overnight experience 150 miles away from home.

Michael described sharing a cabin with 6 other boys, ages 8–10, and their 22-year-old camp counselor, Ben. Michael recalled that Ben initially was very nice to him and bought him candy and other gifts from the canteen. On the second day of camp, Michael said, "Ben got funny with me. He kissed me all over, stuck his hotdog between my legs and squeezed my hotcakes." Michael witnessed Ben abuse the other boys in the cabin. The campers tried a variety of methods to deal with this experience. They tried to avoid Ben (hiding under the bed until Ben left the cabin, and changing their clothes under the covers of their bed), used humor in talking about him (calling him Ben-Gay, and writing a song about him), and labeling him in homosexual terms.

The counselor smoked marijuana in the cabin and offered it to the campers. The campers were threatened that they would not be believed by camp authorities and would be sent back home to be punished by their parents if they disclosed the activity. Additionally, the counselor threatened to reveal their marijuana use if they told.

The crisis intervention with Michael focused on his concerns about his own sexuality and gender identity ("Can you catch being gay?"). He would draw himself without clothes and included prominent genitalia and large breasts; he drew the counselor as an imposing figure with outstretched arms, an erect penis and large breasts. Breasts were drawn on his cartoon characters with this statement, "Charlie Brown is nice but is always getting his ass kicked in," indicating the projection of his own vulnerability and victimization. He referred to Tarzan as "getting gay with Bo Derrick," and another time, in reference to marriage, said that he "was not going to get married just to do *that*, but to have someone cook for him," suggesting cabin conversations between Ben and the campers.

Michael was preoccupied with sex. Initially, all of his human figure drawings involved prominent genitalia. He also drew individual pictures of genitalia with such captions as "dicky" and "pussy." His language and swearing were highly sexual. Michael expressed great fear of Ben, who was white, stating that if he was ever seen in a "white people's neighborhood, I'll run away from him." His aggression was noted in his wanting to take karate lessons so he could "kill Ben," and he stated that if he ever saw Ben again, he would "knock him out with a lucky punch because he got gay with me."

As treatment progressed, Michael's aggressive and avoidant behavior subsided. His school behavior improved and he became asymptomatic. He was discharged after three months of treatment, with telephone follow-up arranged with the mother.

IMPLICATIONS

Mental Health Policy

Follow-up of the camp case revealed the following. Michael's mother was angry and dismayed that a professional with the responsibility of caring for children would violate his position of authority by sexually abusing them. While she was employed by the sponsor of the summer camp program and hesitant to make a complaint, she wanted to protect other children from this counselor. She contacted the director of the agency, reported the incident, and asked for the names of the other children who shared the cabin with Michael, in order to contact their mothers to be certain they were receiving treatment. However, the director refused to give her these names, stating that agency policy on confidentiality prevented such practice. Because he never gave a satisfactory explanation for the incident or of any investigation of the report, the mother asked the nurse counselor what she should do.

With the mother's permission, the nurse called the camp director. He was defensive over the report and said, "I was at the camp the entire summer, and if any such incident occurred, I would have heard about it at that time from the campers." He went on to explain that "the accused camp counselor was a graduate student in social work and as a professional would never molest children and risk ruining his career." The director also made two additional points: (1) that latency-age children fantasize about sexual relationships with adults; (2) there is an overreaction and undue interpretation about sexual contact by adults with children. He agreed to confront the camp counselor with the accusation and stated he would not be rehiring him the following summer. (The counselor denied molesting the campers.)

Michael's mother, not satisfied with the agency's response and believing Ben was a threat to children in the future, contacted local law enforcement officials in the neighboring state where the camp was located. A detective traveled to Boston to interview Michael. However, the boy was unable to talk about the victimization, and the detective felt there was inadequate evidence to proceed with criminal charges. The detective said the complaint would be kept on file.

The following year, Ben received his graduate degree from a prominent social work school and is currently practicing in a major metropolitan agency.

What are the policy implications in this case? Clearly, the agency professionals resisted investigating the complaint and responded with the notion that the exploitation did not occur and that the boy's claims were reasonably explainable. Some professionals do, under a cloak of compassion, minimize and confuse issues and justify acts of exploitation, easily blaming the victim and pointing a finger at colleagues, accusing them of hysteria.

To deal with policy implications requires grappling with the question raised by Carolyn and Eli Newberger (1986): How is it possible for adults to justify having sex with children? The Newbergers give case examples of a variety of professionals who have the welfare of children as their primary responsibility, yet use their positions for the sole purpose of gratifying their desires for sex with children. They then transcend the cases and reflect on the response of the immediate social institutions responsible for addressing the offenses. Their point is that sex is a powerful force, and in our society there is great effort to control sex. Yet when a case is opened up for public reaction, everyone's interests are served except those of the victims. It is their thesis that this level of self-interest reveals the level of moral development operant, and therefore the predictable behaviors.

Using Kohlberg's (1977) stages of moral orientation, the Newbergers derive their own hierarchy of moral response to children. Abusive and exploitative behaviors emanate from dominant self-interest. Taking this same paradigm, they suggest the institutional insensitivity follows similar cognitive constructs. They suggest that the rage reaction and thirst for arrest block the moral imperative that adults are responsible for the well-being of children.

The polarization of self-interest and responsibility blinds efforts to bring just and considerate actions to incidents of child sexual abuse. A classic example is a case where a young girl disclosed a sexually abusive relationship with her father. When it came time for the trial, the child refused to testify against her father. The judge ordered the girl to be put in jail for contempt of court, illustrating the level of moral confusion of the court (the girl is victimized first by the father and second by the court). Another example is a case of a mother who stops her estranged husband from visiting the children because of his history of molesting his children and is imprisoned for interfering with the visitation rules. A third example of this type of confusion of using rules of law rather than evaluating ethical and pragmatic aspects of the sexual abuse of children is the judge who orders a severely abused, institutionalized daughter to live with her father when he remarries, assuming the father will stop his abusive behavior because of his new wife. This type of polarization reflects the immature morality conflicts that do nothing to address the problems of sexual abuse of children. Rather, this division allows sexual exploitation to be carried out at the most prestigious levels of our society. What is perpetuated is confusion and unwitting collusion with the offender. The professional who offends certainly knows the choices he is making. He can make these choices only when he is confident that what he is doing is supported at some level in society.

In the case example, the camp director refuses to investigate and the child's complaints are disqualified. While it is true that there can be damage due to false accusation, it is equally true that victims of abuse are damaged by the lack of response of self-monitoring professional groups. It appears that professional boards are hesitant to investigate complaints, but then act with conviction once a member has been identified as transgressing sexually. There is a naive belief regarding the behavior of the offending professional, with a tendency to excuse, make exceptions, blame the victims, and/or minimize the consequences of the assault. Much of this is based on ignorance of the fact that pedophilic behavior is deeply ingrained and can be manifested by individuals of all levels of intelligence and social accomplishment. The belief patterns of those who sexually molest children are deeply supportive of their behavior. They believe themselves entitled to their sexual proclivity and claim that no harm comes to the child from it. Furthermore, they are convincing, especially to the child, that it is the child's fault, responsibility, and desire for the liaison, even when the victim is arbitrarily selected. When confronted with their behavior, they are clever and bold in denying and confusing others, especially colleagues and adults, as to who is responsible and what happened, going to great lengths to intimidate and confuse the child and the child's parents. When the offender is in a position of trust, as is a physician, money and influence outweigh, most often, the resources of the victim. Consequently, pursuit of the offending professional is dropped or avoided when obstacles to due process are repeatedly encountered.

Professional boards can and should take some responsibility in responding to reports of professional misconduct. First, professional boards, committed to monitoring professional practice, must be prepared to investigate claims of sexual abuse of children. Procedures that are thorough, just, and fair for the claimant and the accused need to be established.

Once the sexual transgression has been established, procedures need to be in place to deal with the offending professional, and decisions need to be made regarding the continuation of the accused's practice. In addition, there should be an interstate registry of disqualified professionals. Too often an institution, to protect itself, allows the professional to resign. Later, in another setting, it is learned that the offending professional's behavior has been known for many years, throughout many agencies.

Careful investigation needs to be carried out in the face of an accusation to make sure the professional has not been implicated in the past. This is a difficult task, but it can be done with care as well as thoroughness. By the same token, the pattern of accusation by the victim needs to be investigated. This means that investigative procedures need to be coordinated with law enforcement activities.

Since victims can charge the professional in a civil suit as well as in a criminal case, cooperation is imperative. Furthermore, the investigation must be seen as benefiting the victim and the professional. If the professional is innocent, this is imperative to establish. If the professional is not innocent, for his or her sake as well as that of others, the behavior must be stopped.

Important to the discussion of implications for policy is the area of legislation. If existing laws are inadequate to protect children against sexual exploitation by professionals, new legislation should be formulated (Davidson, 1983). This would require a review of current state and federal statutes as well as an examination of the role of professional associations in responding to reports of professional misconduct.

Practice

There are two important components of mental health implications for practice: (1) understanding the dynamics of adult abusive behavior, in order to evaluate that such activity can occur, and (2) understanding the impact of such abuse on the developing child, in order for treatment to be effective. The dynamics of child molesters must be appreciated if intervention has any chance of restricting their behavior.

In treating the perpetrator, the deeply ingrained characteristics of behavior, attitude, fantasy, and drive to molest children must be confronted until sufficient dissonance is set between the thought of the act and committing the act. A first step is reducing the arousal level toward children. Next, the complex levels of thought justifying the acts must be challenged, with the result that the offender recognizes, emotionally as well as intellectually, that his behavior hurts, and is harmful, destructive, and egocentric. This treatment phase is critical and no doubt confronts the offender with the rudiments of his or her own prior abuse and neglect as a child. The offender's early failures to engage and participate in pleasant and constructive relationships often precipitate grief and sadness; however, the hope is that the identification of one's vulnerability enhances empathy toward the child, thus reducing the desire to act out sexually. Rehabilitation and socialization toward alternative, positive life experiences is the final phase of intervention.

The education and training of mental health professionals include not only didactics about healthy and deviant behaviors but also an awareness of the self and its influence in the professional relationship. Although the topic of professionals acting upon their sexual feelings within the therapeutic setting has been addressed and a stringent code against such behavior has been developed, it is known that it does occur. Various reasons may exist for such occurrences. For example, the normalizing of sexual activity in various settings and with various persons may have blurred professionals' ability to identify or differentiate sexually abusive colleagues. Thus, mental health implications in this area need to be addressed within curriculum and training guidelines as well as in the supervisory process.

Two facets of training for mental health professionals need to be underscored: (1) training needs to focus on assessment, intervention, and legal testifying in behalf of victims, and (2) training needs to explore and address the moral and ethical responsibilities of professionals toward their relationships with clients. Issues surrounding sexual responses need to be addressed throughout training. Posttraining requirements should encourage peer review, supervision, and consultation. This not only helps develop the professional, but also reduces isolation and a tendency to meet interpersonal needs within the client-professional relationship.

Treatment of childhood sexual abuse is a neglected area in clinical training and textbooks. This neglect reflects the unwitting conclusion that sexual molestation does no harm to children. This societal acceptance of sexual molestation of children is echoed in professional education. It has been only since the early 1980s that the truly negative impact of sexual abuse of children has begun to be documented through research. Thus, models of intervention and their effectiveness need to be introduced, evaluated, and practiced.

Research

Research implications may be reviewed in terms of the adult abuser, the victim, and the criminal justice system. Research on the similarities and differences of professionals who sexually abuse in relation to other types of sex offenders could be undertaken. Experience with child victims suggests that sexually exploiting professionals are similar in their methods, manner of self-defense, and pursuit of exploitation to other compulsively and chronically sexually exploitative people, such as rapists and pedophiles, not usually thought of as being within the professions.

Research is needed on the child witness and the criminal justice system. Even though clinicians, police, and prosecuters may believe that sexual abuse has occurred, evidence may be lacking for criminal prosecution. Difficulties emerge in several areas. First, there is often an inability to obtain hard evidence of sexual abuse, such as photographs of a child in a compromising situation with the offender. Second, cases most often rest solely on the child's testimony. Evidence gained from the child's initial disclosure is often disqualified in court because the interviews were deemed leading or did not establish the child's capacity to distinguish right from wrong or reality from fantasy, or did not distinguish the child's capacity to recall past events with accuracy. Third, the process of facing the accused and the cross-examination creates stress for children. This threat often results in the child's recanting the initial accusation. There is need to explore court proceedings that can protect the child and at the same time not undermine fundamental principles of our legal system (Feron, 1985).

All of these difficulties, in addition to many others, have the potential for negative impact on the child victim. Disclosure plus litigation creates a high level of stress. Research is needed to study the impact of this stress upon recovery from victimization. In addition, research is needed to define methods of investigation and litigation that do not negatively impact on the child.

The criminal prosecution of child sexual abuse cases has an emotional cost to the child. The initial emotional and behavioral reactions demonstrated by the child can be prolonged or intensified when legal proceedings are involved. The literature is replete with case documentation by clinicians, prosecutors, and experts in child sexual abuse that children suffer additional psychological harm due to insensitive legal procedures. When decisions are made to prosecute, the required recounting of their experiences to police and court personnel may frighten children and leave them with the impression that they are guilty (Berliner and Barbieri, 1984).

The defendant-oriented adversarial court system in which the Constitution's Sixth Amendment guarantees the right of the accused to face his accuser places additional responsibility on the child. A child witness does not have any constitutional rights to protection during the investigation or the trial, as the defendant does. But the court does have an obligation to protect the child from undue harm. System-induced trauma to the child witness is appearing as an important issue for the medical, legal, mental health, and social service group (Conte, 1984).

Insensitive interactions, poor interviewing techniques, and mismanagement of cases can result in further trauma to the victim, as well as contribute to delays in prosecution and therapeutic intervention for the child. For those who travel the long and winding court road, major problems can occur in the courtroom in general and with the court appearance of the child witness in particular. While researchers have not investigated whether court proceedings interfere with children's ability to recount what happened, there are good reasons to believe that court appearances inhibit the chances of obtaining accurate and complete testimony from children. Some appropriate topics for research are the long delay between the sexual abuse event(s) and testifying, and its effect on the child's recall; the stressful nature of the courtroom for the child, such as the unfamiliarity of the courtroom, the presence of the defendant, and difficulty understanding questions asked; the increased stress, and the child's increased suggestibility; and the child's loss of confidence, with concomitant decrease in credibility as witness (Goodman and Helgeson, 1985).

In summary, sexual abuse of children by professionals is nested in a complex of social-system relationships that, while establishing rules saying abuse is taboo, confuse the issue by unwittingly supporting abusive acts. This is done by naively anticipating their occurrence and/or minimizing their negative impact. Mental health implications for this problem include a convergence of policy, practice, and research initiatives.

REFERENCES

Berliner, L. & Barbieri, M. D. (1984). The testimony of the child victim of sexual assault. *J Social Issues, 40*(2), 125–37.

Burgess, A. W. (ed.). (1984). *Child pornography and sex rings.* Lexington, MA: Lexington Books.

Burgess, A. W., Groth, A. N., & McCausland, M. P. (1981). Child sex initiation rings. *Am J Orthospychiatry, 51*(1), 110–19.

Burgess, A. W. & Hartman, C. R. (eds.). (1986). *Sexual exploitation of patients by health professionals.* New York: Praeger.

Burgess, A. W., Hartman, C. R., McCausland, M. P., & Powers, P. (1984). Children and adolescents exploited through sex rings and pornography. *Am J Psychiatry, 141*(5), 656–62.

Conte, J. R. (1984). Progress in treating sexual abuse of children. *Social Work* (May-June), 258–63.

Davidson, H. A. (1983). *Child sexual exploitation: Background and legal analysis.* Washington, D.C.: American Bar Association.

Feron, J. (1985, October 25). No indictments in sex abuse case at West Point. *New York Times*.

Goodman, G. S. & Helgeson, V. S. (1985). Child sexual assault: Children's memory and the law. In J. Bulkley (ed.), *Papers from a national policy conference on legal reforms in child sexual assault cases*. Washington, D.C.: American Bar Association.

Kohlberg, L. (1977). Recent research in moral development. New York: Holt, Rinehart, and Winston.

Newberger, C. M. & Newberger, E. (1986). When the pediatrician is a pedophile. In A. Burgess & C. Hartman (eds.), *Sexual exploitation of patients by health professionals*. New York: Praeger.

8

Sexual Abuse by Professionals: A Case Study of the Interaction between Legal and Cultural Factors in Seeking Criminal Prosecution and Civil Damages

Paul J. Hebert

This case study involves the handling of 13 children's claims against the Catholic Diocese of Lafayette, Louisiana, and a Catholic priest, Father Gilbert Gauthe, who was accused and convicted of abusing these and other children over the course of 7 years. All of the cases were filed in the 15th Judicial District Court, for the parish of Vermilion, Louisiana, and were either settled out of court or during the course of the selection of the jury.

Father Gauthe sexually molested more than 35 minor children over the course of a 5-year period as pastor of a small rural church in the parish of Vermilion, Louisiana. The knowledge of this particular claim was brought to the author's attention by a client in June 1983. Shortly thereafter, within the course of three working days, the priest was removed from his position as pastor, and since then has been institutionalized in a variety of religious-oriented mental health facilities. In 1984, Father Gauthe was convicted of several crimes involving minor children, resulting in a 20-year sentence without parole and his voluntary consent to chemical castration by means of the drug Depo Provera.

It is important to note that this occurred in an area of southwest Louisiana that has a predominantly Catholic population. It has obviously been an extremely emotional case not only from the standpoint of the victims and their parents but also from the position of the defendant, the Catholic Church.

The handling of a child sexual abuse claim is extremely difficult with only one client; however, when there are several clients sexually abused by the same professional, the emotions are heightened. Further, the problems become magnified. Initially, the different types of personalities involved make the case extremely difficult to handle in a normal fashion. Although the handling of a claim can, in some respects, be compared with a regular tortious injury (such as an auto accident), the emotional factors involved present a large number of problems that have to be dealt with by the attorney personally as the claim is being prosecuted. The most important point to deal with on behalf of the client is the removal of the perpetrator from his professional role. This was not as difficult in the case of Father Gauthe as it may be in the case of another professional (such as a psychologist or a lawyer), since the institutional Church, after being presented with information and factual evidence, took immediate action to remove the priest from his appointed position. Even so, the span of three days, which was due to administrative delay, caused me a great deal of mental concern because of the fear of reprisal against the perpetrator.

Obviously, in the case of a professional abuser, we are often dealing with a nonfamily member as the perpetrator. It is therefore important that the attorney be prepared to face serious emotional questions relating to the physical reaction by the parents or guardians of the minor child against the perpetrator. This issue was of paramount importance in Vermilion and required immediate action to avoid physical conflict and the possibility of resulting crimes. We have seen a recent example in the press of a perpetrator being killed in an airport by a father who suspected this professional (a karate instructor) of abusing his minor child. As an aside, that case ended with the jury in Baton Rouge, Louisiana, finding the father guilty of manslaughter. He was sentenced to five years in prison, two of which he will serve. While the father's anguish over the abuse of his child was understandable, light sentences such as these may further encourage vigilante actions, thereby endangering the lives of those who are accused.

In Father Gauthe's case, the initial fear of physical violence was very great and required immediate attention by the institutional Church. This will always be the initial confrontation in all cases involving professional abuse, regardless of setting. Specifically, the institution, when informed, should, if the facts are substantiated, take appropriate action to protect not only the child victim but also the perpetrator of the crime. Once the attorney has successfully removed the perpetrator from the community and has received the assurance from his employer that he is in an appropriate facility or has been arrested and placed under bond, the attorney must direct his clients toward the criminal and civil prosecution of that claim.

PRACTICAL PROBLEMS IN THE CRIMINAL PROSECUTION OF PROFESSIONAL PERPETRATORS

Initially, the counsel or attorney for child abuse victims has to recognize that there are two methods of proceeding to resolve the rights of the victim and the rights of the state. The criminal prosecution of a perpetrator is one option, and is dependent on the facts of the case and the state laws that have been enacted controlling this situation.

However, criminal prosecution as an initial step is painstakingly slow and contains many formal legal proceedings. These proceedings tend to reduce the confidence of the parents and minor victims that justice will be the outcome of this process. Nevertheless, in a crime such as the one committed, it was not very difficult for the parents and victims to realize the importance of proceeding with the criminal process. This is especially true when it became apparent to them that this particular pedophile had molested children in the course of his professional duties as a priest in three other Church parishes prior to his placement in Vermilion Parish.

In these cases the criminal indictment of the defendant priest was not submitted or rendered to a grand jury until some 14 months after the initially reported incident. The reasons for this were twofold.

The priest and the institutional Church initially generated a great deal of emotion among the parents and children in making the choice of proceeding criminally against a priest. Normally the anger and frustration surrounding such crimes allow the client to immediately and strongly pursue criminal charges. However, that is easier said than done, and it may be that the child abuse claim against a "professional" is often delayed because of the professional's image not only in the community but also in the eyes of the parents and victims.

Further, there are the normal fears of any child victim witness in the criminal prosecution of a claim. The publicity surrounding such cases, along with the possibility of courtrooms and grand jury testimony, makes it extremely difficult to prepare the child victim for these anxious and difficult events. Nevertheless, the anxiety can be lessened, and has been reduced by the education of parents as to the occurrence and effect of sexual abuse. It is becoming readily apparent that the educational process that is ongoing relative to sexual abuse of minor children is aiding those children and their parents in making the decisions to criminally prosecute a professional. For the children involved in this case, it also was of great benefit that the district attorney's office provided investigators who were compassionate to the circumstances of their abuse. These investigators did their job not only professionally but also in a manner that protected the confidentiality of the child victims.

Some of the advantages and disadvantages of criminal proceedings are listed below.

Advantages of the criminal proceeding include the following:

1. The victims are protected from further abuse or fear of abuse.
2. Civil litigation claims are solidified because the criminal investigation and indictment in most cases establish that abuse occurred.

3. In most cases, it will carry the burden of publicity for the victim, especially when an institution is a defendant, since the minor victim's identity is very well guarded by criminal statutes.
4. The successful conclusion of a criminal proceeding lessens the victim's future concerns over risk of confrontation with the perpetrator.

Among disadvantages of the criminal proceeding are the following:

1. The process is extremely slow.
2. The awkwardness of the criminal proceedings and the rights of the perpetrator as established by our Constitution often leave the victims feeling that they are on trial.
3. There is an influx of strangers, who may not be educated as to the affects of child abuse, handling the investigation in, for example, the district attorney's office.
4. It is difficult to have the minor child victim express accurately the crimes that occurred.

PROCEEDINGS AGAINST A WELL-ESTABLISHED INSTITUTION FOR CIVIL DAMAGES

Since the inception of the claims in June 1983, there have been rapidly increasing numbers of claims against institutions arising out of sexual abuse by their professional employees. In fact, at present, in southwest Louisiana approximately ten other claims involving either minor children or majors who claim to have been sexually abused by other priests are pending. In this particular case, the initial steps in handling the claim were not originally directed toward civil liability and damages. It was only after the clients came to realize that the institutional defendant, the Church, would not admit any wrongdoing for the actions of this priest, nor make an effort to contact the parents of children possibly abused by this priest, that civil litigation was discussed.

Institutional liability, however, is not automatic. There must be a connection between the professional abuser and his or her employment activities. However, if it is possible to establish that foundation, then the imposition of liability against the institution is established by a variety of legal doctrines (such as respondent superior, where the employer is liable for the acts of the employee in the course and scope of his or her employment). In addition, if it is possible to establish that the superiors or administrative officers of the institution had knowledge or should have had knowledge of the propensities of the professional toward such acts, then one may impose direct liability not only on the institution but also on the particular officers of the defendant corporation.

In this particular case, it took approximately eight weeks to realize that the resolution of the claim as previously stated was not going to be accomplished, and at that point investigative work was begun to determine whether legal liability could be imposed. In this situation it did not take long to uncover a variety of incidents where the priest had perpetrated similar acts against minor children in other Church parishes, the knowledge of which had been presented to Church superiors over the course of seven years. However, the most significant finding was that this particular priest had been treated by a psychiatrist in 1977 for these exact problems.

As the attorney representing these children, it was imperative for me to realize that the effects of this priest's abuse included significant damages to my clients that were especially heightened due to the authorization and omnipotent appreciation they had of the priest.

Before proceeding with the civil suit, it is necessary to confirm, through the psychologist treating the claimant, the acts of abuse. The nature of such claims carries with it a great deal of publicity, and failure by the attorney to properly investigate the claim or accusations is tantamount to malpractice. Therefore, it is mandatory that the child victim be psychologically evaluated and treated for several months before civil litigation is commenced. This statement is made strongly because when a child has been abused by a professional such as a priest/teacher, it often takes this much time to get an accurate picture of what has occurred.

We must realize that in many cases the child victim, when abused by a professional, is not able to trust other professionals. It therefore becomes extremely difficult to establish a normal relationship with the client whereby he or she is able to discuss the circumstances that occurred. It is imperative that immediate medical treatment for the victim be provided, and that this treatment include the family.

As the civil claim develops against a defendant institution, it is important that the attorney prepare his or her clients for the reaction of the public, which has limited knowledge of the facts and the particulars involved in the claim. This is obviously true when the entity is the predominant religious faith in the community. From my experience, it is important that publicity of the victims should be protected against by the attorney at all costs. This goal was accomplished by sealing the records with a court order. This was contested by opposing attorneys, and the Louisiana Supreme Court upheld the seals insofar as the confidentiality of the victims was concerned, and further prevented public inspection of the records without prior court approval. Client communication with the media is not recommended in cases where an institutional defendant is involved, since the clients are not prepared to deal with the media, nor are they capable of making decisions spontaneously without adequate preparation. The claim that is being presented may involve a request for damages on behalf of the parents as well as the child, and the effect of the publicity must be considered in the overall presentation of the case. Generally, publicity may provide some benefit through educating the public, but in most cases it creates a serious misunderstanding of the true facts of the incident. It is therefore recommended that attorneys who handle such cases be prepared to deal with the media directly, protecting their clients from this exposure and further requesting that the media seek interviews with the institutional defendants and make this expression known to the public.

The advantages of the prosecution of a civil case are numerous:

1. Immediate medical attention will, in most cases, be provided to the family and victim.
2. The possible recovery of monetary damages will provide some method of redressing the wrong that has been committed against the child victim and the family.
3. The education of the family and the child victim as to the cause and effects of child abuse reduces the possibility of further occurrences.
4. Through conferences with medical personnel, attorneys, social workers, and other professionals the minor victim's ability to trust will be reestablished.
5. The professional will be removed from his or her occupation.
6. Additional violence by either the victim or parents against the perpetrator will be prevented.

CONCLUSION

Eleven of the child victims in this case have had their claims settled either prior to filing of the lawsuit or during the selection of the jury. The amounts of these settlements are not available for public disclosure. Nevertheless, it is clear that without the legal profession's involvement in these cases, it would have been very difficult, if not impossible, for the parents of the victims to properly address the issues we have discussed here and obtain any satisfactory resolution.

Part III

Legal Sanctions for Professional Misconduct

9

Failure to Report Child Abuse: Legal Penalties and Emerging Issues

Howard Davidson

> Any person [who is] required . . . to report known or suspected child abuse . . . who knowingly and willfully fails to . . . shall be guilty of a misdemeanor and shall be civilly liable for the damages proximately caused by such failure.[1]

Since the first state mandatory child abuse and neglect reporting laws were enacted in the early 1960s, there has been a steady increase in the number of "mandated" professionals who are obligated to report known or suspected child maltreatment. Since 1967, all states have had such laws, and in most of these states physicians, dentists, interns, nurses, psychologists, teachers and other school personnel, social workers, law enforcement officers, and personnel in childcare programs are now specifically identified as being required to report.

To address the major legal impediments that have inhibited reporting, (a) every state has provided statutory immunity to the reporter, thus providing an absolute defense to the professional who is sued as a consequence of fulfilling in good faith the reporting obligations; (b) most states have abolished the doctor-patient and therapist-client privilege in all child abuse-related situations; (c) many states have laws that shield the reporter from having his or her identity revealed; and (d) a few states provide protection to reporters from any job-related sanctions based on the decision to report, and preventing any supervisor from interfering with the making of the report.

CIVIL LIABILITY FOR FAILURE TO REPORT

In 1970, a five-month-old boy was brought to a hospital in San Luis Obispo, California, on several occasions with what appeared to be nonaccidental injuries. Each time he was released to his mother and her boyfriend.

Finally, after he had suffered permanent brain damage in a beating, his father filed suit for $5 million against the nonreporting doctors. In 1972, the suit was settled when the doctors' insurance companies agreed to establish a $600,000 trust fund to provide lifelong care for the now severely retarded, institutionalized boy. This may have been the first failure-to-report lawsuit in the country to be filed and resolved.

The earliest, and still most significant, reported appellate court decision to suggest that nonreporters could be held legally responsible for injuries later sustained by a child after negligently failing to report child abuse was *Landeros* v. *Flood*.[2] In this medical malpractice action, a guardian *ad litem* filed suit on behalf of an 11-month-old girl who in 1971 had been examined by a physician in a hospital and released without any child abuse report having been made. Soon after, her mother's common law husband beat the child severely, resulting in painful permanent injuries. The claim against Doctor Flood and the San Jose Hospital was that there was an improper diagnosis of the child's condition at the time of her earlier examination, and that proper medical treatment would have included reporting her as exhibiting "the medical condition known as the battered child syndrome."

In this case, the California Supreme Court recognized that a mandatory child abuse reporting law existed in 1971, that in that same year another California court had allowed expert testimony on the "battered child syndrome," and that the syndrome had then become an accepted medical diagnosis. In the years previous to the *Landeros* decision, several legal commentators had written persuasive articles supporting the theory of malpractice liability for failure to report child abuse, and by 1976 the court was prepared to state that both a physician and a hospital could be held liable for injuries sustained by a child if they failed to diagnose and report the battered child syndrome.

However, it is interesting to note that the reporting law applicable to the *Landeros* situation required a report *only* where a child was brought before a physician "for diagnosis, examination or treatment" and where "from observation of the minor" there *appeared* to be nonaccidental inflicted injuries. That law has since been revised, but in 1976 the court construed this language as requiring proof before a finding against the doctor could be made that (a) the doctor had *actually observed* the child's injuries and (b) the doctor had formed the *opinion* that they were intentionally inflicted and yet didn't report. Today, most state reporting laws require only "reason to suspect" or a "suspicion" of abuse, so a nonreporting physician can be held civilly liable without proving his or her actual observation of the injuries and a conclusion that they were inflicted (that is, what his or her state of mind was). In short, because of the language used in the law at that time, the *Landeros* case suggested that the doctor could only be held liable if he *intentionally* rather than negligently failed to report.

In 1981, the U.S. Court of Appeals in New York issued another important opinion related to the failure to report child abuse. Here, a federal civil rights action seeking damages had been brought on behalf of a teenage girl who, it was claimed, had continued to be sexually abused by a foster parent because workers in a private agency supervising the placement failed to report child abuse pursuant to the New York State reporting law.[3] The court held that the placement agency's failure to report to the Department of Social Services an expert's conclusion that the child was sexually involved with her foster father resulted in her remaining in the abusive home for several more years. Such actions were considered by the court as appropriate evidence of a violation of the child's civil rights. In addition, the court ruled that a lower court hearing this case was wrong in excluding from evidence a memo from the public child protection agency that reminded private placement agencies of their duty to report suspected abuse and suggested that agency directors review the reporting law with their staff.

An issue in all these failure-to-report suits is the legal concept of "proximate cause." Simply stated, defendants in these cases typically assert that even if the failure to report is conceded, some other intervening act (unanticipated continued abuse) should relieve the nonreporting of liability, particularly since the professional could not have known for certain what would ultimately happen to the child. In *Landeros*, the court concluded that if the professional not reporting should have "reasonably foreseen" that the child's caretaker would resume abuse, then liability could still be applied. The proximate-cause test can become a critical factor in some failure-to-report cases. For example, in a $1 million wrongful death suit filed in the Richland County, South Carolina, Court of Common Pleas, a hospital staff's failure to diagnose and report physical abuse of a child admitted to the facility was alleged to have resulted in further abuse of the child, who "was caused to and did take his own life."[4] It is likely that in such a case the hospital would argue that the child's suicide was an intervening act that the hospital staff could not have reasonably foreseen and that this should absolve them of liability.

JUDICIAL INTERPRETATIONS OF THE REPORTING OBLIGATION

Although the laws on child abuse reporting are not without weaknesses, which will be addressed later, there are no reported court decisions that have frustrated their intent by rendering them unconstitutional or by nullifying them as violative of the principle of professional privilege, of confidentiality, or of the privacy rights of patients. On the contrary, in the case of *People* v. *Stritzinger*,[5] the California Supreme Court held that the state's mandatory reporting law took precedence over the psychotherapist-patient privilege due to the interest of the state in detection and prevention of child abuse. One year later, a California Court of Appeals upheld the reporting law from a challenge that it unconstitutionally interfered with a person's right to seek treatment for an illness and forced that person to become a witness against himself. In this case, *People* v. *Younghanz*,[6] the court affirmed a father's conviction for child molestation that was based on disclosures he made at a clinic following a warning by a physician that the law required him to report such a revelation.

In *State* v. *Odenbrett*,[7] the Supreme Court of Minnesota upheld a man's child sexual assault conviction that was based on his revelation of the abuse to a health center therapist who then reported to the child protective services agency. Again, the defendant's claims of a breach in the physician-patient privilege and a violation of his right to privacy were denied. One other interesting challenge to mandatory reporting laws should be noted. In a rare written judicial decision arising out of a challenge to a criminal prosecution for failing to report child abuse, the Denver, Colorado, County Court held that the mandatory reporting law was not unconstitutionally vague or overbroad in requiring a report of sexual abuse based only on "reasonable cause to know or suspect" abuse. In so holding, the court was affirming that a mandated reporter must report even a mere suspicion, rather than only actual knowledge, of abuse. In that case, *People* v. *Poremba*,[8] the court also rejected the defendant's arguments that (1) the reporting law violated his right to equal protection under the law, since only certain professionals were required to report, and (2) that the term "mental health professional" in the reporting law was not specifically defined, and thus people like the defendant (a psychologist) could not be sure the law applied to them.

The *Poremba* case is one of the few written court decisions based on a criminal prosecution of a person for failure to report child abuse. Extensive research disclosed only three other published cases in this area.[9] These are all appellate court decisions that in some way relate to a prosecution for failure to report, but they do not thoroughly analyze the issue or even uphold a lower court conviction for failure to report. The dearth of related litigation suggests that criminal prosecutions for failure to report are indeed as rare as most suspect; although such prosecutions have been threatened or initiated by local district attorneys, convictions and actual penalties are almost unheard of. Criminal penalties for failure to report do exist legislatively in all states except Maryland, Mississippi, North Carolina, and Wyoming. The extent of potential penalties ranges from a maximum fine of up to $1000 (in California and Massachusetts) to up to a year in jail (in Rhode Island). All of these criminal laws make failure to report a misdemeanor rather than a felony.

A number of interesting lawsuits have been brought to challenge certain reporting practices under the laws. In *April K.* v. *Boston Children's Service Association*,[10] the U.S. District Court in Massachusetts refused to accept a contention that a parent's civil rights were violated because a child abuse report was made without the reporter having had contact with the involved children or the alleged perpetrators.

In a suit entitled *Planned Parenthood Affiliates of California* v. *Van de Kamp*,[11] a California Court of Appeals ruled that the state's mandatory reporting law did *not* require health care professionals treating children under 14 for pregnancy or sexually transmitted diseases to report as "abused" such children who have been involved in voluntary consensual sexual activities rather than actual sexual abuse.

In California a child under 14 cannot *legally* consent to sexual contact, and thus any such contact was, in the opinion of the state attorney general, technically abuse. The attorney general had issued a formal opinion that persons treating or counseling a child under 14 for prenatal care, an abortion, or sexually transmitted disease (or where a child seeking contraceptives indicated that (s)he had been sexually active) *must* report the child as abused. The stated reason for this was that the crime of "lewd and lascivious acts" with a child under 14 could reasonably be considered by the professional to have occurred in such situations.[12] On September 13, 1985, the court issued an order temporarily enjoining the implementation and enforcement of this opinion, awaiting further legal action in the case, and on May 21, 1986, the court restrained enforcement of the child abuse reporting law as it applies to voluntary sexual conduct of minors under age 14.

Another case in which reporting laws were challenged through a lawsuit is *Pennsylvania State Education Association* v. *Commonwealth*.[13] Here, the court ruled that the mandatory reporting law did *not* apply in cases where teachers were the *alleged perpetrators* of child abuse. The court held that where the law required reports of abuse committed by "a person responsible for the child's welfare," this phrase was not contemplated by the Pennsylvania legislature to include public school teachers. That phrase, or one similar to it, appears in many state child abuse laws, as well as the federal Child Abuse Prevention and Treatment Act (42 U.S.C. Sec. 5101). Thus, under the rationale of this case, abuse by school employees, daycare center staff, or institutional personnel might be considered to fall outside of many mandatory reporting laws. To remedy this, Congress in 1984 amended the federal act to encourage states to include under their mandatory reporting laws abuse committed by persons providing "out-of-home care." States are slowly beginning to amend their laws accordingly. Unlike Pennsylvania, there are a number of states where the child abuse reporting laws apply when *any person* inflicts a physical injury on a child.[14]

Another gap in the effective scope of the mandatory reporting laws concerns revelations of abuse that are made by perpetrators during their counseling, therapy, or other treatment. In a number of states, the reporting obligation applies only to professionals who learn of abuse in the course of examining, attending, or treating *a child*. Thus, in those states, an admission by an adult that he has molested a child need *not* be reported if the recipient of this admission has not *also* seen the child in a professional capacity. This is a powerful barrier to reporting by psychologists, psychiatrists, and other therapists. Indeed, in *State* v. *Groff*,[15] a court decided that a psychiatrist could not be convicted under the state's criminal failure-to-report law because he was not "serving children" (the words used in the reporting law), but was treating the abused child's father.

Still another factor that once inhibited the reporting of abuse relates to professionals who see abusing adults in federally supported alcohol and drug abuse programs. Federal laws and regulations had restricted disclosure of information concerning patients in these facilities.[16] Several official state attorney general opinions also pronounced that federal substance abuse treatment laws preempt their state's mandatory child abuse reporting law,[17] but the Iowa opinion suggested that mandatory reporting would still be required if the report did not reveal any adult or child named in the report *as a patient in the facility*. The Minnesota Supreme Court, in *State* v. *Andring*,[18] ruled that the federal alcohol and drug abuse law did *not* preempt the state's reporting law, since the latter was mandated by still another federal statute (the Child Abuse Prevention and Treatment Act). Congress has since amended the federal Public Health Service Act so that confidentiality and privacy provisions "do not apply to the reporting under State law . . . of suspected child abuse or neglect."

PROFESSIONAL ETHICS AND DISCIPLINARY SYSTEM ISSUES

An American Bar Association (ABA) survey of professional association ethical opinions and licensing body actions disclosed a few interesting matters that are related to failure to report child abuse. The New Jersey State Bar issued an ethics opinion[19] that responded to the following dilemma. An attorney was retained by a woman who was the subject of an action by a child welfare agency to remove custody of her children. According to the opinion, if in the course of his representation, an attorney learns of facts that demonstrate the "continuing unfitness of the mother," his misrepresentation to the court of the mother's fitness would "probably constitute fraud on the court," and the attorney should "disclose his information" to the agency.

The Missouri State Bar took a different approach to a variation on this dilemma.[20] In the course of a divorce action, an attorney for a mother learned from both the mother and one of her children of child abuse committed by the father. Soon after, the mother asked the attorney to dismiss the divorce action because she and her husband had gotten back together. According to the opinion, if an attorney "believes that there is a present danger of the acts of child abuse being repeated in the future," the attorney *can* (the opinion does not say "must") reveal the information received from the child, but *not* information revealed exclusively by his client, the mother.

The Alabama State Bar issued an opinion based on still another variation of the lawyer's duty to reveal knowledge of child abuse.[21] An attorney was appointed by a court to represent a child as guardian *ad litem* in a sexual abuse case. Shortly thereafter, the child's mother revealed to the attorney that in *another proceeding* she was going to seek to stop visitation by the allegedly abusive father. The attorney asked the Bar for an opinion as to whether he could testify about the abuse revelations by his child client at the hearing on visitation. The opinion stated that as guardian *ad litem* the attorney could testify if he considered it to be in the best interests of the child to do so, despite the fact that the child was too young to intelligently waive the lawyer-client privilege. However, the opinion did include a caution that in order to testify, the attorney would have to conclude that *if* the child had the capacity to waive the privilege, she would do so.

Finally, the State Bar of Michigan Professional and Judicial Ethics Committee issued an opinion involving an attorney who had been appointed as guardian *ad litem* for a child in a sexual abuse case.[22] Here, the attorney, while preparing the case, learned that a counseling agency previously contacted by the family had illegally failed to report the abuse, thus allowing it to continue. He asked the Bar whether he could ethically represent that child in a second case, a damage action on behalf of the child against the counseling agency for failure to report. The Bar said that this was permissible, and that the attorney could assume the representation in the second case on a contingent fee basis.

The ABA survey did not produce any cases of disciplinary action taken against an attorney for failure to report child abuse (only three states—Mississippi, Nevada, and Ohio—include attorneys in their mandatory reporting laws). However, the Washington State Medical Disciplinary Board did indicate that action had been considered against one physician who failed to report possible abuse, but that in August 1985 this doctor was merely counseled that "you recognize the necessity for compliance in reporting child abuse [and] . . . that you modify your rationale in such cases."

In a letter to the ABA from the Utah Division of Occupational and Professional Licensing, the respondent noted that in the past ten years one physician was disciplined by the Utah Physician's Licensing Board for failure to report. In this case, which involved a child under the physician's care who had been abused by the child's parent, the doctor was reprimanded. Finally, the Louisiana State Board of Board Certified Social Work Examiners reported that hearings on two social workers who failed to report abuse led to a Board sanction that they be required to "complete additional education in the area of child abuse."

In the field of education, the California Commission on Teacher Credentialing has asserted that it will "take a hard line" on disciplining teachers and school administrators who fail to report suspected child abusers in the schools, including dismissals in appropriate cases.[23] This position was taken after revelation of a well-publicized Los Angeles elementary school case in which the district attorney was investigating failures to report suspected molestation by a teacher and parents from that school had filed a $110 million suit against the Los Angeles Unified School District.

LEGISLATIVE REFORMS

Several states have enacted unusual laws to further encourage reporting of child abuse by professionals. In California, all persons entering into employment after January 1, 1985, as a teacher, childcare worker, or medical practitioner, as a prerequisite of employment must sign a statement on a form provided by the employer that they have knowledge of the mandatory reporting law and will comply with its provisions.[24] Under another California law, a court-appointed attorney for a child in an abuse case is required to report to the court any potential civil action against a professional who failed to report that abuse, and consideration may then be given to appropriate legal action against the nonreporter.[25]

In Florida, since March 1, 1985, all school boards have been required to prominently post notices that all school employees have a duty to report child abuse, including on the notice a toll-free phone number to be used in reporting.[26] As a result of another Florida law, as of March 1, 1985, all of the state's hospitals and public health facilities must have written protocols that incorporate reporting responsibilities into their official policies.[27]

Illinois has enacted two relevant laws. In the first, any physician who willfully fails to report suspected child abuse or neglect must be referred to the state's Medical Disciplinary Board for potential action.[28] In the second law, failure to report abuse or neglect has been added to the list of reasons for revocation or refusal to review the license of a childcare facility.[29]

CONCLUSION

Surveys of professionals provide a number of reasons for their nonreporting of child abuse. Some of these include a failure to identify abuse caused by a lack of education on the subject; a belief that reporting will do no good for the child and family, and may even do harm, given some negative perceptions about the functioning of child protective service agencies; and a concern that reporting is a betrayal of trust and a breach of the professional relationship that will sever the therapeutic ties that could have helped the abuser to correct his/her behavior while overseeing the safety of the child.

None of these barriers to reporting can be removed through legislative action or selective litigation against the nonreporter. There are, however, a few additional legal reforms not mentioned earlier that might help encourage more reporting:

1. A requirement that child protective service agencies provide feedback to the reporter on the actions taken as a consequence of the report, thus helping reporters to better understand the response of these agencies
2. An extension of the principle of immunity from liability as a result of reporting, which would encompass all other activities the reporter might have to undertake as a result of a report, such as involvement in the investigation, providing access to relevant treatment records, participation in case consultations with prosecutors and multidisciplinary teams, and testifying in court
3. The right to be reimbursed by the state for attorney's fees that might be incurred by the reporter as a result of a lawsuit brought against him/her for the reporting
4. The creation of a special legal cause of action for the reporter to sue anyone who takes any adverse job-related action against him or her for exercising the legal obligation to report.

Of course, legislative policy changes in the area of reporting alone will not cure the fundamental distrust and dislike that many professionals have for the child protective system. Thus, policy makers must also be attentive to the need to improve the legislative framework, which will assure the prompt delivery of appropriate services to abused children and their families, the prompt resolution of child abuse-related judicial proceedings, and the full protection under the law of the rights of children, parents, and professionals alike who become involved in the complex process of state intervention in the family.

NOTES

1. Sec. 12, *Child Protection: A Guide for State Legislation* (HHS, 1983).
2. 551 P.2d 389 (Cal. 1976).
3. *Doe* v. *N. Y. City Department of Social Services*, 649 F.2d 134 (1981).
4. *King* v. *Providence Hospital*, no. 85CP405037, filed November 6, 1985.
5. 668 P.2d 738 (Cal. 1983).
6. 202 Cal. Rptr. 907 (Cal. App. 4 Dist. 1984).
7. 349 N.W.2d 265 (Minn. 1984).
8. 7 FLR 2142 (1981).
9. *State* v. *Boucher*, 468 A.2d 1227 (R.I. 1983); *Florida* v. *Groth*, 409 So.2d 44 (Fla. App. 1981); *Gardner* v. *Sheriff*, 571 P.2d 109 (Nev. 1977).
10. 581 F.Supp. 711 (1984).
11. 226 Cal. Rptr. 361 (1986).
12. Opinion of the Cal. Attorney General, no. 83-911 (June 1, 1984).
13. 449 A.2d 89 (Pa. Cmwlth. 1982).

14. For instance, Cal. Penal Code, sec. 11165(g).
15. 409 So.2d 45 (Fla. App. 1981).
16. 42 U.S.C. sec. 4582; 21 U.S.C. sec. 1175; 42 C.F.R. Pt. 2.
17. Iowa Attorney General Opinion no. 83-11-3; Cal. Attorney General Opinion no. 83-812.
18. 342 N.W.2d 128 (Minn. 1984).
19. No. 280, 1974.
20. Informal opinion 6, July 28, 1978.
21. Ethics Opinion RO-85-99, September 27, 1985.
22. CI-1016, July 9, 1984.
23. *Education Week*, August 21, 1985, p. 8.
24. Cal. Penal Code, sec. 11166.5.
25. Cal. Welf. and Inst. Code, sec. 318(d).
26. Fla. Stat. Ann., sec. 230.23 (18).
27. Fla. Stat. Ann., sec. 339.005.
28. Ill. Stat., ch. 23, sec. 2054.02.
29. Ill. Stat., ch. 23, sec. 2218. Also, in Maryland, there are several recent laws affecting professionals who fail to report. Police officers can lose their certification, school employees can be dismissed, and physicians, social workers, and nurses can lose their licenses if they knowingly fail to report suspected child abuse. Md. Code art. 41, sec. 4-201(d) (7); Occ. Code, sec. 14-504(27), 18-310(15), and 7-313(a).

10

Civil Damages Suits against Professionals in Cases of Child Sexual Abuse

Ross Eatman

The treatment of child victims in the investigation and criminal prosecution of sexual abuse cases has been the subject of sweeping legal reforms since the early 1980s.[1] These reforms generally were intended to sensitize the criminal justice system to the special needs of child victims and to minimize the trauma children suffer through their involvement with the criminal justice system.[2] In a parallel development, sexual assault victims generally (and others affected by criminal victimization) have increasingly sought redress against criminal perpetrators through civil litigation.[3] Presumably, the heightening of public awareness of child abuse, the increase in reports of such abuse, and the vigorous criminal prosecution of offenders will be reflected in a greater number of civil damages suits against abusers of children.

A civil damages suit affords a victim relief not available through other means. A primary objective of a civil damages suit is to procure financial compensation for the victim. The benefits of a damages suit accrue directly to the victim, unlike disciplinary or criminal sanctions, which usually focus more on punishment of the perpetrator. The sexual abuse of a child may cause physical and emotional trauma requiring long-term therapy. The compensatory element of a damages award may mitigate the impact of such injuries by covering the victim's expenses. A punitive damages award may serve to deter future abuse. Finally, a successful result in a civil damages suit may serve as a vindication of the victim's rights and as a clear legal pronouncement of the abuser's fault. As with a conviction in a criminal case, this may be especially significant for child victims, since as a result of the disclosure and investigation of the abuse, a child may perceive himself or herself as the wrongdoer rather than as the victim.[4]

In bringing a civil damages action, a victim initiates proceedings that more closely approximate legal "self-help" than do other types of proceedings. The plaintiff initiates a civil action by bringing suit, and with counsel determines which witnesses and evidence to introduce in support of his or her claim. In the criminal justice system, on the other hand, the prosecutor has the discretion to dismiss a case and, in the first instance, to determine whether to process the victim's complaint for prosecution. Where the perpetrator of abuse is a professional or licensed caregiver, disciplinary and licensing review boards may also fail to serve the victim's interest adequately.

A child victim's parents (or guardian) and counsel, however, should carefully assess the potential impact of civil litigation on the child before initiating a lawsuit on the child's behalf. A civil damages suit may require the child's protracted involvement with the legal system. Civil litigation may involve extensive discovery and pretrial proceedings, a long trial, and an appellate process that could last for years, especially if a retrial is required. During the early stages of the civil proceedings, counsel must examine various procedures—such as the sealing of records, obtaining of protective orders,[5] closure of proceedings,[6] and other means of minimizing public exposure—that may protect the child's privacy. The emotional impact of the proceedings on the child should also be an important factor in assessing alternatives to a full litigation process. A reasonable pretrial settlement, for example, might serve the objectives of a damages suit, offering the child a certain and final resolution and obviating the child's unnecessary participation in legal proceedings.

This chapter addresses various legal issues that may arise in civil damages suits brought against professionals who abuse children and against entities or institutions with which the professionals are affiliated. Some special rules pertain to litigation of sexual abuse cases and to treatment of child witnesses in general.[7] Few special legal rules, however, apply solely to child sexual abuse by professionals. In most respects, professionals who abuse children stand in civil litigation as any other abusers or tortfeasors.

For the purposes of this chapter, the term "professional" encompasses a broad range of occupations and includes diverse occupational practices, obligations, and affiliations. Professionals do, however, share certain characteristics relevant to these cases. Professionals may be subject to a licensing authority and ethical and professional codes. They are often protected by insurance coverage, and frequently have significant personal financial resources. Professionals are often affiliated with institutions that may have a role in the legal proceedings. Most important, a professional has a trust or authority relationship with a patient or client, especially when that client is a child.

Likewise, the child victims of such abuse may share certain characteristics. A child victim of sexual abuse may not immediately recognize his or her injury or the wrongfulness of the adult conduct. Even if the child recognizes the injury or the impropriety of the conduct, the nature of the abuse and the status of the offender may prevent or delay the child's disclosure of abuse.[8] Finally, children generally trust adults or recognize adult authority, and may have a greater respect or fear of adult caretakers, especially doctors, teachers, and other professionals.

It is in the special nature of professional obligations and in the trust with which professionals and their affiliated institutions are held (especially by children) that one can discern the themes that link the various legal issues discussed below.

CAUSES OF ACTION

This section addresses basic tort theories of liability under which a child victim of sexual assault may recover from the abusing professional. A child victim's parents or caretakers may themselves have a cause of action for damages they incurred as a result of the professional's abuse of the child.[9] A child may also have a cause of action for the damages caused to family relationships. Discussion of these related causes of actions, however, is beyond the scope of this chapter.

Intentional Torts

A sexual assault victim may sue his or her abuser for a variety of "intentional torts," including assault, battery, intentional infliction of emotional distress, and fraud or deceit. The special circumstances of a professional's abuse of a child may undermine the utility of traditional defenses to intentional torts. A defense that a victim consented to the defendant's allegedly tortious conduct, for example, is a legitimate and common defense to a tort action for assault and battery. A consent defense, however, may be inappropriate when a professional has sexually victimized a child. Every state has criminal statutes prohibiting sexual contact or intercourse with minors under a prescribed age.[10] A minor's consent to sexual activity does not constitute a defense to the criminal sexual assault charge, since minors under the statutory age are deemed presumptively incapable of such consent.

Under the approach taken in the *Restatement (Second) of Torts*, courts can best serve the legislative purpose of these criminal statutes by holding that the consent of an underage minor to sexual acts is also ineffective as a defense to a civil action arising out of the conduct. The restatement states:

Consent to Crime

1. Except as stated in Subsection (2), consent is effective to bar recovery in a tort action although the conduct consented to is a crime.

2. If conduct is made criminal in order to protect a certain class of persons irrespective of their consent, the consent of members of that class to the conduct is not effective to bar a tort action.[11]

The criminal statutes fixing the age of consent to sexual intercourse "obviously are intended to protect a limited class of persons against their own lack of judgment, and so against their own consent."[12] Although these criminal statutes "expressly make their violation only a criminal offense, they are construed as a legislative declaration that females below the stated age are incapable of giving a consent effective to bar a civil action for assault and battery."[13] Thus, in any civil damages suit for assault and battery of a child under the age of consent, the judge may appropriately instruct the jury that the victim's consent is no defense to the action.

Evidence pertaining to the victim's acquiescence in, or assent to, the conduct may, however, in some cases be relevant in assessing the damages suffered by the victim. When the victim is a minor close to the age of consent, for example, the voluntariness of the victim's participation (though not sufficient as a defense to assault and battery) might nonetheless be a legitimate issue for a jury assessing the nature and extent of the victim's injuries. A defendant's offer of such evidence, of course, may be foreclosed by strategic considerations, since an assertion that the victim voluntarily participated implicitly acknowledges the defendant's own tortious participation.

Even if the consent defense were not categorically rejected, and the jury were allowed to consider such a defense, it would likely be unpersuasive. A professional's sexual involvement with a minor in his or her care invariably requires the abuse of trust or authority that, when compounded by a large age difference between perpetrator and victim, is inherently coercive. A victim's consent might, however, be relevant in establishing the measure of compensatory damages or in weighing the appropriateness of awarding punitive damages.

Negligence

Although an intentional tort action would seem to be the most appropriate vehicle for a professional's sexual abuse of a minor, many plaintiffs also proceed on a negligence theory. One major reason for this is that a professional's liability insurance policy generally covers injuries arising from the professional's negligent conduct, but often excludes coverage for the professional's intentional misdeeds.[14] A civil plaintiff could thus benefit from the insurance coverage if he or she prevails in a negligence action, whereas the plaintiff might be required to satisfy a successful intentional tort judgment out of the professional's personal assets.

A suit against a professional for negligence in his or her professional capacity is a suit for "professional negligence" or "malpractice." As in any negligence claim, the plaintiff must establish that the professional owed a duty of care to the plaintiff, breached that duty, and thereby injured and damaged the plaintiff. When sexual abuse is the basis of a malpractice claim, special legal issues may arise during litigation.

Expert testimony, for example, is ordinarily required to establish the appropriate standard of professional care in assessing the professional's duty and conduct under given circumstances.[15] Expert testimony is necessary for two reasons: first, to acquaint a fact finder with specialized knowledge that may be essential to a decision; and second, to allow the fact finder to measure the professional's conduct against the conduct of the reasonable practitioner in the field. Expert testimony, however, might not be required to establish that a professional's sexual assault of a patient or client violates the professional's duty of care.[16] In most circumstances the blatant impropriety of such conduct would seem to eliminate the need for expert testimony.

It is also possible that civil plaintiffs will offer into evidence written professional codes of conduct and ethical guidelines in proving their malpractice cases. In showing that professional standards expressly prohibit sexual misconduct, a plaintiff may argue that he or she is entitled to have a judge instruct the jury that the professional's violation of the professional standards constitutes negligence per se.[17]

As is true of the defenses to intentional torts, the defenses to negligence may be unavailable in an action arising out of a professional's sexual misconduct with a minor. The relevant defenses to negligence—contributory (or comparative) negligence and "assumption of the risk"—are grounded in the notion that the allegedly negligent actor should not bear sole responsibility for damages caused wholly or partly by the plaintiff's own conduct. Assumption of the risk is essentially a negligence analogue to the intentional tort defense of consent. The defense operates as a complete bar to the plaintiff's recovery if the defendant proves that the plaintiff proceeded to encounter a known risk of harm, thus relieving the defendant of his or her legal duty to the plaintiff.

A plaintiff does not assume the risk of harm from the abuser's conduct unless the plaintiff "knows of the existence of the risk and appreciates its unreasonable character."[18] The plaintiff's assumption of the risk is judged by a subjective standard; and if the plaintiff, because of "age, or lack of information, experience, intelligence, or judgment," does not understand the risk involved in the defendant's conduct, he or she will not have assumed the risk of harm from such conduct.[19]

The criminal statutes prescribing the minimum age of consent to certain sexual acts should be construed to render a child under that age incapable of knowingly assuming the risk in a negligence action based on sexual abuse.[20]

A child who is sexually victimized by a professional to whom he or she is entrusted probably has no meaningful opportunity either to refuse or to consent to the act.

The same reasoning should govern a defendant's attempt to raise a contributory or comparative negligence defense,[21] defenses that operate either to bar or to reduce the plaintiff's recovery when the plaintiff's negligent conduct contributes to his or her own injuries. In some circumstances, however, the issue of contributory negligence may be submitted to a jury, as in *Anonymous* v. *Berry*,[22] in which the jury was allowed to consider a contributory negligence defense in weighing a malpractice claim against a psychiatrist for the psychiatrist's sexual intercourse with a 17-year-old schizophrenic patient. The jury found that the plaintiff had not been contributorily negligent. Similarly, evidence of the voluntariness of the victim's participation may be considered relevant in establishing the measure of compensatory damages or in weighing the appropriateness of awarding punitive damages.

INSURANCE

Many professionals are insured for acts they perform in their professional capacities. A professional is not absolved of civil liability merely because he or she is uninsured—the professional, like any other tortfeaser, is personally obligated to pay any court judgment against him or her. A defendant, however, may not have sufficient resources to pay a large damages award, and a professional's liability coverage thus provides an important source of recovery for an injured plaintiff. Further, the terms and scope of an insurance policy may determine which theories of recovery the plaintiff (victim) pursues in legal pleadings. Finally, the availability of insurance coverage is a significant factor in settlement negotiations.

If the professional is affiliated with an institution or supervising entity, that entity's insurance coverage may play an important role in civil litigation. Whether institutional insurance is available to a plaintiff will depend both on the institution's relationship with an allegedly abusive professional and on the institution's knowledge, participation, or acquiescence in the acts allegedly constituting abuse.[23] It is reasonable to expect that as victims increasingly resort to civil damages suits, the applicability of certain insurance provisions, both in individual malpractice policies and in institutional insurance policies, will be addressed specifically in the context of child sexual abuse. It is also reasonable to assume that insurers may alter the language or structure of their policies to avoid responsibility for these acts that are clearly outside of the professional's legitimate activities.

Insurance coverage thus affects a victim's financial compensation, a professional's personal liability exposure, and the exposure and financial integrity of institutions or supervisory entities affiliated with an abusing professional. Insurance policies usually contain specific exclusions designed to delineate the insurer's responsibilities and to apprise the insured party of risks outside the coverage of the policy. Courts have already addressed the applicability of certain exclusions to acts of sexual misconduct perpetrated by professionals.

Intentional Acts or Damages Exclusions

A standard clause in both homeowner's and professional liability (malpractice) policies denies coverage for claims arising out of intentional acts committed by the insured party. Such clauses may exclude either coverage for injuries arising out of an intentional act or coverage when the insured party actually intended to inflict damage or injury in so acting.

An insurer is likely to contend that sexual abuse (especially of a child) is within an intentional acts or injuries exclusion, and hence is not covered under a policy. In *Horace Mann Insurance Co.* v. *Independent School District No. 656*,[24] the Minnesota Supreme Court interpreted such an "intentional damages" exclusion to relieve an insurer of any obligation to pay for injuries arising out of a high school teacher's alleged sexual abuse of a 16-year-old student. Both the teacher's professional liability policy, obtained through the state educational association, and his homeowner's policy contained such exclusions.[25] The court held that the insurer's denial of coverage was proper under the exclusion, since an intent to inflict injury could be inferred from the nature of the teacher's acts.[26] The same court ruled, in cases involving the sexual abuse of children[27] and of a disabled adult,[28] that under an intentional acts or damages exclusion, an insurer had no obligation either to defend or to indemnify the insured person for claims arising out of sexual abuse.

The argument has been raised that even in the absence of an intentional acts exclusion, an insurer should not be required to pay for civil consequences of an insured's intentional and criminal wrongdoing, since such coverage, by insulating the wrongdoer, would violate public policy. The New Jersey Supreme Court, in *Ambassador Insurance Co.* v. *Montes*,[29] rejected this argument, reasoning that insurance coverage benefits the innocent third person (the victim), and that the insurer could recover from the wrongdoer any amount it was required to pay to the injured victim.

Sexual Misconduct Exclusion

In their professional liability policies, some insurers have specifically excluded coverage for sexual misconduct. The primary malpractice insurance carriers for both the American Psychological Association and the American Psychiatric Association have included such clauses in their professional liability policies, in response to the growing number of claims alleging improper sexual contact between therapists and their patients.[30] Such conduct, even between a therapist and a consenting adult patient, is proscribed by professional ethical standards and, in some states, by criminal statutes.[31] Until very recently, the American Psychiatric Association nonetheless provided malpractice coverage for sexual misconduct cases out of concern for wrongfully accused psychiatrists and, conversely, a concern for the victims of justifiably accused practitioners.[32] Now, however, its carrier will refuse to pay claims for "undue familiarity," but will continue to pay for the psychiatrist's legal defense of such a claim.[33]

If other professionals who regularly deal with children—teachers, pediatricians, clergy, daycare workers—become the target of more claims alleging sexual abuse, their professional liability policies may reflect this increase in a specific exclusion for sexual misconduct. As a consequence, victims would be afforded no protection by the professional's liability insurance coverage.

Activities Outside of Professional Services

When there is no specific exclusion for sexual misconduct, insurers have nonetheless tried to deny coverage on the grounds that the professional, by engaging in sexual conduct, is not providing a "professional service" within the ambit of malpractice policy protection. This issue has been addressed in cases in which a therapist had improper sexual relations with a patient. In both *Zipkin* v. *Freeman*[34] and *Vigilant Insurance Co.* v. *Kambly*,[35] state appellate courts found that policies covering injuries arising from services the psychiatrist "rendered or failed to render" were broad enough to encompass the therapist's sexual relations with an adult patient. A Florida court, in *Anonymous* v. *Berry*,[36] held that a psychiatrist's sexual intercourse with a minor patient during therapy constituted "treatment" within the scope of a malpractice policy, and hence the conduct was covered by the policy. In contrast, the Minnesota Supreme Court, in *Smith* v. *St. Paul Fire & Marine Ins. Co.*,[37] held that a physician's sexual assaults of minor patients were solely for the satisfaction of the doctor's prurient interests and therefore did not relate to his "providing or withholding of professional services."[38] Under the *Smith* approach, a victimized patient is afforded no protection by the professional's liability policy, even though the injuries were inflicted in the course of, and through the doctor's exploitation of, the professional relationship.

In *Hertogs* v. *Employers Mutual Liability Company of Wisconsin*,[39] a New York appellate court adopted a position that might accommodate both the victim's and the insurer's legitimate interests. The court held that under the "professional services" clause of a professional liability policy, an insurer had no obligation to defend or indemnify a doctor for "fornication therapy" that the doctor admitted was improper and unrelated to the treatment of his patient.[40] The court, however, acknowledging that a professional liability policy serves to protect not only the professional but also his unwitting victims, stated that the patient (victim) might have the right to proceed against the insurer, since at the time she submitted to the doctor's sexual advances, she believed it was appropriate medical therapy.[41] The practical impact of such a decision is that the innocent victim might still recover from the insurer, which could, in turn, seek indemnification from the doctor for any liability it incurred as a result of the doctor's intentional and wrongful conduct.[42]

Punitive Damages

An insurer may specifically exclude coverage for punitive damages arising out of a malpractice claim. When there is no specific disclaimer or exclusion, however, "courts . . . have been virtually unanimous in holding that . . . the [liability insurance] contract includes indemnity against such damages."[43] Insurers have argued that since the purpose of punitive damages is to punish the wrongdoer and deter future misconduct, it is inappropriate to relieve the actor of liability by shifting the financial burden to the liability insurer. Since punitive damages may be awarded only when the wrongdoer's conduct was grossly negligent, reckless, wanton, or intentional, the shifting of liability, according to liability insurers, may actually encourage such conduct or, at the least, fail to deter it.[44]

This public policy argument has been rejected by courts: "[Nor] is there any . . . evidence that contracts of insurance to protect against liability for punitive damages have such an 'evil tendency' to make reckless conduct 'more probable' or that there is any substantial relationship between the fact of such insurance and such misconduct."[45]

Some commentators have observed that in the absence of a specific policy exclusion, liability coverage for punitive damages conforms to an insured's "reasonable expectations" under the consumer-oriented approach that many states use in interpreting insurance policies.[46] Finally, the courts' willingness to uphold specific punitive damages exclusions weakens the insurers' position, since the failure to include such an exclusion could be viewed, under a contract view, as implicitly acknowledging coverage for punitive damages.

A punitive damages award is particularly appropriate in damage suits against a professional for sexual abuse of a child. The victim's youth, the exploitation of the trust relationship used to facilitate the abuse, and the reckless or intentional nature of the acts all enhance the probability that such damages will be awarded. Since sexual abuse often will not be accompanied by lasting physical damage or injuries, a punitive damage award, along with a compensatory damage award for emotional pain and suffering, may comprise a large component of any total award. Thus, a punitive damages exclusion in a professional liability policy could have serious consequences for a victim's remedy.

INSTITUTIONAL DEFENDANTS

Institutional involvement in the sexual abuse of children, apart from its staggering social implications, raises a range of vexing legal issues. The variety of institutional settings and conditions in which a professional sexually abuses a child is as broad as the spectrum of professional/institutional interactions. Counties, school boards, state and private hospitals, clinics, licensing boards, daycare centers, and even the Catholic Church are among the entities that have been called upon to defend civil damages suits for child sexual assault.

A suit against an institution or supervising entity in such cases serves a number of purposes, the primary one being to encourage institutional responsibility. Suit against an institution affiliated with the abuser also affords a victim practical benefits. If an institution, through legal precepts, is liable for its agent's acts, the plaintiff may satisfy any money judgment against the institution if the abuser is insolvent or has insufficient assets. If the institution itself is determined to have injured the plaintiff through its own negligence, the plaintiff may satisfy a judgment against either the institution or the abuser. The availability of institutional insurance may enhance the opportunity for a victim to recover fully for his or her injuries and may also facilitate pretrial settlements.

An institution's liability for a professional's abuse of a child in the institution will turn upon numerous factors, including the institution's legal relationship with the professional; the institution's legal obligation to those entrusted to the care of the professional; and the institution's knowledge of, and acquiescence or participation in, the events constituting or contributing to the abuse.

When the abuse is perpetrated by an individual in an institutional setting (or with institutional affiliation), the institution or entity may incur liability either vicariously (for the acts of its agent or servant) or as a result of its own negligence. Although both theories are grounded in negligence, vicarious responsibility imputes the negligent conduct of an actor to the supervising entity, even if that entity has been free from fault. The institution or entity, through its acts or omissions, may itself owe and breach a duty of care to the plaintiff, in which case it can be found liable for its own negligence.

Under a vicarious liability theory, a supervising entity (or even an individual charged with the oversight of the wrongdoer) may in some circumstances be held responsible for the wrongful acts of an individual merely because of its relationship with the wrongdoer. The most common of these relationships, anachronistically designated the master-servant relationship, deems a master (employer) legally responsible for the acts of a servant (employee) in the course or scope of the servant's employment.[47] The legal relationship between the individual and the entity can be established by law, by contractual agreement, or by the circumstances of their interaction.

At least two obstacles may prevent the imposition of vicarious liability on an institution for a professional's sexual abuse of a child. Vicarious liability, as exemplified in the master-servant liability theory, is premised in part on the assumption that the supervising entity either controls, or has the right to control, the performance of the servant.[48] By virtue of their special knowledge, professionals are often considered to be independent contractors whose performance the hiring or supervising entity has no power to control. Physicians (other than interns and residents), for example, have traditionally been characterized by courts as independent contractors (rather than hospital employees) when treating hospital patients, since the physician's specialized training makes supervision of them impracticable. The general rule is that an employer is not vicariously liable for the acts of an independent contractor.[49] Thus, a professional who functions as an independent contractor in an institutional setting may not expose the institution to vicarious liability through his or her actions.

Even if the professional's legal status does not preclude the institution's vicarious liability, the nature of a sexually abusive act may hamper recovery from an institution. In the master-servant context, vicarious liability generally applies only to those acts committed by the servant in the course or scope of his or her employment. The scope-of-employment inquiry focuses on whether the servant's act was of a kind that the servant was authorized to take, whether the act was committed within authorized time and space limits of the employment, and whether the act was motivated by a purpose to serve the master or by the personal motives of the servant.[50] Courts have held the master vicariously liable even for the intentional torts of a servant when the servant's "purpose, however misguided, is wholly or in part to further the master's business."[51] For a master to be vicariously liable for a servant's use of force, however, the use of such force must not be "unexpectable" in light of the servant's duties.[52] The nature of the servant's employment, that is, must be such that the servant's use of force on a third person is sufficiently foreseeable to deem it within the scope of the servant's employment.

Courts have frequently held that certain criminal acts, among them sexual abuse of a child, are so outrageous as to be "unexpectable" or unforeseeable, and hence not within the employer's or master's scope of risk.[53] A California court considered the connection between a school janitor's employment duties and his sexual assault on a child during school hours so attenuated as to leave no basis upon which a jury could find that the janitor acted in the scope of his employment.[54] Similarly, a security company was not vicariously liable for its employee's rape of an occupant of the building the company was employed to protect, since the employee's action was neither in furtherance of the agency's business nor within the scope of his employment.[55]

A professional's sexual abuse of a child, in the absence of special circumstances making such an act foreseeable, may be of a character that is considered presumptively outside of the professional's scope of employment. Because it is a criminal, intentional act that presumably serves the abuser's purposes rather than the employer's, the scope-of-employment requirement may negate the imposition of vicarious liability. The question of whether the employee's act was within the scope of his employment, however, may be a question of fact for the jury's consideration under appropriate circumstances.[56]

In a limited class of cases, a master may incur liability for acts the servant commits outside the scope of the servant's employment. Where the master has undertaken a duty to protect the plaintiff from harm and in attempting to fulfill this duty employs a servant who nonetheless harms the plaintiff, the master will not be insulated from liability merely because the servant acted outside the scope of his employment.[57] Under this theory of liability, the master is said to owe a "nondelegable" duty to the plaintiff and incurs liability commensurate with the scope of the duty undertaken.[58] The nondelegable duty theory is, in essence, a hybrid theory, since it combines elements of vicarious liability with an element of the master's own negligence. The master, that is, owes a duty of care to the plaintiff, but it is through the servant's act, rather than the master's, that this duty is breached.

The same premise that underlies the nondelegable duty—the master's or institution's express or implied undertaking of a special duty to protect the plaintiff—also is apparent in the common law rules governing "common carriers." At common law, certain entities—innkeepers, railroads, and hospitals, for example—as "common carriers," were considered to owe an enhanced duty of care to their customers, passengers, or patients, a duty that protected third parties even from the servant's intentional and personally motivated assaults.[59] A vestige of the common carrier duty is present in *Nazareth* v. *Herndon Ambulance Service, Inc.*,[60] in which a Florida appellate court held that an ambulance service could be liable vicariously for a sexual assault and battery perpetrated by its ambulance driver upon a passenger being transported to the hospital. The applicability of the nondelegable and common carrier duties to child sexual abuse cases is discussed in more detail below.

Vicarious liability, where applicable, provides a plaintiff with an alternative financial source (a supervising individual or institution) for recovering a judgment against an insolvent or unavailable abusing professional; it does not, however, entitle an injured plaintiff to double recovery. Further, the victim's recovery against an institution or entity on a vicarious liability theory is in some respects fortuitous, since the intricacies of the entity's relationship with the abusing professional may be determinative of the entity's liability.

Even if the institution or entity cannot be held responsible solely on a vicarious liability theory, it may owe an independent duty to potential victims to minimize or prevent such acts, or at least to ensure their earliest disclosure. Such a theory recognizes that the entity's own negligence or recklessness, rather than merely the fault of the abuser, may also have contributed to the plaintiff's injuries. The institution, for example, may be negligent in failing to instruct or supervise an individual working in its ranks[61] or in entrusting certain tasks to an individual who poses a risk of harm to third parties. The utility of this approach in sexual abuse cases is significant, since the institution or entity charged with oversight of the professional may be in the best position to prevent abuse or its recurrence. A victim, however, must still prove all of the elements of a negligence claim against the institution, establishing that the abuse was a reasonably foreseeable consequence of the institution's conduct and that the institution's acts or omissions were a proximate cause of the abuse.

Allegations that an entity or institution negligently hired, retained, or supervised an abuser have led to plaintiffs' verdicts or settlements in a number of child sexual abuse cases. A Virginia county school board, its members, and school officials were sued for negligence in continuing to employ a school bus driver-janitor after parents complained to the school that the bus driver had fondled their children.[62] The driver, who was dismissed after the complaints, was rehired 2 years later and was the target of further complaints before he was eventually dismissed again. In an ensuing criminal prosecution, the driver was convicted of 9 sex-related offenses against 7 children and given a 104-year prison sentence.[63] The civil suit, brought by parents of 12 children allegedly molested by the driver, resulted in a large settlement.

In a well-publicized Louisiana case, a Catholic priest was accused of sexually molesting young boys through exploitation of his professional position.[64] The priest was ultimately convicted of criminal charges, and civil damage actions against the priest, the Church, and Church officials have resulted in numerous out-of-court settlements. Although the Church denied prior knowledge of the priest's proclivities, the plaintiffs' lawyers and others contend that the Church's awareness was clearly established. Their research established that parents in other parishes had complained to Church superiors of other acts of sexual misconduct by the priest. The Church apparently was also aware that the priest had been treated by a psychiatrist for his sexual preoccupation with young boys.

Another priest from the same diocese, who was transferred several times within the diocese, was eventually suspended from his clerical duties because of allegations of sexual misconduct with minor boys.[65] The priest later left the state and was hired to counsel boys in a medical center's substance abuse program. When the priest was fired from the program because of similar allegations of sexual misconduct, the medical center claimed that it had received no adverse information when checking the priest's references.[66]

The circumstances surrounding *Evans as Next Friend of D.M.* v. *Rippy*[67] provide an egregious example in institutional abdication of responsibility. Malpractice actions were brought against a board-certified child psychiatrist who allegedly mistreated children during treatment by administering drugs to them and physically and sexually abusing them. An investigation revealed that unresolved complaints against the psychiatrist alleging sexual misconduct were on file in the local medical society's records. The ensuing controversy forced the psychiatrist to leave the area, after which he moved to North Carolina and was allowed to head a children's unit in a state hospital. The abusing psychiatrist also had disclosed to a psychiatrist treating him (prior to his own board certification as a child psychiatrist) his predilection for young boys.[68]

In all four cases, institutional or supervisory failures served to perpetuate abuse and to enlarge the pool of victims. Since these entities or institutions are often in a position to prevent or limit the abuse, it is important to address the parameters of institutional responsibility in such situations. *Evans* v. *Rippy*, because it arguably involved institutional failure at several junctures, is a good case with which to examine some of the preliminary issues.

A further investigation in *Evans* v. *Rippy* might have supported a theory of institutional liability on any of these grounds:

- A private hospital's negligence in failing to discover the malpractice, investigate complaints, and prevent further abuse (negligent hiring, retention, and supervision)
- A medical society's negligent failure (and the failure of its officers in their official capacities) to investigate apparently legitimate complaints and take disciplinary or protective measures
- A state hospital or hiring entity's negligence in failing to investigate adequately the background of a psychiatrist before appointing him to a children's unit.

An entity's liability to third parties under a negligence theory for such acts or omissions depends largely on the legal interpretation of "duty." Duty, in the context of a negligence action, simply addresses the question of "whether the defendant is under any obligation for the particular plaintiff."[69] The scope of such duty, however, cannot be precisely defined except as "an expression of the sum total of those considerations of policy which lead the law to say that the particular plaintiff is entitled to protection."[70] The value to society of the entity's activities, the nature of the risk to potential plaintiffs from such activities, and the practical and financial burdens on institutions posed by legal accountability are among the policy considerations weighed by courts in determining the scope of negligence duties.

There should be little doubt that a school owes to its students, a church to its parishioners, and a hospital to its patients the duty to protect them when the entity has actual knowledge or a reasonable suspicion that a professional in its ranks is abusing children. In *Evans*, the failure of an institution's internal supervisory or oversight mechanism allowed abuse to persist; a pedophile who had professional access to children under these conditions in essence inflicted systemic abuse as effectively as if the institution sanctioned it. A hospital thus contributed to the victimization of those it was designed to treat. Similarly, the Catholic Church, in the Louisiana cases, and the school board officials, in the Virginia case, failed to act on information readily available to them, causing further hardship to children and parents they were supposed to serve. No public policy interests are contravened by holding an institution or entity legally accountable under such circumstances, since the institution is aware of the risk of abuse, could easily take steps to prevent future abuse, and would itself be best served by so doing.

It may be appropriate for courts to hold that entities entrusted with the care of children, such as schools, pediatric clinics, and daycare centers, owe an enhanced duty of protection to the children.[71] Such a duty, like the nondelegable and common carrier duties, might be justified on the grounds that the entity has undertaken a special role in the care of its young students, patients, or clients, one that protects the child from the risk of sexual abuse at the hands of an adult.

It is more difficult to justify imposition of liability for an institution's or entity's failure to protect from abuse those other than its own clients or constituents. Phrased in negligence terminology, the issue is to what extent an institution or entity owes a duty to those it does not serve directly. An institution or entity may indeed be in the best position to warn others of a professional's abusive propensities; it cannot, however, be burdened with a duty to warn the world at large of such a risk. In *Evans*, the private hospital, the medical society, and the state hospital might have viewed their duties as fulfilled upon severing their ties with the abuser. The adequacy of such a view, however, must be questioned when the abuser is allowed to resume his activities, without obstacles, in a new location.

Legal accountability, through a broader interpretation of the duty component of negligence, might encourage institutions to exercise greater responsibility in the exercise of ancillary functions. Medical professionals, for example, who serve on peer review boards, medical malpractice panels, and professional conduct boards should have a heightened awareness of the public risks of allowing an abusing peer to continue practicing without restriction. It may, therefore, not be unreasonable to impose on them (or other similarly situated individuals, institutions, or entities) a legal duty to advise or warn licensing authorities, professional organizations, or prospective employers of substantiated allegations of misconduct and abuse.[72] The extent of such a duty, and its merits under particular circumstances, must be addressed in a case-by-case approach.

NOTES

1. R. Eatman and J. Bulkley, PROTECTING CHILD VICTIM/WITNESSES (1986); J. Bulkley, *Evidentiary and Procedural Trends in State Legislation and Other Emerging Legal Issues in Child Sexual Abuse Cases*, 50 Dick. L. Rev. 645 (1985).
2. J. Bulkley, RECOMMENDATIONS FOR IMPROVING LEGAL INTERVENTION IN CHILD SEXUAL ABUSE CASES (1982).
3. *See, e.g.*, Daily Breeze, May 20, 1985 (Torrance, Ca.); Los Angeles Times, May 21, 1982.
4. J. Goldstein, A. Freud, and A. Solnit, BEFORE THE BEST INTERESTS OF THE CHILD (1979).
5. *See, e.g.*, FED. R. CIV. P. 36.
6. Note, *First Amendment Right of Access to Civil Trials After Globe Newspaper Co.* v. *Superior Court*, 50 U. Chi. L. Rev. 286 (1984).
7. *See* Eatman and Bulkley, *supra* note 1.
8. MacFarlane, *Diagnostic Evaluations and the Uses of Videotapes in Child Sexual Abuse Cases*, PAPERS FROM A NATIONAL POLICY CONFERENCE ON LEGAL REFORMS IN CHILD SEXUAL ABUSE CASES (1985); Berliner and Barbieri, *The Testimony of the Child Victim of Sexual Assault*, 40 J. Soc. Issues 2 (1984).
9. RESTATEMENT (SECOND) TORTS, secs. 701–704 (1977).
10. J. Bulkley, CHILD SEXUAL ABUSE AND THE LAW (1985).
11. RESTATEMENT (SECOND) TORTS, sec. 892, comment D (1977); *see id.*, sec. 61.
12. W. Prosser, LAW OF TORTS 107 (4th ed. 1971).
13. RESTATEMENT (SECOND) OF TORTS, sec. 483, comment g (1977).
14. *See infra* notes 24–29 and accompanying text.
15. Prosser, *supra* note 12, at 164.
16. *See, e.g., Hammer* v. *Rosen*, 165 N.E.2d 756 (N.Y. Ct. App. 1960).
17. RESTATEMENT (SECOND) OF TORTS, secs. 288B, 496F (1977).
18. *Id.*, sec. 496D.
19. *Id..*, comment (c).
20. *Id.*, sec. 496F; *see also* sec. 496F, comment(d).
21. *Id.*, sec. 483, comment(g).
22. No. 78-8182 (Fla. Duval City Cir. Ct. March 14, 1979).
23. *See infra* text accompanying notes 47–72.
24. 355 N.W.2d 413 (Minn. 1984).

25. *Id.* at 415, 417.

26. *Id.* at 416; *see also CNA Insurance Co.* v. *McGinnis*, 282 Ark. 90, 666 S.W.2d 689 (1984).

27. *State Farm Fire and Casualty Co.* v. *Williams*, 355 N.W.2d 421 (Minn. 1984).

28. *Estate of Lehmann* v. *Metzger*, 355 N.W.2d 425 (Minn. 1984).

29. 76 N.J. 477, 388 A.2d 603 (1978).

30. Simon, *Sexual Misconduct of Therapists*, Trial 46 (May 1985).

31. *Id.* at 51.

32. *Id.* at 50.

33. *Id.*

34. 436 S.W.2d 753 (Mo. 1968).

35. 319 N.W.2d 382 (Mich. App. 1982).

36. No. 78-8182 (Fla. Duval City Cir. Ct. March 14, 1979).

37. 353 N.W.2d 130 (Minn. 1984).

38. *Id.* at 132.

39. 89 Misc.2d 468, 391 N.Y.S.2d 962 (N.Y. Sup. Ct. 1977).

40. *Id.* at 965.

41. *Id.* at 966.

42. *See also* RESTATEMENT (SECOND) OF AGENCY, sec. 401, comment (d) (1957).

43. Lambert, *Commercial Litigation*, 35 ATLA L. J. 164, 182 (1974).

44. *Id.* at 183.

45. *Harrell* v. *Travelers Indemnity Co.*, 567 P.2d 1013, 1017 (1977).

46. Lambert, *supra* note 43, at 182.

47. RESTATEMENT (SECOND) OF AGENCY, sec. 219(1) (1957).

48. *Id.*

49. Prosser, *supra* note 12, at 468.

50. RESTATEMENT (SECOND) OF AGENCY, sec. 228 (1957).

51. Prosser, *supra* note 12, at 494.

52. RESTATEMENT (SECOND) OF AGENCY, sec. 245 (1957).

53. *See, e.g., Gambling* v. *Cornish*, 426 F.Supp. 1153 (N.D. Ill. 1977).

54. *Alma W.* v. *Oakland United School Dist.*, 123 Cal. App. 133, 176 Cal. Rptr. 287 (Cal. App. 1981).

55. *Rabon* v. *Guards Mark, Inc.*, 571 F.2d 1277 (4th Cir. 1978), *cert. denied*, 439 U.S. 866 (1978).

56. *Lyon* v. *Carey*, 533 F.2d 649 (D.C. App. 1976).

57. RESTATEMENT (SECOND) OF AGENCY, sec. 214 (1957).

58. *Id.*, sec. 214(a) (1957).

59. Prosser, *supra* note 12, at 180.

60. 467 So.2d 1076 (Fla. App. 1985).

61. RESTATEMENT (SECOND) OF AGENCY, sec. 213 (1957).

62. Virginian-Pilot, June 7, 1984 (Norfolk Va.), at 1.

63. *Id.*

64. Hebert, *Sexual Abuse by Professionals: A Case Study of Extralegal Factors in Seeking Criminal Prosecution and Civil Damages*, Ch. 8 in this volume.

65. Spokesman Review and Spokane Chronicle, Feb. 9, 1986, at 1, col. 1.

66. *Id.*

67. 23 ATLA L. Rep. 62 (March 1980).

68. *Id.* at 62.

69. Prosser, *supra* note 12, at 324.

70. *Id.* at 325–26.

71. *Durate* v. *State*, 84 Cal. App.3d 729, 148 Cal. Rptr. 804, 811 (Cal. App. 1978); *Cotton* v. *Collinsville Community School Dist. No. 10*, no. 5-84-0455 (Ill. App. Oct. 29, 1985); *Butler* v. *Circulus, Inc.*, 557 S.W.2d 469 (Mo. App. 1977).

72. Three Massachusetts physicians, for example, wrote laudatory letters of recommendation for a physician who just days before had been convicted of rape. The letters made no reference to the conviction, and at least one of the authors believed that the conviction did not have any bearing on the felon's abilities as a doctor. Under such circumstances, the authors of the reference letters took an affirmative step to mislead a prospective employer, and potential injuries to the felon's future patients might be deemed a foreseeable consequence of the recommending physicians' action. Boston Globe, Feb. 4, 1982.

11

Disciplinary Proceedings against Professionals for Sexual Abuse of Children

Josephine Bulkley and Ross Eatman

Sexual abuse of children is now a recognized national problem. Although many children are abused by parents or other family members, both research and recent reports suggest that a significant number of cases involve other adults a child knows and trusts.[1] Indeed, adults often use their professional status to gain access to children and use their position of authority and trust to sexually abuse a child. There is a wide variety of professionals who have close and regular contact with young children, including schoolteachers, daycare center employees, pediatricians, and mental health professionals.

If a professional sexually abuses a child, not only may he or she be subject to criminal proceedings or civil lawsuit like other adults, but he or she also may be subject to state administrative disciplinary proceedings to suspend or revoke his or her license to practice. The professional further may be subject to ethical sanctions of professional associations, societies, and institutions that "potentially might have teeth by eliminating career opportunities, staff privileges at various institutional facilities, and so forth."[2]

In general, most professionals, such as doctors, teachers, and lawyers, must conform to high ethical standards. The conduct of attorneys, for example, must be kept "beyond reproach and above suspicion," whether the attorneys are acting in their professional or their private capacity. Most states also have passed statutes requiring a license to practice as a professional as a means of protecting the public from unscrupulous, immoral, incompetent, and unsafe practitioners. Under the state's police power, a state legislature has the authority to regulate a professional through the requirement of a license.[3] Under most licensing statutes, professional licensing boards are established to meet society's need to have professional groups licensed and disciplined in order to protect citizens from harm.[4] A second purpose of licensing is to protect the integrity of a profession and to establish and enforce professional standards.[5]

State licensing laws usually set out licensing requirements, create a licensing board (a majority of whose members are generally members of the profession), establish grounds for revoking or suspending a license, and set forth procedures for disciplinary proceedings. In the case of attorneys, however, although a disciplinary board may make findings and recommendations, only a court has authority to determine whether an attorney is guilty of an act constituting a ground for disbarment or suspension.[6]

Most laws provide for loss or suspension of a license for unprofessional, immoral, or dishonorable conduct, or for an act involving moral turpitude. Many laws also provide for loss of a license for conviction of certain types of crimes, including a crime involving moral turpitude or a sex offense. Clearly, sexual abuse of a child by a professional in the adult's professional capacity would be a ground for license revocation. However, a professional also may lose his or her license if the conduct occurred in his or her nonprofessional activities if the conduct is indicative of moral unfitness for the profession.[7] Generally, for a valid license revocation, courts have held that the due process clause requires a rational relationship or logical connection between the private conduct and job performance, and that the conduct is likely to have an adverse effect upon or endanger the professional's relationship with clients, patients, or students.[8]

Courts also are concerned about whether a professional's private conduct has harmed the integrity of the profession or has engendered public notoriety.[9] Certain types of private sexual conduct, such as homosexual acts, adultery, or prostitution involvement, have been held not to constitute moral unfitness where there is no evidence that the conduct would negatively affect the professional's job performance or the relationship with clients, patients, or students.[10] However, in a case where a doctor's license was revoked for alcoholism, the court held that there was a rational connection between alcoholism and the good judgment necessary to provide quality care, although there was no direct evidence that the alcoholism affected either his relationship with patients or his job performance.[11]

If a professional sexually abuses a child outside his professional dealings but has regular, close contact with children in his profession (such as a teacher or pediatrician), it seems clear that his private conduct might endanger children in his professional capacity. In one case, an elementary school teacher who had sexually abused his stepdaughter lost his teaching certificate.[12] The court noted that there was a connection between the teacher's immoral conduct and his job performance, even though the conduct occurred at home.[13]

Moreover, even professionals such as lawyers, who may have little or no contact with children, have access to their clients' children. In one case, a lawyer molested a number of his clients' children aged 10 to 12 years old.[14] As noted earlier, courts also are concerned that sexual abuse of a child (or similar behavior) reflects poorly on the integrity and reputation of the professional, even if the professional has little or no contact with children and the conduct has no effect on the professional's job performance or competence.[15] For example, in a Florida case, a court disbarred an attorney who had sexually molested his stepdaughter for many years, and who subsequently divorced her mother and married her.[16] The court rejected the argument that a man's personal life "should not gauge his abilities as an attorney, but that his personal life should be his own, free from inroads upon it by those charged with policing the bar."[17] The court stated that he should not be accorded the protection of the bar in pursuit of the profession upon which he had brought dishonor.[18]

However, the fact that the behavior is unlikely to adversely affect a professional's competence may result in a disposition other than revocation of a license. In a case where a lawyer was convicted of molesting a child, the state bar disciplinary board decided that the attorney had committed an offense of moral turpitude.[19] The board suspended the lawyer from practice for three years, but stayed the suspension and placed him on probation under intense supervision by the board for three years. He also was granted probation for three years in the criminal proceedings and was ordered not to associate with children under 18 years unless in the presence of an adult, and to undergo psychiatric treatment. The court noted that witnesses indicated that the attorney's performance was of the highest professional caliber, and that he was seeing a psychiatrist, who testified that he would be unlikely to commit future sex offenses with children. The attorney also admitted his behavior and expressed remorse. The court indicated that supervised probation in this case would adequately protect the public and the profession.

INTERACTION OF CRIMINAL PROCEEDINGS AND DISCIPLINARY ACTIONS

It is not necessary that a professional's misconduct constitute a criminal offense (or subject him or her to civil liability) to warrant the bringing of a disciplinary proceeding for revocation of a license. It is sufficient that the misconduct demonstrates the individual's unfitness to practice his or her profession or that it brings "reproach on the profession or injures it in the favorable opinion of the public."[20] Similarly, if a criminal proceeding is brought but results in an acquittal or dismissal, the lack of conviction generally does not prevent the institution of a license revocation proceeding.[21] One court stated that a complaint for disbarment of an attorney may be made either before or after a criminal prosecution, and whether or not the prosecution was successful.[22] Courts have indicated that license revocation actions and criminal proceedings are distinct and independent, with different purposes and results.[23] Further, a criminal prosecution requires a much higher standard of proof. For these reasons, a professional normally cannot successfully challenge as res judicata (double jeopardy) the bringing of a disciplinary action where there has been an acquittal involving the same case.[24]

If a professional's misconduct occurs as part of his or her professional activities, disciplinary proceedings may be instituted before or after resolution of a criminal prosecution. When a professional's misconduct occurs outside his or her professional activities, however, courts have held that the disciplinary proceeding normally should be deferred until after a criminal determination has been made.[25] This rule is not absolute, however. The U.S. Supreme Court indicated in an 1883 case:

> It is apparent that whilst it may be the general rule that a previous conviction should be had before striking an attorney off the roll for an indictable offense committed by him when not acting in his character of an attorney, yet that the rule is not an inflexible one. Cases may occur in which such a requirement would result in allowing persons to practice as attorneys, who ought, on every ground of propriety and respect for the administration of the law, to be excluded from such practice. A criminal prosecution may fail by the absence of a witness, or by reason of a flaw in the indictment, or some irregularity in the proceeding; and in such cases . . . the proceeding to strike from the roll may be had. But other causes may operate to shield a gross offender from a conviction of crime, however clear and notorious his guilt may be—a prevailing popular excitement, powerful influence brought to bear on the public mind or on the mind of the jury, and many other causes which might be suggested; and yet, all the time, the offender may be so covered with guilt, perhaps glorying in it, that it would be a disgrace to the court to be obliged to receive him as one of its officers, clothed with all the prestige of its confidence and authority.[26]

Professionals faced with pending criminal and disciplinary proceedings have unsuccessfully raised constitutional claims that the refusal of licensing authorities to stay disciplinary proceedings until the criminal case is resolved violates their Fifth Amendment privilege against self-incrimination and their substantive due process right. In one case, a teacher contended that because he wished to remain silent at the disciplinary proceeding in order to preserve his Fifth Amendment privilege in an imminent criminal case arising out of the same conduct, he was denied the opportunity to present evidence in his own defense at the disciplinary proceeding.[27] The court rejected his argument, observing first that the loss of the opportunity to testify in the board proceeding because of a fear that such testimony would later be used in a criminal proceeding did not violate his Fifth Amendment right and, second, that the refusal of the board to await the outcome of the criminal case did not violate the teacher's due process right. Another court likewise rejected an attorney's contention that a disciplinary board's refusal to stay its proceedings pending the disposition of a related criminal charge violated his due process rights.[28]

Although an acquittal or lack of a conviction is not a bar to revocation of a license, conviction of various crimes, including a crime involving moral turpitude, may be proof of a professional's unfitness or immoral conduct sufficient to justify revocation of a license. Many state statutes provide that conviction of a crime of moral turpitude is a ground for disbarment, revocation of a teaching certificate, or revocation of a medical license.[29] Some licensing statutes for teachers and lawyers also make conviction of a sex offense a ground for revocation.[30] The conviction may be used as evidence in several ways in a license revocation proceeding. The conviction may simply constitute evidence of the professional's misconduct or offense involving moral turpitude. In a case involving a physician convicted of statutory rape of a patient, the doctor alleged that the crime of statutory rape does not per se involve moral turpitude.[31] The licensing statute provided that a conviction is conclusive evidence *only* of the fact that the conviction occurred, and that the licensing board was authorized to determine if a particular crime constitutes an offense involving moral turpitude. The licensing board found that the doctor's sexual acts with his child patient did constitute an offense involving moral turpitude.

In other jurisdictions, however, courts have held that conviction of a crime involving moral turpitude is prima facie evidence of an attorney's unfitness to continue in the legal profession.[32] This means that the burden then shifts to the professional to prove that the conviction does not show the professional's unfitness. Finally, some licensing statutes and courts state that a conviction for a crime of moral turpitude is conclusive evidence of guilt and unfitness to practice, and automatic revocation is justified without further inquiry into the charges; such a conviction would constitute a per se or automatic forfeiture of a license.[33] Some courts have held that this approach is a violation of the due process clause in failing to provide notice and a hearing prior to revocation.[34]

PROCEDURAL REQUIREMENTS AND DUE PROCESS

Statutes that confer upon administrative agencies or bodies the power to suspend or revoke a license usually specify the procedural requirements for such disciplinary actions. The provisions of a specific licensing act may be supplemented by other statutory provisions governing either all license revocation proceedings or all state administrative proceedings.[35] Most states, for example, have an administrative procedure act (APA) that governs state administrative proceedings, and a particular licensing statute may incorporate by reference certain provisions (such as notice or judicial review of agency action) of the state's APA.[36]

The procedures for conducting a formal disciplinary proceeding differ from criminal or civil judicial proceedings. All three share the objectives of determining whether an individual committed certain acts in violation of a rule or statute, and what the appropriate disposition should be. A disciplinary action, however, is an administrative proceeding, and although characterized sometimes as quasi-criminal, civil, or quasi-judicial,[37] nonetheless is less formal than a judicial proceeding. Disciplinary actions are not governed by the same rules of evidence or other legal requirements. For example, disciplinary actions are not usually barred by statutes of limitations that apply to civil or criminal proceedings.[38] A disciplinary action is conducted before a licensing board, often made up primarily of professionals, or before a hearing officer, rather than before a judge or jury. Although disciplinary proceedings are less formal than judicial proceedings, they must be conducted in strict or substantial conformity with the statutory procedures, and a board decision revoking a license may be reversed for failure to adhere to mandated procedures.[39]

The procedures for conducting disciplinary proceedings not only must satisfy statutory requirements for administrative proceedings but also must be conducted in accordance with the Fourteenth Amendment due process requirements. Courts have consistently held that a licensing statute vests the professional with a protected property interest in his or her license.[40] The state, through the licensing body, may not arbitrarily deprive the professional of this interest without providing procedural due process safeguards. Procedural due process requires, at a minimum, that a person facing deprivation of a protected interest be provided with notice and an opportunity for a hearing appropriate to the nature of the case.[41] Since a licensing statute usually affords the licensee some procedural protections, the due process analysis often focuses on whether the procedures are sufficient to adequately protect the licensee from an erroneous deprivation of his or her protected interest in the license.

Due process requires that the licensing authority give the professional fair notice of the disciplinary proceeding, including a description of the incidents or charges upon which the proceeding is based.[42] The U.S. Supreme Court held that an attorney was denied due process in disbarment proceedings when his disbarment was based on a charge of misconduct not contained in the notice of the proceedings.[43] The notice must be sufficiently clear and timely to allow the professional to prepare a defense to the charge. One court found that a teacher had received adequate notice of a disciplinary action when the notice, while not specifying the exact date of the incident giving rise to the proceeding, nonetheless apprised him of the charge and conduct at issue, notified him of the pending hearing, and afforded him an adequate opportunity to prepare his defense.[44]

Professionals subjected to disciplinary proceedings have also challenged sufficiency of notice on the ground that statutory standards of conduct are so vague or indefinite that they could not know in advance what types of conduct were prohibited. Statutory language authorizing disciplinary measures against teachers for "immorality," "immoral conduct," and conduct demonstrating that the teacher is "unworthy to instruct [youth]"[45] have been held not to be unconstitutionally vague, since persons of ordinary intelligence would know that the conduct at issue in each case was sufficiently egregious as to fall within the statutory proscription. Statutory requirements that attorneys conduct themselves in a "temperate and dignified" manner and refrain from "dishonest, unprofessional, or immoral conduct," and that a physician comport himself with "good moral character" have also survived constitutional vagueness challenges.[46] The general view is that "the legislature is not required to define with particularity the acts which constitute unprofessional conduct" and that broad standards are acceptable.[47]

Due process also requires that a professional have an opportunity to appear and be heard on the charges and to present a defense to them.[48] One court held that an attorney was denied due process when, because he was incarcerated, he was unable to attend his disbarment proceeding and the attorney representing him at the proceeding was not allowed to present any evidence in the client's behalf.[49] A physician who was imprisoned at the time of a revocation action against him was also held to have been denied due process because he was unable to attend the proceeding.[50]

Due process generally requires a hearing before a professional's license may be suspended or revoked, but there may be limited conditions under which a prompt postsuspension hearing will satisfy due process concerns. The postponement of remedial action until after notice and a hearing may not be necessary if a professional's continued practice would expose the public to unreasonable danger, and some statutory schemes authorize summary actions in such circumstances, provided the professional is given a prompt postsuspension hearing.[51] Such procedures are disfavored, however, and a preference is expressed for presuspension hearings.[52]

At the hearing, the professional must be allowed to present a defense to the charges. The professional has a right to present evidence at such a hearing, and due process generally requires that the professional have the opportunity to confront and cross-examine adverse witnesses, especially when alleged misconduct is the basis of the proceeding.[53] It is the licensing board's function to determine both the competence and the sufficiency of the evidence before it.[54] Such hearings, because they are characterized as administrative or quasi-judicial, need not strictly adhere to civil or criminal rules of procedure, or technical rules of evidence, and can be conducted with less formality than is required in adversarial judicial proceedings.[55] A professional's due process rights may nonetheless be violated if, for example, the revocation of a physician's license is based primarily on hearsay evidence,[56] and courts have stated that evidence must be sufficiently relevant and reliable as to justify its admission at the hearing.[57]

In a disciplinary proceeding the licensing authority bears the burden of proof, but due process does not require that the evidence constitute "proof beyond a reasonable doubt," as is required in criminal cases.[58] Proof by a "preponderance" or "fair preponderance"[59] of the evidence has been held to satisfy due process, although some jurisdictions require proof by "clear and convincing evidence,"[60] a standard more demanding than the preponderance standards but less stringent than the burden of proof in criminal cases. The evidence must clearly establish the professional's guilt of the charges competently and probatively, and the hearing officer or board must support its decision with findings. Although it has been said that the hearing body's findings must be specific enough to allow meaningful review by a court, a general finding may be acceptable. One court held that a finding that a dentist was "guilty as charged in said accusation" was adequate to justify suspension of his license for his guilt of the charged conduct.[61] Another case held that specific written findings were not necessary to support a teacher's dismissal.[62]

The professional has a right to proceedings that are fair, free from prejudice or fraud, and conducted before an impartial tribunal.[63] Professionals subjected to disciplinary proceedings have contended that licensing authorities are unable to make a fair and impartial assessment of the evidence when they serve both investigative and adjudicative functions in a case. The U.S. Supreme Court has held, however, that while due process requires a fair tribunal in administrative adjudicative proceedings, the combination of investigative and adjudicative functions does not, in itself, create an unconstitutional risk of bias.[64] The court noted that in the absence of evidence to the contrary, members of administrative boards are "assumed to be . . . [men and women] of conscience and intellectual discipline, capable of judging a particular controversy fairly on the basis of its own circumstances."[65]

Many statutes provide a party with a right of appeal or right to petition for judicial review of a licensing authority's disciplinary ruling.[66] Generally, a party seeking such judicial review must first exhaust all available administrative remedies. Courts have found professional disciplinary proceedings reviewable even in the absence of specific statutory authority.[67] Further, a state's APA may provide the necessary authority where specific authority in the relevant licensing statute is lacking.

Although it varies by jurisdiction, the scope of such review is generally limited. The prevailing view (applicable to judicial review of most administrative decisions) is that the reviewing court does not substitute its judgment for that of the administrative body, reviewing the administrative decision only to determine whether the procedures followed conformed to statutory requirements and upholding an administrative ruling if it is supported by substantial evidence adduced at the administrative proceeding.[68] Under this scope of review, the court does not assess the credibility of testimony or weigh conflicting evidence, but modifies or reverses the administrative decision only if the decision is erroneous as a matter of law, is arbitrary or capricious, or is not supported by substantial evidence.[69]

Several states provide for de novo review of disciplinary decisions, affording the court more latitude in reviewing the administrative ruling. Under one type of de novo review, the court determines whether the board's findings were contrary to the clear preponderance of the evidence rather than whether there was substantial evidence to support the findings.[70] Another type of de novo review allows the court to receive evidence, review the record of the administrative proceeding, and reach its own independent judgment on the merits.[71]

EFFECTIVENESS OF DISCIPLINARY PROCEEDINGS

Based upon a survey of state licensing boards for physicians, psychologists, and social workers, it appears that very few complaints are made to, or disciplinary actions taken by, state licensing authorities for abuse of children by these professionals.[72] Furthermore, according to a March 1985 *New England Journal of Medicine* article, disciplinary actions in general are rarely filed against physicians throughout the country.[73] It was indicated that in 1982, for example, California had more than 50,000 licensed physicians and only 144 disciplinary actions were taken; in 1982 New York had more than 40,000 doctors with only 51 disciplinary actions. Five states had *no* disciplinary actions against physicians in 1982.

More distressing are statistics regarding lawyers. According to one commentator, "Surveys of bar procedures in major states reveal that *some 90% of complaints are dismissed without investigation*, and national statistics reflect that of grievances falling within disciplinary jurisdiction, *less than 30% result in public sanctions and only .8% in disbarment*" (emphasis added).[74] Further, of 108 cases involving disbarment for nonprofessional misconduct from 1976 to 1981, only 3 percent represented sexual misconduct.[75] It is difficult to believe that no more than a few lawyers in the United States sexually abused a child during that time or were convicted of child sexual abuse. Finally, based upon a survey of therapists who said they had sexual contact with their patients, the number of actual cases was significantly higher than the number of recorded complaints to licensing boards and the number of civil lawsuits.[76]

From the above data, it is difficult to tell if some complaints were resolved informally (for instance, an admission by the professional with certain conditions imposed, such as probation and treatment). The figures may reflect only formal disciplinary hearings. Nevertheless, it appears that professional disciplinary proceedings rarely seem to be instituted for any type of misconduct. A 1975 article emphasized this point: "A lawyer, whether acting in his professional capacity or otherwise, is bound by disciplinary rules of the Code of Professional Responsibility. Bar associations are notoriously reluctant to disbar or even suspend a member unless he has murdered a judge downtown at high noon in the presence of the entire Committee on Ethical Practice."[77] In discussing lawyers, another commentator stated that "every major analysis of the disciplinary structures has found them grossly insensitive . . . to serious professional misconduct. . . ."[78]

Indeed, it appears that complaints of professional misconduct often are never even investigated. As noted above, 90 percent of lawyer complaints are never investigated. Further, a case reported in the *American Trial Lawyers Association Reporter* revealed that a number of complaints that had been filed with a medical board in Florida about a doctor's sexual abuse of child patients never had been resolved.[79]

With all professions, there traditionally has been a desire to be independent from government control,[80] and for the profession to be reluctant to take action against a member of its own group. In a 1981 article about teachers who abuse children, it was noted that a teacher convicted of sexually abusing a number of children was widely supported by teachers throughout the town, with bumper stickers distributed proclaiming his innocence and fund-raising dinners sponsored for him.[81] The article noted that if a professional is uncovered as a child abuser, the profession will close ranks to protect the person and its own. Moreover, the public has placed fundamental trust in professionals such as doctors, teachers, or psychologists, who are presumed to possess high moral standards, and the professions have made their own efforts to promote high moral character, honesty, trustworthiness, and integrity in their members.

At one time, it was believed that professionals did not require regulation for several reasons.[82] First, they were thought to possess unique skills and knowledge that laypeople could not evaluate or regulate. Second, they were thought to possess a higher degree of morality in which the public could place complete trust and confidence. Third, it was believed the profession itself could deal with the occasional incompetent or unethical practitioner. In recent years, however, these beliefs have been eroded. The general public is now much more knowledgeable. It is now recognized that there are some incompetent professionals. And the professions frequently have failed to act against their own members for misconduct.[83]

With greater awareness of the problem of child sexual abuse, legal actions have become much more common. At one time, for example, criminal prosecutions were rarely instituted in these cases. Like criminal prosecutions, license revocation proceedings also may become more common. In a case involving sexual relations between a psychiatrist and an adult patient, the dissent suggested that a licensing proceeding may in fact be a better mechanism for dealing with such misconduct than a civil damages action.[84]

It appears that with most professions, where misconduct such as sexual abuse of a child is also a criminal offense, licensing authorities are likely to wait until the outcome of a criminal prosecution. The advantage of this approach is that the availability of a conviction should make it easier to revoke the professional's license in a disciplinary proceeding. This, however, creates the problem that an individual alleged to have sexually abused a child in his or her professional practice may continue practicing for many months after the complaint is made, until the criminal proceeding is terminated.

If a disciplinary proceeding occurs before a criminal trial, however, the professional may be able to discover and use information from the disciplinary proceeding to aid in his or her criminal defense. Moreover, if a disciplinary proceeding precedes a criminal or civil trial, it is also possible that disclosures made by the professional can be subpoenaed and used against him or her in judicial proceedings.[85] As noted previously, this may not be a violation of his or her Fifth Amendment privilege against self-incrimination, but it may inhibit a professional's acknowledgment of the offense, preventing informal resolutions and necessitating a full-blown hearing. These problems have been addressed in some state licensing statutes by provisions prohibiting the discovery of any information in the disciplinary proceeding for use in a subsequent criminal or civil action.[86]

Another issue in disciplinary proceedings involves the type of discipline imposed. Judicial decisions indicate that licensing authorities impose conflicting dispositions after it has been proven that the professional is unfit based upon sexual abuse of a child. Where the abuse would have no adverse effect upon the individual's practice and occurred outside the professional sphere, revocation may not necessarily be the appropriate disposition. Suspension of the license with treatment may be a better alternative. On the other hand, it may be wise to revoke the medical license of a pediatrician or a teacher's certificate if the professional is found to have abused several children (either as part of or outside professional work).[87] However, it appears that dispositions may not always reflect this type of logical reasoning. In some cases the results seem too lenient, while in others they seem too harsh.

In a Washington State case, for example, a doctor's license was suspended after he was convicted of sexually abusing a female child, but the order was stayed as long as he had contact with girls only when a responsible adult who knew of his conviction was present.[88] In another case in which the licensing board found that a pediatrician had sexually molested a boy, the doctor's license was suspended for 30 days, and he was placed on probation with the requirement of chaperoned examinations of boy patients for 10 years.[89] On the other hand, sexual offenders who are considered to have a mental problem and to be in need of treatment may be unduly punished by multiple legal proceedings potentially resulting in a prison sentence, a monetary civil damages award, revocation of their license to practice their profession, and professional association sanctions.

The problem of multiple proceedings when a professional sexually abuses a child not only affects the professional but also may cause repeated trauma to the child, who may be a witness in each proceeding. When a family member abuses a child, it has been noted that the child victim is often subjected to insensitive legal procedures in both juvenile court and criminal proceedings.[90] If a professional sexually abuses a child, the child may be involved in five different proceedings.

CONCLUSION

Only recently has there been acknowledgment that children are sexually abused by unrelated adults they know and trust. These include professionals, such as doctors, teachers, and others. Disciplinary proceedings are necessary in order to limit a professional's continued access to children. Even though a criminal action may prevent a professional's contact with children (through imprisonment or no-contact orders as a condition of probation), many criminal cases involve relatively short sentences. Neither criminal nor civil judicial proceedings have the authority to revoke a practitioner's license, and thereby permanently cut off a professional's access to children. Moreover, aggressive pursuit of disciplinary proceedings is necessary to maintain the public's continued confidence and trust in professionals who deal with children. Parents should not have to fear sending their children to daycare, school, or a doctor's office. As a doctor noted in a 1985 article, "The overwhelming majority of physicians are competent and honest professionals. By identifying and disciplining the few who are not, we meet our public and professional responsibilities."[91] Another pediatrician and child abuse expert underscores the need for effective use of disciplinary proceedings to deal with sex offenders who use their professions to abuse children:

> When the pediatrician is a pedophile, the interests and needs of many parties are compromised: the children's needs to be free of abuse and exploitation and to trust adults to whom they must turn for care; the medical profession's needs to maintain its standards for care and its status within the community; the community's needs to trust those on whom they rely for the care of their children and to maintain the social order.[92]

NOTES

1. Russell, *Incidence and Prevalence of Intrafamilial and Extrafamilial Sexual Abuse of Female Children*, 7 Child Abuse and Neglect 133 (1983); Finkelhor, SEXUALLY VICTIMIZED CHILDREN (1979).

2. Stove, *Patient/Therapist Sex—The Legal Perspective*, 2 Psychiatric News 18, 19 (1976).

3. 70 C.J.S. *Physicians and Surgeons* sec. 6 (1948); 7 Am. Jur. 2d *Attorneys at Law* sec. 2 (1980).

4. Feinstein, *Special Report: The Ethics of Professional Regulation*, 312 New Eng. J. Med. 801, 802–804 (1985).

5. *Id.*

6. 7 Am. Jur. 2d *Attorneys at Law* sec. 27, 28 (1980).

7. 7 Am. Jur. 2d *Attorneys at Law* sec. 67 (1980).

8. Annot., 78 A.L.R.3d 735, 739 (1977); Note, *Disciplining Attorneys for Nonprofessional Conduct Involving Alcohol and Sex*, 1975 Ariz. St. L. J. 411 (1975).

9. Annot., 36 A.L.R.3d 735, 739 (1971); Note, *supra* note 8, at 423–24.

10. Note, *supra* note 8, at 428; *Morrison* v. *State Bd. of Educ.*, 82 Cal. Rptr. 175, 461 P.2d 375 (1969); 7 Am. Jur. 2d *Attorneys at Law* sec. 69 (1980).

11. *Grannis* v. *Board of Medical Examiners*, 96 Cal. Rptr. 863, 872 (Cal. App. 1971).

12. *Tomerlin* v. *Dade Co. School Bd.*, 318 So.2d 159 (Fla. Dist. Ct. App. 1975).

13. Annot., 78 A.L.R.3d 42 (1977).

14. *In re Karin*, 262 N.W.2d 162 (Minn. 1978).

15. 7 Am. Jur. 2d *Attorneys at Law* sec. 40 (1980); Note, *supra* note 8, at 423–24.

16. *Florida Bar* v. *Hefty*, 213 So.2d 422 (Fla. 1968).

17. *Id.*

18. *See also In re McDonald (II)*, 239 S.E.2d 83 (S.C. 1977).

19. *In re Safran*, 554 P.2d 329 (Cal. 1976).

20. Annot., 36 A.L.R.3d 735, 738 (1971).

21. 7 Am. Jur. 2d *Attorneys at Law* sec. 25, sec. 83 (1980); 70 C.J.S. *Physicians and Surgeons* sec. 17 (1948).

22. *See* 76 A.L.R. 674, 675 (1932).

23. Annot., 76 A.L.R. 674, 675–76 (1932).

24. Annot., 81 A.L.R. 1196, 1198 (1932).

25. Annot., 90 A.L.R. 1111, 1112 (1934); 70 C.J.S. *Physicians and Surgeons* sec. 72 (1948).

26. *Ex parte Wall*, 107 U.S. 265 (1883); 7 Am. Jur. 2d *Attorneys at Law* sec. 72 (1980); Annot., 76 A.L.R. 674 (1932).

27. *Lang* v. *Lee*, 639 S.W.2d 111, 113 (Mo. App. 1982).

28. *Devita* v. *Sills*, 425 F.2d 1172 (3rd Cir. 1970).

29. 7 Am. Jur. *Attorneys at Law* sec. 74 (1980); 70 C.J.S. *Physicians and Surgeons* sec. 16 (1948).

30. *See, e.g.*, Cal. Educ. Code sec. 12912, 13207 (West. Supp.).

31. *Bernstein* v. *Bd. of Medical Examiners*, 22 Cal. Rptr. 419, 204 Cal. App.2d 378 (5th Cal. Dist. Ct. App. 1962).

32. Annot., 81 A.L.R. 1196 (1932).

33. *See id.* at 1198–99; Herbsleb, Sales, and Overcast, *Challenging Licensure and Certification*, 40 Am. Psychologist 1165 (1985).

34. *Greenfield* v. *Hamrick*, 341 So.2d 136 (Ala. 1976); Herbsleb, Sales, and Overcast, *supra*, note 33, at 1174.

35. Cooper, 2 STATE ADMINISTRATIVE LAW 492 (1965).

36. Davis, ADMINISTRATIVE LAW TREATISE (1979). *See, e.g.*, Ga. Code sec. 43-11-47(b) (1982) (dentist licensing statute incorporates emergency action and summary suspension provision of other state administrative laws).

37. 7 Am. Jur. 2d *Attorneys at Law* sec. 87 (1980).

38. 7 Am. Jur. 2d *Attorneys at Law* sec. 89 (1980); *see Appeal of Plantier*, 494 A.2d 270 (N.H. 1985).

39. *See, e.g.*, *Neal* v. *Bryant*, 149 So.2d 529 (Fla. 1962).

40. *In re Polk License Revocation*, 449 A.2d 7 (N.J. 1982); *Re Cappoccia*, 59 N.Y.2d 549, 466 N.Y.S.2d 268, 453 N.E.2d 497 (1983); see also *Woods* v. *District of Columbia Nurses' Examining Bd.*, 436 A.2d 369 (D.C. App. 1981) (holding that right to practice one's profession is a *liberty* interest meriting procedural due process protections).

41. *Mullane* v. *Central Hanover Trust Co.*, 339 U.S. 306, 313 (1950).

42. *Re Ruffalo*, 390 U.S. 544 (1968).

43. *Id.*

44. *Shurgin* v. *Ambach*, 83 A.D.2d 665, 442 N.Y.S.2d 212 (1981).

45. *Weissman* v. *Board of Education*, 547 P.2d 1267 (Colo. 1976); *Tomerlin* v. *Dade County School Bd.*, 318 So.2d 159 (Fla. Dist. Ct. App. 1975); *Kilpatrick* v. *Wright*, 437 F.Supp. 397 (D. Ala. 1977).

46. *Committee on Professional Ethics & Conduct of State Bar Ass'n* v. *Durham*, 279 N.W.2d 280 (Iowa 1979); *Appeal of Plantier*, *supra*, note 38; *In re Polk License Revocation*, 90 N.J. 550, 449 A.2d 7 (1982).

47. 70 C.J.S. *Physicians and Surgeons* sec. 17 (1948).

48. *Missouri ex rel. Hurwitz* v. *North*, 271 U.S. 40 (1925).

49. *Giddens* v. *State Bar*, 28 Cal.3d 730, 170 Cal. Rptr. 812, 621 P.2d 851 (1980).

50. *State ex rel. Munch* v. *Davis*, 143 Fla. 236, 196 So.2d 491 (1940).

51. National Association of Attorneys General, DISCIPLINARY ACTION MANUAL FOR OCCUPATIONAL LICENSING BOARD (1978); *see* Ga. Code 43-11-47(b) (1982). See also *Burleigh* v. *State Bar of Nevada*, 643 P.2d 1201 (Nev. 1982).

52. *Greenfield* v. *Hamrick*, 341 So.2d 136 (Ala. 1976).

53. *Lenihan* v. *Commonwealth*, 165 Ky. 93, 176 S.W. 948 (1915); see also *Willner* v. *Committee on Character & Fitness*, 373 U.S. 96 (1963).

54. 70 C.J.S. *Physicians and Surgeons* sec. 18(d)(1948).

55. *Giddens* v. *State Bar*, *supra* note 49; *Morra* v. *State Bd. of Examiners of Psychologists*, 212 Kan. 103, 510 P.2d 614 (1973); 61 Am. Jur. 2d *Physicians, Surgeons and Other Healers* sec. 112 (1981); 7 Am. Jur. 2d *Attorneys at Law* sec. 90 (1980).

56. *See Masters* v. *Bd. of Dental Examiners of Cal.*, 15 Cal. App.2d 506, 59 P.2d 827 (1936).

57. *In re Polk License Revocation*, 449 A.2d 7 (N.J. 1982).

58. *Re Mayberry*, 295 Mass. 155, 3 N.E.2d 248 (1936); 7 Am. Jur. 2d *Attorneys at Law* sec. 95 (1980).

59. *Re Cappoccia*, 59 N.Y.2d 549, 466 N.Y.S.2d 268, 453 N.E.2d 497 (1983); *In re Kincheloe*, 157 S.E.2d 833 (N.C. 1967).

60. *Gonzalez* v. *Comm'n. on Judicial Performance*, 33 Cal.3d 354, 657 P.2d 372, 188 Cal. Rptr. 880 (1983), *app. dismissed* 464 U.S. 1033 (1984); *Contra in re Polk License Revocation*, 449 A.2d 7 (N.J. 1982).

61. *Barron* v. *Bd. of Dental Examiners of State of Cal.*, 44 Cal. App.2d 790, 113 P.2d 247 (1941).

62. *Pryse* v. *Yakima School Dist.*, 30 Wash. App. 16, 632 P.2d 60 (1981).

63. *Gibson* v. *Berryhill*, 411 U.S. 564 (1972).

64. *Withrow* v. *Larkin*, 421 U.S. 35 (1975).

65. *Id.* at 55.

66. 70 C.J.S. *Physicians and Surgeons* sec. 18(g) (1948).

67. *See, e.g.*, *Laisne* v. *California State Bd. of Optometry*, 19 Cal.2d 831, 123 P.2d 457 (1942).

68. *Penn-Delco School District* v. *Urso*, 382 A.2d 162 (Pa. Comm. 1978).

69. *Bovino* v. *Bd. of School Directors of Ind. Area School*, 377 A.2d 1284 (Pa. Comm. 1977); *In re Cutshaw*, 432 P.2d 474 (Ariz. Ct. App. 1967); *Morra* v. *State Bd. of Examiners of Psychologists*, 510 P.2d 614 (Kan. 1973).

70. 70 C.J.S. *Physicians and Surgeons* sec. 18 (1948).

71. *See, e.g.*, *Reagan* v. *Bd. of Directors, Republic School Dist.*, 4 Wash. App. 279, 480 P.2d 807 (1971) (modified by later state and case law). See also *Pryse* v. *Yakima School Dist.*, 30 Wash. App. 16, 632 P.2d 60 (1981).

72. *Survey of State Licensing Board Disciplinary Actions for Professionals' Abuse of Children*, unpublished (American Bar Association, 1985).

73. Feinstein, *supra* note 4.

74. Rhode, *Moral Character as a Professional Credential*, 94 Yale L.J. 491, 547 (1985).

75. *Id.*

76. *See* Hays, *Sexual Contact Between Psychotherapist and Patient: Legal Remedies*, 47 Psychological Rep. 1247 (1980).

77. Note, *supra* note 8, at 411.

78. Rhode, *supra* note 74, at 547.

79. 23 ATLA L. Rep. 62 (1980).

80. Feinstein, *supra* note 4.

81. Bridgman, *Teachers Who Abuse Children Often Escape, Justice Study Finds*, Education Week, May 9, 1984.

82. Feinstein, *supra* note 4.

83. *Id.*

84. *Patient-Therapist Sex—The Legal Perspective,* 2 Psychiatric News, 18–19 (1976).

85. Sinnett and Linford, *Processing of Formal Complaints Against Psychologists*, 50 Psychological Rep., 535–44 (1982).

86. *Id.*

87. *Tomerlin* v. *Dade Co. School Bd.*, 318 So.2d 159 (Fla. Dist. Ct. App. 1975).

88. Survey, *supra* note 72.

89. Newberger and Newberger, *When the Pediatrician Is a Pedophile*, SEXUAL EXPLOITATION OF PATIENTS BY HEALTH PROFESSIONALS (A. W. Burgess and C. R. Hartman, eds., 1986).

90. Bulkley, RECOMMENDATIONS FOR IMPROVING LEGAL INTERVENTION IN INTRAFAMILY CHILD SEXUAL ABUSE CASES (American Bar Association, 1982).

91. Feinstein, *supra* note 4.

92. Newberger and Newberger, *supra* note 89.

Part IV

Beyond Legal Sanctions

12

Structural Reconciliation of Therapeutic and Criminal Justice Cultures

Jon R. Conte

The failure of mental health, medical, and other professionals to report cases of suspected child abuse has been described as a problem almost since mandatory reporting laws were introduced. Comparisons of the assumed rate of victimization based on incidence studies and the actual rate of cases investigated by child protection agencies in the various states is assumed to be proof of a nonreporting problem. Actual data on the extent of the nonreporting problem are very difficult to obtain, although nonreporting has been the subject of some research over the years (see, for instance, Saulsbury and Campbell, 1985; Attias and Goodwin, 1984; Muehleman and Kimmons, 1981). Social sanctions (such as disapproval or a reluctance to refer cases) for advocating the nonreporting of child sexual abuse are such that it is difficult to get many professionals to describe their reporting behavior or to discuss the context in which they frame their actions.

Clinical experience suggests that at least some professionals exhibit a reluctance to report some cases of suspected sexual abuse. Their subsequent behavior in the face of this reluctance is not known. Current proposals for appropriate responses by the state, other professionals, and society at large to the nonreporting problem have tended to focus on the behavior of reporting (for instance, increasing and actually delivering sanctions against the professional who fails to report or increased training on the mandate to report, the rationale for reporting, and penalties for nonreporting). Generally, the professional who is reluctant to report is looked upon in negative terms in these efforts. For example, he or she may be described as someone

The author thanks Howard Levy, M.D., Mt. Sinai Hospital Medical Center, Chicago; Detective Scott Keenan, Chicago Police Department; and John Goad, Illinois Department of Children and Family Services, for their comments on earlier versions of this chapter.

more afraid of legal suit by alleged offenders than concerned with protecting children, or as someone unable to deal with the discomfort of interacting with a client after reporting the client's abuse of a child.

Little research is currently available that describes the extent and nature of the nonreporting problem across the United States. Nor is it completely clear what the reasons are for professional reporting behavior. In a situation characterized by so many unknowns, it may be helpful to take a broader look at the "problem" before rushing toward recommendations directed at changing professional behavior (for instance, by the increased use of penalties for nonreporting). This chapter will suggest that understanding the context of professional reluctance to report some cases of child sexual abuse may be helpful in deciding how to respond to nonreporting of cases (if in fact that is a major problem). More important, such an understanding may help inform social policy regarding how to respond to the sexually abused child. Recommendations for future action also are offered.

From the outset it should be understood that the context of professional reporting described in this chapter is based on the author's experience and not on research actually describing the presence of certain dimensions described below. Nor should anything in this chapter be taken to advocate the nonreporting of cases. While there are numerous legitimate concerns that in part support a reluctance to report, nonreporting presents its own problems to clients who are left in abusive situations or who fail to receive the social and mental health services that would help correct the abusive situation and the effects of such abuse in the life of the abused children and her/his family. Experience also suggests that there are personal reasons for some professionals' reluctance to report that are largely self-centered and in no way directed toward the interests of clients (for instance, fear of being sued by angry former clients). It is toward the reporting behavior of these professionals that many of the proposed responses (such as professional disciplinary actions) are directed. However, as described below, there are a number of legitimate professional concerns that are client-centered and that should not be confused with these personal, less admirable reasons.

RELUCTANCE TO REPORT

Professional reluctance to report cases of childhood sexual victimization may be based on motives that are essentially derived from a sincere concern for clients. These motives are based in part on the professionals' firsthand experiences in reporting previous cases, on their contact with the reporting mechanisms (either police or child protection agencies), and on professional socialization and training, which define the intent of professional intervention in cases of child sexual abuse. There are at least four aspects of the current scene that define the context in which professional reluctance to report may be understood.

Criminalization of the Problem

In an important paper prepared for the Surgeon General's Workshop on Violence, Newberger (1985) traces the evolution of interest in child abuse to its current heavily legalistic formulation. In its simplest and perhaps most expressive form, contemporary interest in maltreatment of children is, as Dr. Newberger points out, interest in finding fault. Much of intervention is directed toward determining who did what, to whom, when it was done, and who witnessed it.

From the outset of the rediscovery of child sexual abuse in the late 1970s, there has been recognition that sexual abuse of children is inherently a medical, mental health, social service, and legal problem. Consequently, numerous professionals are likely to be involved in these cases. Conte (1984a) has suggested that between the late 1970s and the 1980s much professional energy has been directed toward reducing the danger of system-induced trauma resulting from intervention of numerous professionals.

Considerable early debate raged between those who advocated a strong role for the justice system in dealing with these cases (see, for instance, Berliner and Stevens, 1984) and those who opposed such involvement (see, for example, MacFarlane, 1978). It should be noted that those advocating strong involvement of the justice system in child sexual abuse cases made such an argument because the justice system appears necessary to encourage sexual offenders to acknowledge their problem and to enter and remain in treatment (see, for instance, Conte, 1984b). It is currently not clear exactly what actually happens to most identified offenders (whether they actually enter and remain in treatment or how long, if at all, they serve in prison).

More to the point here, the criminalization of child sexual abuse has resulted in a number of problems for professionals who provide service to them, which is part of the reason for the general professional reluctance to report cases.

Increasing the Burden of Proof

In a desire to reduce the potential trauma of multiple interviews by a number of professionals, it was proposed that multidisciplinary teams should investigate cases. Under this model of investigation, police, child protection workers, and medical personnel jointly interviewed and investigated allegations of child sexual abuse. One of the apparent results of these teams, in some cases, has been the tendency of professionals to defer the finding of whether abuse took place to the professional acting under the highest burden of proof. This means that the child protection worker will unfound an allegation if the police officer does not feel there is sufficient evidence to support criminal charges. This happens even though the intent of child protection legislation and current law is that child protection and law enforcement operate on different standards of evidence.

Intent of Child Protection

From its earliest historical beginning, this society has approached the idea that the state may intrude into family life with the greatest reluctance. State intervention into family life because of child abuse was, and still is, to be for the sole purpose of determining if, in fact, children are at risk. If they are at risk, the state is to provide those services necessary to alter the conditions that caused state intervention in the first place. The burden of proof required to support a finding of child abuse was intended to be less than that to support criminal charges because the intent of intervention was to offer help, not punishment.

It is currently difficult to get an accurate picture of what actually happens to cases of alleged sexual abuse. No national data are available that describe the services provided or consequences to children and their families. Clinical experience suggests that most cases do not, in fact, receive the services that are the ultimate justification and purpose of state intervention under child protection laws. It is clear that many states provide no funding for treatment. The failure to provide services to sexually abused children removes the moral and legal basis for intervention by state child protection agencies. Without services, cases may as well be investigated by the police.

Emphasis on Professional Procedures

Sexual victimization of children often involves the child, the child's significant others, and professionals in adversarial legal processes in criminal or family court. Although it is not currently clear how many of the total number of known cases of child sexual abuse ultimately result in some kind of adversary process, it appears that it is actually a small proportion. However, because these cases often involve younger children, multiple victims and offenders, allegations and counterallegations, such cases are inherently complicated.

In many of these cases around the country, the central focus of attention has become the procedures employed by mental health professionals to identify victims, support disclosure, and determine the veracity of child victims' statements. Therapists are criticized because their interviewing procedures and techniques do not meet scientific standards applied to psychological tests (such as reliability).

The issues involved in the current debate surrounding the extent to which interviewing techniques or, more generally, any adult intervention can permanently alter a child's report of events are complicated (see, for instance, Jones, 1987). They involve both issues of human behavior (such as suggestibility of young children) and trial strategy (such as whether a defense attorney can get a jury to believe something that may or may not be scientifically accurate). For our purposes here, the point is that the framing of the issue as a question of professional practice, rather than of what has really happened to the children involved, has fundamentally distorted how professionals view many of the cases involving young children, multiple victims, and multiple offenders.

Mental health professionals are trained to relate to a client, and to encourage expression and the recounting of the client's story. An understanding of reality, of what actually happened or did not happen to the client at some time in the near or distant past, is not initially the therapist's major concern. An understanding of what is real may help direct therapy, but it is the client's understanding of, or memory of, "reality" that is the initial core of the beginning phases of treatment.

As practiced by many attorneys, the adversary process allows questioning of professional practice, efforts to discredit witnesses, and the presentation of theories of events intended to influence the judgment of juries, even though they may be virtually without scientific support. Accounts of cases involving these elements have received considerable media attention in many parts of the country, and the cases in Jordan, Minnesota, and southern California have received national attention (see, for instance, *Chicago Tribune*, 1984).

Mental health professionals aware of the considerable and inherent conflict between forensic and therapeutic practice are understandably reluctant to become involved in legal processing of cases. Professionals aware of the great costs to clients of such involvement have to think carefully—indeed, be reluctant—to see their young clients become involved in a process where they may become the targets of an adversarial legal process.

CHILD PROTECTION AS A "BLACK BOX"

For many professionals, child protection agencies are "black boxes" into which one puts reports of abuse and from which no information about the agency's response or decisions is forthcoming. The processes employed in making decisions, the evidence used to make them, and the internal mechanisms employed to help ensure that the decisions are good ones are completely unclear. Experience in reporting abuse varies considerably across professionals who make reports, child protection workers who receive them, and those who investigate them. Many professionals have had the experience of having a report not accepted by the child abuse hot line one day and accepted the next, the only difference being that they talked to a different child protection worker on the second call. It is not clear what accounts for this variation, since there has been no systematic study of child protection decision making in sexual abuse cases. Indeed, some variation is unexplained and is perceived by potential reporting professionals as capricious, a function of poor training, or the result of the individual bias of a child protection worker.

It seems likely that an individual professional's prior experience with reporting cases of child sexual abuse is an important component of current attitudes toward reporting. The ways that public child protection agencies handle these experiences may have considerable influence over future reporting behavior. Several illustrations present some of the typical problems in how these experiences are handled (it should be noted that there are numerous examples of ideal handling as well).

Lack of Feedback

In many situations, the rationales for ultimate decisions are never communicated to the reporting professional. By definition, when a professional makes a report of sexual abuse, he or she has reason to suspect that a child has been sexually abused. When the child protection agency investigates the professional's suspicion and determines the allegation to be unfounded, there is an inevitable difference of professional opinion. If the reasons for unfounding the case were made clear to the professional and, when appropriate, there were a means to appeal the decision, it is likely that many reporting professionals would understand the processes far better than many do at present. Such feedback may also serve to increase a sense of collaboration between the child protection agency and professionals likely to report child abuse.

Lack of Consistency

Most professionals who have made reports have experienced the situation that subsequent reports of the same allegation may result in different decisions. It is not clear why this happens, although in part it seems to be a function of getting a different worker, making enough "fuss" over a case to call attention to it, or creating an organizational problem that can be resolved only by founding the case. These are obviously not good reasons to determine that an allegation of abuse is founded, yet they do occur with some frequency.

CONSEQUENCES OF REPORTING

The consequences of reporting allegations of child sexual abuse are not clear. There are currently no regional or national data describing what happens to cases in terms of prosecution, removal of offenders or children from the home, services provided, or immediate and long-term consequences of reporting to child victims, offenders, or their families. Unfortunately, in the absence of data, what seems to form professional attitudes about reporting are cases that result in adverse consequences. Although it is not clear how commonly they occur, some of the typical adverse consequences are discussed below.

Investigation and Adjudication Without Treatment

It is clear that sexual abuse places a child at risk for psychosocial difficulties, both as a child and later in life (see, for instance, Conte, 1985). It is also generally recognized, although research support for this belief is not available, that investigation can cause disruptions in life-style and other traumas to a sexually abused children that may produce psychosocial difficulties in their own right. Investigating and determining that, in fact, a child has been sexually abused, but doing nothing to reduce the known risks for immediate and long-term psychosocial consequences of sexual victimization, could be regarded as a form of state-initiated child abuse (or at least child neglect). Not only does it remove the foundation of child protection, but it seems to risk increasing the victim's sense of betrayal and victimization, as well as leaving him or her an easy target for retribution by the alleged offender.

Removal of the Perpetrator from the Home

In many cases, perpetrators who admit abuse are removed from the home, while those who deny it are allowed to remain. There is the risk that current practices result in the most treatable offenders (those who admit the abuse and take immediate steps to assume responsibility for the abuse) suffering more adverse effects than offenders who deny the abuse and fight the allegations. There appears to be considerable risk that those who cooperate with the system by acknowledging the victimization of a child may suffer harsher consequences than those who refuse to cooperate by denying the allegations.

RECOMMENDATIONS

The explosion in the number of reports of child sexual abuse appears to have far outstripped many communities' capacities to respond meaningfully to these cases. Some public social service agencies lack the trained manpower always to complete an investigation in a sensitive and efficient manner.

Many communities lack the specialized mental health services necessary to assist sexual abuse victims and the adults who share and influence their lives. Funding of treatment is scarce. The placing of blame for this situation is complicated and involves a number of social policy decisions since the late 1970s (deprofessionalization of child protection positions, support for investigation over treatment, emphasis on punishment rather than treatment).

Blame seems to offer little in the way of corrective response to the problems all professionals face in dealing with these cases. Corrective response to the failure of some professionals to report cases of suspected child sexual abuse (for instance, through sanctions) may be useful in those cases where the failure is driven by self-serving concerns of the professional. Society will make a great mistake if it believes that the reluctance of all professionals to report emanates from these "baser" motives. Indeed, much can be learned about how to improve society's response to victimized children by recognizing that some of this professional reluctance is based on the higher principles of professional judgment and dedication.

The context surrounding the reluctance to report described in the previous pages suggests several recommendations for how to deal with the "problem." These recommendations are outlined in the remainder of the chapter for the purpose of discussion. Many will require substantial changes in current law, agency practice, and professional conduct.

Relink Investigation and Treatment

Advocates for victims have to do a better job of articulating for the public the immediate and long-term psychosocial consequences of the failure of states to provide meaningful treatment to victims. Public pressure to increase state funding of treatment resources can be initiated only by advocates and not by state agency administrators. Agency administrators often operate under political constraints established by elected officials who may not have the needs of sexually abused children as a priority.

Advocates for victims also can be advocates for state agencies as they articulate the importance of providing treatment and, consequently, of increasing state treatment budgets. Traditional tools of the advocate, such as public education and other public awareness campaigns, legal suits, and efforts to create legislation that would increase the availability of treatment, are all likely to be useful in this regard.

Create a New Subspecialty of the Forensic Therapist

The use of mental health professionals as agents of investigation to determine if children have or have not been sexually abused, does not appear to be a good use of manpower. Not only are most mental health professionals untrained in legal principles, but much of therapeutic training runs counter to the requirements of case investigation, developing evidence, and supporting the credibility of witness and expert testimony.

Consequently, specially trained mental health professionals should serve as forensic therapists whose purpose is the sensitive, trauma-reducing investigation of difficult cases of alleged sexual abuse. These professionals should base their interactions with clients both on sound interpersonal practice and on legal requirements. Standardized procedures, careful attention to documentation, and close supervision of investigation and disclosure processes should be the hallmarks of this subspecialty.

While the availability of this professional expertise would not diminish the responsibility of professionals to report sexual abuse, it would free therapists from the task they are ill-equipped to perform: validating allegations. Because of special expertise, it may also result in better forensic practice.

View the Reporting of Child Abuse as a Professional Collaboration Between Reporter and Agency

State confidentiality laws and policies need to be altered to allow the state agency to report back to mandated reporters the rationale behind the final decision of child protection investigation. Cases may be unfounded for a variety of reasons, including lack of evidence, uncooperative witnesses, or errors. The sharing of information, a characteristic of virtually all collaborative professional practice, would make it possible for mandated reporters to understand why their reports are unfounded. It would also provide an ideal mechanism for the training of reporters.

Other characteristics of collaborative practice are likely to be helpful in improving both reporting and the practice of child protection generally. Many of the concepts and procedures that make up mental health quality assurance efforts would be useful. For example, periodic peer review, conferences on difficult cases that involve child protection workers and mandated reporters, case consultation involving mandated reporters as consultants, and the like would increase reporters' understanding of the difficulties of child protection work and of the internal workings of the "black box" that is child protection. Such efforts should also increase the knowledge of child protection workers.

Continue Efforts to Make Legal Interventions Victim-Sensitive

Current efforts to make involvement with the justice system helpful rather than trauma-producing for the child client should be helpful in reducing some professional reluctance to report. Renewed efforts to create alternatives to incarceration (especially community-based treatment programs) seem especially important in light of current emphasis on punishment responses to adults who have sex with children. Also important are the efforts to make children's appearances in court less trauma-producing. The creation of children's courtrooms, examination of children via closed-circuit television, and increased use of judicial power to control the defense are all steps likely to reassure professionals that reporting of abuse will not result in a trauma-producing experience for the child.

Improve the Quality and Quantity of Public Social Services

Efforts to deal with the reporting "problem" have to recognize at some level that part of the problem is the general deterioration in public social services since the late 1970s. Significantly increasing demand, budgets that have failed to keep up with the demand, deprofessionalizing line positions in many states, unionization of line positions (which makes discipline of problem workers and assignment by expertise rather than seniority difficult), and a host of other problems have in some states contributed to a general decline in the quality of public social services, especially child protection investigations. For example, training of child protection workers is an ongoing problem. In some states, workers receive more training in how to fill out forms than in how to plan and conduct an investigation. Staff burnout and turnover are often high.

Efforts that increase the financial and other supports for public social service should result in improved client services. Such improvements should help reduce some professional reluctance to report.

CONCLUSION

In an age characterized by the search for easy answers and quick fixes, the idea that resolution of the "problem" of nonreporting will require the very efforts that improve client services will not be a popular position. It is far easier to argue that sanctions for nonreporting or increased training of mandated reporters will "fix" the problem. Such a view ignores the many real and important reasons professionals are reluctant to report some cases of child sexual abuse. Ultimately, clients and society in general lose when the highest professional instincts (such as concern for clients) are ignored or reframed as professional weaknesses rather than strengths.

REFERENCES

Attias, R., & Goodwin, J. (1984). Knowledge and management strategies in incest cases: A survey of physicians, psychologists and counselors. Paper presented at the Fifth International Congress on Child Abuse and Neglect, Montreal, Canada.

Berliner, L. D., & Stevens, D. (1984). Clinical issues in child sexual abuse. *Social Work & Human Sexuality, 1*, 93–108.

Chicago Tribune. (1984). *Child sexual abuse*. Reprints of stories running in 1984, available from Chicago Tribune, 435 N. Michigan Avenue, Chicago, IL 60611.

Conte, J. R. (1984a). Sexual abuse of children: A progress report. *Social Work, 29*, 258–263.

Conte, J. R. (1984b). The role of the justice system in responding to child sexual abuse. *Social Service Review, 58* (4), 556–68.

Conte, J. R. (1985). The effects of sexual abuse on children: A critique and suggestions for future research. *Victimology: The International Journal, 10*, 110–30.

Jones, P. H. (1987). Reliable and fictitious accounts of sexual abuse to children. *Journal of Interpersonal Violence*, 1:27–45.

Kulla, R. Personal communication.

MacFarlane, K. (1978). Sexual abuse of children. In J. R. Chapan and M. Getes (eds.), *Victimization of women*. Beverly Hills, Ca: Sage.

Muehleman, T., & Kimmons, C. (1981). Psychologists' views on child abuse reporting, confidentiality, life and the law. *Professional Psychologist, 12*, 631–38.

Newberger, E. (1985). Child abuse. Paper presented at the Surgeon General's Workshop on Violence and Public Health, Leesburg, Va.

Saulsbury, F. T., & Campbell, R. E. (1985). Evaluation of child abuse reporting by physicians. *American Journal of Disease of Children, 139*, 393–95.

13

Toward Community Responsiveness in Childcare Protective Agencies

Marie Leaner

The purpose of this chapter is to describe the experience of the state of Illinois Department of Children and Family Services (DCFS) in responding to recent developments in reporting of child abuse and neglect. As noted in earlier chapters, reporting of abuse and neglect has increased astronomically in recent years, and the ability of child protective services to keep up with this trend has sometimes been outstripped by the enormity of the demands made on the system.

This situation, one of increased expectations of the child welfare system (due to increased awareness and reporting in the community) and absence of corresponding increases in the resources available to the child welfare system, has generated a good deal of tension and misunderstanding between the professional community and the providers of protective services. This chapter is an attempt to describe one state's efforts to deal with these problems and to provide quality protection to children at risk.

THE ILLINOIS EXPERIENCE

In 1980 Illinois began to improve child protection by consolidating 70 different response systems throughout the state into a single unified system. The new system uses one toll-free hot line number, 24 hours a day, 365 days a year, in order to better identify abuse and neglect situations and to help families in need. It also houses the State Central Register, a sophisticated computer system that tracks prior indicated reports of abuse or neglect. If a reporter is doubtful about the spelling of a name, the "Soundex" search system will display similar names along with other identifying data. Displayed in seconds, this information will include the date and nature of the prior indicated reports, the names of all others in the family, the identity of the perpetrator, actions taken by the department, and the name of the department caseworker.

Eight hundred child protection personnel were added to handle investigations and provide casework services to families at risk. At that time, an enormous investment was made to train child protection workers, police, doctors, school personnel, and others in how the new system was designed to work. In order to educate the community, a statewide network of volunteers visited hospitals, police stations, daycare centers, and work places of other professionals who were mandated by the new state law to report suspected cases of abuse and neglect. These volunteers delivered information kits and copies of the new child abuse and neglect law, and showed a brief film describing how the new hot line worked. They not only disseminated information but also acted as a link between child protective services and the community at large.

Additionally, the hot line was publicized in all forms of mass media, particularly radio and television. Spot announcements were made by advertising agencies that donated their time and efforts to the project. At the same time, a full complement of trained social workers was assigned to the hot line to handle additional calls generated by the announcements. Previous experience in other states had indicated that massive publicity campaigns often resulted in system overload, delaying the response to critical calls. In Illinois, preparation for increased community response proved more than adequate.

INCREASING SYSTEM DEMANDS

But to quote a recent movie, "That was then and this is now." By September 1985, the hot line averaged over 750 calls per day, about 6.2 calls per worker per hour. In October, the figure was closer to 567 calls per day. Since that time, the hot line has almost consistently averaged 550 calls per day. Yet, only three in every ten of those calls is a report.

The effect of these increases on hot line staff was easy to anticipate. They were overwhelmed by the influx of calls and were not able to keep up with the dramatic increase. In trying to assess this phenomenon, we examined the calls and noted that over 30 percent of them were from our own staff, who must call to request that additional names be Soundexed, to secure additional information on child abuse and neglect reports, or to document the taking of temporary custody.

Even though there is a separate telephone number for these calls, the number rolls over to the major hot line number when the designated line is busy. Because calls from staff and other nonreporting calls tied up the lines, 10 to 16 percent of all calls were being terminated by callers before they could be answered.

The goal for hot line response is to obtain all requisite information from 90 percent of the calls made when they first come in. In these circumstances, however, it was taking two or more hours to return phone calls of mandated reporters because only 50 percent of incoming calls were being completed when they first came in. It was not unusual for mandated reporters to be called back as much as four hours after they reached out for help on a family's behalf.

That's the bad news. The good news is, first, that the Protective Service Division asked for, and received, $35,000 in additional emergency funding for the final seven months of that fiscal year. This provided for two contractual staff members and two completely separate telephone lines. Second, as of February 1, 1986, hot line staff was increased by one-third. In the following fiscal year, another 17 positions were to be added. Third, a state-of-the-art telecommunications system was purchased, increasing capacity and, hence, ability to respond. By pressing one additional number after reaching the hot line, callers can indicate whether they are DCFS staff, mandated reporters or nonmandated reporters, and the purpose of their call. This system will allow speedier, more expeditious responses to emergency situations and calls from mandated reporters. The anticipated result will be increased confidence and cooperation from these vital allies in protecting children.

OUTREACH TO MANDATED REPORTERS

In addition to enhancing the ability of child protective services to respond to reports, it is important to continue efforts to educate people in the community. To this end, a public education campaign has been designed to explain how the hot line works; to better define, for potential reporters, what does and does not constitute a report; to describe how investigations are conducted; and to provide similar relevant information.

In the five years since the first campaign, there has been considerable staff turnover in community agencies, resulting in a new generation of mandated reporters. Many of these professionals are not aware of the expanded reporting requirements under Illinois law. The amended law has new requirements for reporting as well as new, clearly defined penalties for failure to report.

In order to avoid a statewide crunch in hot line and investigative capacity, the public education campaign is to be implemented in phases, targeting one region every two months. (Illinois has eight regions.) Planned activities include a press conference in each region, announcing the major training initiative of mandated reporters, introducing radio and television public service announcements, and announcing the new regional multidisciplinary teams instituted by the department to better coordinate response to reports of abuse and neglect.

Before the project is undertaken, the hot line will be fully staffed, the new telephone system will be fully operative, and each region will be up to its full complement of child protective service investigators. In order to aid the department in accomplishing such a wide-scale training effort, two coordinators will be hired to train and maintain volunteers, with a focus on setting up a cadre of volunteers in each community with a population of 10,000 or more. The volunteers will be recruited from the Urban League, Junior League, American Association of University Women, and other community resources. After the campaign the volunteers will continue to relate to the local protective service team.

The training curriculum for the mandated reporters includes films, brochures, and complaint forms. All groups of reporters will be involved, with some training being done, as before, at hospitals, police stations, and so on.

Composition of the community-based multidisciplinary teams will reflect the range of treatment resources available to abused and neglected children and their families. Teams will engage in community awareness activities, speaking before local groups, running workshops, and providing training for other involved personnel. They will be the focal point in communities for child advocacy and for the development of additional resources. In addition, each child protection investigative team will have a mandated reporter liaison, who will have regular communication with mandated reporters and will provide ongoing training regarding recognition of abuse and neglect and reporting obligations.

DEVELOPING COOPERATIVE WORKING RELATIONSHIPS

In addition to the training and public information campaign, it is vitally necessary to institute new initiatives to respond to the feelings of resentment generated by lack of feedback to reporters on the outcome of case investigations. For instance, Illinois has commonly used a simple computer-generated form letter to let a reporter know whether a case was indicated or unfounded. No further information is available unless the worker, independently and against the rules, gives the reporter more information about the nature of the investigation or the dynamics of the case. By listening to feedback from the community on such matters, the department will be better able to respond to community concerns and attempt to find solutions to these barriers to a cooperative working relationship.

It is clearly in the best interest of the department to foster the development of more collaborative and less antagonistic relationships with other professionals. These efforts often lead to more effective reporting on the part of allied professionals and aid in the provision of a comprehensive service response to children and families in need. Three additional examples of department efforts to develop such relationships follow.

The first involves working together with coroners and pathologists. Before lobbying efforts with the legislature were successful, it was not possible to share departmental investigative findings with coroners and pathologists, nor were they allowed to share their findings with the department. In order to learn more about serious child injuries, a multidisciplinary task force of coroners and pathologists was convened. As a result of this joint effort, an autopsy protocol has been developed that standardizes the process for conducting child autopsies in Illinois.

This is a real breakthrough. When a child dies in suspicious circumstances, the state will now be in a better position to assess the safety of any other children in the home. In spite of this success, the work of the task force is not done. Currently, they are developing a protocol to help distinguish between accidental and nonaccidental injuries.

The second example of collaborative effort is an agreement with the Illinois State Board of Education. Basically, it calls for acceptance by the hot line of reports of child abuse against school personnel. Previously such reports were handled internally by the school system or as a police matter.

This effort was initiated by the passage of a resolution by the Illinois House Committee in response to increasing numbers of sexual abuse reports involving school personnel. The resolution called for the involvement of the State Board of Education and the DCFS in responding to allegations of sexual abuse of children by school personnel. An agreement was reached, however, not to limit department response to sexual abuse but to respond to all Priority One allegations. These include reports of serious bodily harm, sexual abuse, and other serious kinds of abuse. Responsibility for all other investigations is delegated to the State Board of Education.[1]

A third area of collaboration involves three other state agencies: the Department of Corrections, the Department of Mental Health and Developmental Disabilities, and the Department of State Police. As a result of an analysis of reports received by the DCFS by source, it was determined that almost no reports are received from state-operated institutions. In an effort to improve monitoring in these institutions, agreements were reached to educate corrections, mental health, developmental disability, and state police personnel in how to identify abuse and neglect, when and how one should make a report, and how CPS investigations are conducted.

CONCLUSION

The DCFS has accepted the responsibility for training mandated reporters of child abuse and neglect. Though no agency can expect perfect results, it is hoped that these efforts to educate, train, and communicate with mandated reporters will continue to have a significant impact on the reporting level and will gradually erode the resistance from allied professionals in health, mental health, education, and other fields who believe that confidentiality and the right to privacy supersede the right of children to be protected.

NOTE

1. Effective January 1, 1987, several important changes in the Illinois Abused and Neglected Child Reporting Act and related statutes were made. The new law expands the definition of a person responsible for a child's welfare at the time of abuse or neglect to include health care professionals, educational personnel, recreation supervisors, and volunteers or support personnel in any setting where children may be subject to abuse or neglect. The expanded definition means that the above-named personnel are now reportable as perpetrators of child abuse and neglect.

14
The NEA: Professional Organization and Advocate for Teachers

Lynn Ohman

The NEA, unlike many professional organizations, is also a union. As such, its mission is not only to work to assure the highest possible standards in education but also to act as a representative of and advocate for professionals and others who work in the field of education.

STRUCTURE AND GOALS OF THE NEA

The impact of the organization's structure and goals on the manner in which the issue of professional responsibility is addressed can best be understood through a review of the structure, function, and mission of the NEA.

The NEA is a professional association that has represented members of the teaching profession for over 130 years. Since the late 1960s, NEA has branched out from representing only teachers and administrators to include all types of educational employees. In approximately 35 states NEA has evolved from a "professional association" to become a collective bargaining agent in a formal labor-management relationship with employing school districts. NEA's membership is now 1.8 million, of which about 85 percent are classroom teachers. The remaining 15 percent are college faculty and educational support personnel.

The organization is structured in three tiers. When an individual educator joins a local NEA affiliate, he or she also joins a state-level organization and the national organization. As the national organization, NEA operates as a "parent" organization to the state and local chapters. The state and local tiers function as separate entities, setting their own goals and policies. These

---

The opinions expressed in this chapter are those of the author and do not necessarily reflect the policies of the National Education Association.

policies might include whether to support preemployment criminal checks on teachers and automatic revocation of certification in instances where teachers are convicted of felonies.

NEA policies are established at an annual meeting that is attended by approximately 8500 delegates. To the extent that the national organization can influence its state and local affiliates, it will. However, these affiliated organizations may set courses of their own that differ from, or at times are at odds with, those of the national NEA.

REPORTING CHILD ABUSE

Bearing this structure in mind, the first issue to be addressed evolves from NEA's sensitivity to the problem of child abuse and its concerns about how to reduce the harm this abuse inflicts on the nation's children. In this regard, the NEA and its state and local affiliates have developed a national program for teachers and parents on how to detect abuse and to encourage reporting of abuse. For the educators, in particular, the responsibility to report abuse and neglect, as mandated by state laws, is outlined.

To underscore the importance of child protection, the NEA has adopted two formal policy resolutions dealing with the ethics of reporting child abuse and the protection of teachers who are sued as a result of their work-related activities, including criminal charges of abuse. These positions have been accepted generally by NEA's state and local affiliates.

Essentially NEA believes that all children should be protected from any form of abuse or exploitation, and that all school personnel are in a position to observe and recognize abuse that has been inflicted on children.

To this end NEA supports enactment of federal, state, and local legislation that (1) provides school personnel with immunity from legal action in reporting abuse, (2) requires school personnel to report abuse, and (3) provides due process for school personnel accused of child abuse.

In July 1984, NEA launched an in-service training program for teachers and other school personnel on the subject of detecting and reporting child abuse. The in-service program is designed around a mixed-media kit that includes leaflets for parents, and audio and visual materials for conducting workshops. Materials focus on detecting child abuse, informing educators about whom to contact to report a suspected incident of abuse, how to follow up in writing, and the protection available to teachers under state statute (if any protection is available) in subsequent lawsuits by angry relatives or other individuals who may be charged as perpetrators of abuse. The materials are directed not only at the ability to identify abuse and neglect, but also at the educator's responsibility to report abuse.

This project was fueled, in part, by a concern of NEA that teachers have not known how to recognize child abuse, have not been made aware of their legal responsibilities to report abuse, or have not understood the consequences of nonreporting. Telephone conversations with the legal staff of several NEA affiliates confirmed that virtually every NEA state affiliate has attempted to set up a reporting awareness program through local field staff representatives.

BARRIERS TO REPORTING

Nevertheless, barriers to reporting abuse are significant. Mandatory reporting laws, even with their stated protections of indemnity, are probably not sufficient to remove the social barriers from reporting. Some of these barriers are listed below:

- Abuse may be difficult to detect.
- An educator's concern about maintaining the integrity of a confidential relationship may outweigh his or her concern that reporting to government authorities be done immediately. For example, an educator may wait to identify a child by name until a student can be brought to recognize the importance of involving a social welfare agency.
- Concern about reprisals, in the form of civil litigation by parents or other individuals, may discourage reporting. Even though the reporting statutes require that reporters be indemnified, protection from personal financial loss dispels only part of an educator's concern. Involvement in a lawsuit, particularly in a community where the incident of child abuse and its subsequent reporting may be highly publicized in the local press, is very traumatic.
- Many may fear reprisals by school administrators, particularly if the suspected perpetrator is another school employee.

Juxtaposed against these social barriers to reporting instances of abuse is the very real concern that educators may be charged criminally if they fail to report suspected abuse to the proper authorities.

CASE STUDIES IN REPORTING

The following three examples are case studies in which educators have been charged criminally with nonreporting. In Nevada, a guidance counselor was convicted of a misdemeanor but the conviction was subsequently overturned. In Colorado, criminal charges against a high school sociology teacher were dropped one week before trial. In Michigan, a principal was charged with not reporting suspected abuse by his school's janitor. The facts in the first two cases are interesting in that they highlight some of the ethical considerations educators must face in deciding when to break a student's confidence and report suspected abuse to the government authorities.

An NEA member who is a guidance counselor in the Reno, Nevada, area was advised on February 1, 1985, by a 14-year-old female student of an isolated incident of sexual abuse that occurred approximately 6 years prior to the student's conversation with the counselor. The incident involved the student's stepfather, who was residing with the student and her mother at the time the incident occurred. The student expressed no fear of reoccurrence of the incident. The stepfather was living in Mexico at the time the guidance counselor and the student spoke.

The guidance counselor promptly advised the student's mother of the incident of sexual abuse. The guidance counselor also involved the student in individual and group counseling. Under the circumstances, the guidance counselor concluded that there was no imminent danger to the student of further abuse and therefore no duty to report the incident to the local social services agency. Eight days later the counselor reported the incident. On the same day the incident was reported, the student and a friend consumed an overdose of pills. Upon questioning at the county medical center, the student claimed that she had attempted suicide as a result of the incident of sexual abuse that had occurred six years earlier.

A criminal complaint and arrest summons were filed by the district attorney's office on July 1, 1985. The guidance counselor was convicted in mid-September of failing to report abuse. An appeals court overturned this decision in January 1986.

The arguments in defense of the guidance counselor, which were used to appeal the lower court's decision, were that the purpose of the statute is to remove children from situations in which there is a present danger that they will be abused, and that the state reporting statute requires that the individual "knowingly and willfully" failed to report.

The guidance counselor made a judgment that there was no imminent danger, since the incident had taken place six years before and the stepfather was residing in Mexico. Furthermore, the counselor informed the student's mother immediately and made arrangements for therapy.

The Colorado case involves a high school sociology teacher who was conducting a special unit on child abuse as part of a regular sociology course. A student who was not enrolled in the course asked to audit the child abuse unit. The sociology teacher agreed. The student subsequently asked to speak to the sociology teacher in confidence. The student reported to the teacher that her father occasionally beat her when he had too much to drink. The teacher encouraged the student to report the alleged abuse to the local social services agency. She refused, but agreed to come back the next morning to talk with the teacher. The teacher telephoned the social services agency and reported the conversation he had had with the student, but refused to give the student's name.

The social services agency responded by sending a police officer to the school the following day. The teacher refused to cooperate with the police officer by identifying the student, but was able to persuade the student to talk by telephone with a social worker who was able to talk the student into filing a report. Immediately after this report was filed with the social service agency, the police issued a summons for the teacher's arrest for failure to report.

The local prosecuter subsequently filed criminal charges and attempted to settle through plea bargaining. The teacher refused to settle. One week before the scheduled trial the charges were dropped in the "interest of justice."

In Michigan, an elementary school principal was charged in December 1986 by the local prosecutor with failure to report suspected child abuse by the school janitor. Apparently two young students complained to the principal that they had been sexually molested by the janitor. Their report followed a film presentation to all the students at the school on how to detect abuse. When the principal failed to report the incident, the parents of one of the children informed the police, who issued a summons for the principal's arrest, charging failure to report abuse to the Michigan Department of Social Services. The principal's stated reason for not reporting the abuse was that he questioned whether there was sufficient cause to believe the incident had taken place. Both the principal and the janitor were placed on administrative leave pending the outcome of the police investigation.

In the first two instances, it seems fairly clear that the teachers were caught between a rock and a hard place—by a well-intentioned reporting statute and a zealous local prosecutor. Although the intent of the state statutes—to encourage reporting abuse, and as early as possible—is undeniably a positive public policy, charging the offending teacher may not have been entirely in keeping with the spirit of the public policy. In the Colorado case, the teacher's wrongdoing was not subversion of the reporting statute but his judgment as to the best way to handle the situation. The local prosecutor ultimately agreed, and dropped charges, but not before the teacher was subjected to adverse publicity and the threat of a misconduct termination by school administrators. In the Nevada instance, the teacher's conviction was found to be inconsistent with the intent of the statute. The Nevada State Education Association supported the teacher's appeal to the intermediate state court in Nevada.

The Michigan case is interesting in that it highlights the difficult situation that a school employee may find himself in concerning the suspected activities of another school employee. The facts, however, are more troubling in the sense that the educator may have overlooked an instance of abuse.

The response of the NEA and its state and local associations to a member who is charged with nonreporting is to protect the member's right to a due process hearing. Consequently, in the first two instances, the Colorado Education Association and Nevada State Education Association hired lawyers to protect the members during the criminal investigation, and to represent the member during the trial. These organizations will also defend the member if any subsequent disciplinary action is indicated by the school district.

In the last instance, the principal is not a member of the association and consequently is not entitled to legal assistance from NEA or its affiliates. However, had the individual been a member, similar defense benefits would have been available.

In summary, NEA actively supports involvement of teachers and other educators in reporting child abuse. Educators must be concerned, however, about the personal consequences of reporting abuse to government agencies. Although most state statutes provide indemnification for reporters of abuse, there is still considerable personal risk involved for the individual who reports. NEA's organizational response is (1) to educate teachers regarding their responsibility to recognize and report child maltreatment; (2) to defend members in criminal proceedings (at minimum to reimburse fees through insurance); and (3) to make sure that the school district does not unfairly discriminate against a member for reporting abuse or, for that matter, not reporting abuse.

TEACHER MISCONDUCT

The second concern for NEA is what to do in situations where members are charged with abusing children. Although there are no reliable statistical data, for example, on how many educators are charged criminally, how many of these cases are successfully prosecuted, and how many are successfully defended, reports made to the Office of Legal Services Programs from NEA state affiliates around the country, and the limited secondary data available to NEA through its liability insurance program, suggest that the number of instances in which educators are being charged with child abuse is increasing.

This is obviously a more complex problem for NEA as a labor/professional association that has as one of its chief missions the protection of educators' job rights, but that in no way condones classroom teachers who abuse children.

Turning back for a moment to the formal policy resolutions of the association, NEA has taken the position that when any criminal action is instituted against any educator that is subsequently dismissed or in which the individual is ultimately exonerated, the board of education should reimburse the educator for legal fees and expenses incurred in the defense.

Connecticut appears to be the only state in which school districts are mandated to defend or reimburse an individual who is charged criminally as a result of work for the school district. While 42 states have statutes providing a range of protection from very limited to fairly complete for educators who are involved in civil litigation as the result of their work, protection by employing school districts in criminal matters is extremely rare.

In its role as a professional association, the NEA provides members with liability insurance protection for both criminal and civil matters. Protection in civil matters is up to $1 million plus attorney's fees and costs. Coverage relating to criminal matters is more limited. Consistent with NEA's policy resolution, coverage is restricted to reimbursement for legal fees and costs *if* an individual is exonerated of charges. There is one exception to this exoneration requirement. If the criminal charges stem from disciplining a student, the liability insurance program reimburses regardless of exoneration. The reimbursement limit under the policy is $25,000.

For example, if an individual member is charged with criminal assault in connection with child abuse, is exonerated, and the parents of the child subsequently file a civil action against the educator, the NEA liability protection program will reimburse the attorney's fees and expenses in the criminal matter and will undertake the defense of the teacher in the civil litigation. Finally, if the teacher is subsequently reprimanded by the school district or the district moves to terminate the teacher for "conduct unbecoming" or "moral turpitude," NEA, through its state affiliates, will defend the teacher in the job rights problem with the school district.

Based on limited claims data from the NEA insurance program and observations by the state affiliate staff responsible for administering job rights programs, it appears that there has been an increase since 1978 in the number of cases in which educators have been accused of abusing students. There also appears to be a corresponding increase in the number of criminal cases in which charges are dropped or the individual is exonerated, since the insurance program generally reimburses only when the individual is cleared. However, it is important to stress that these insurance program data are very inconclusive.

Observations of NEA state affiliate general counsels and directors of legal programs, however, support the concern that there has been a troubling increase in nuisance charges against teachers. They speculate that increases in the abuse-related charges generally, and in nuisance charges specifically, stem essentially from three factors:

1. General increase in the awareness of child abuse as an issue about which the public should be concerned, including what activities constitute child abuse, and removal of taboos about reporting abuse
2. Implementation of state laws requiring reporting of abuse by certain professionals
3. Increased awareness by children of child abuse reporting as an avenue allowing them to "get back" at teachers.

Whatever the reasons for the increase in the number of cases involving educators, NEA and its state affiliates are more frequently being asked by members to become involved in defending teachers. Furthermore, a disturbing number of these charges turn out to be unsubstantiated. This is not to suggest that all instances in which a teacher is charged criminally should be discounted. There are, of course, instances where the charges of abuse against educators are warranted. In these situations, although NEA and its affiliates may protect the due process rights of the individual in a subsequent tenure hearing or certification revocation proceeding, the member will not receive financial assistance in defending a criminal proceeding. The insurance program reimburses only if exonerated. Furthermore, if the individual is terminated or his or her certificate is revoked, the individual will no longer be entitled to membership in the association. However, where the charges of abuse are unfounded, even the process of investigating the charges may result in irreparable harm to the educator's career. In California, for example, the general counsel reports that kindergarten and primary school teachers feel "frozen" and disoriented in their teaching styles as a result of their concern about exposure to allegations of abuse. In Colorado, male elementary school teachers are being counseled not to touch students at all. (The problem does not seem to be as severe for female elementary teachers.)

Although school district responses typically vary, a teacher who is under investigation for a criminal violation involving child abuse is often placed on administrative leave, with pay. In some instances, the teacher may be removed from a classroom or "contact" position pending the outcome of the investigation. It is unrealistic to assume that the investigation can be kept secret, since the teacher is usually removed from the classroom. Even if the local prosecutor decides not to press charges, the teacher is already identified in the community as being accused of abusing a student. (Kansas has attempted to deal with the secrecy problem by requiring police to be in plain clothes when conducting investigations on school grounds.)

CASE STUDIES OF UNFOUNDED REPORTS

The following cases represent recent examples of allegations made by students that proved to be unfounded but resulted in stigmatization of the teacher.

The first involves a Maryland fourth grade classroom teacher during the 1984–85 school year. The incident took place in October. While the teacher was on playground duty, she attempted to stop an altercation between two children, and in the process picked a child up off the ground and jammed her thumb into the child's neck. There were about 100 children on the playground at the time and two other faculty members.

The student went home and complained to his mother that his throat hurt, telling her of the incident on the playground. The mother took the child to a pediatrician, who examined the child. The pediatrician confirmed there was a bruise on the child's neck, but indicated there was no damage to the child. After examining the child and listening to the mother, the pediatrician reported the incident to the local child services agency as suspected abuse.

Following this report, the local police and the social services agency conducted an extensive investigation that lasted for several months. The teacher who was accused of abuse, the other faculty members who were on the playground, and the principal were interrogated, along with several of the students who were present. A report was given to the state attorney's office in late April. On June 24th after the conclusion of the school year, the state attorney's office decided not to press charges, agreeing with the teacher that no abuse had taken place. The results of the investigation indicated that the student was unhappy with the teacher's treatment of some of his friends. The investigation also suggested that the bruise may have been inflicted during the fight that the teacher had been breaking up, and not by the teacher at all.

Meanwhile, the teacher, in a small community on the Eastern Shore, spent almost the entire school year with the threat of a felony charge hanging over her head. At the conclusion of the matter, a letter was placed in her personnel file indicating she should not touch children. The attorney's bill for the investigation amounted to almost $6000, which was paid by the Maryland State Teachers Association, and subsequently reimbursed by the insurance carrier.

In another situation in Maryland in 1984, an elementary school principal was visited by a kindergarten child, along with the child's mother. The child reported that she had been abused sexually on the playground by teenage boys. The incident was alleged to have taken place in daylight, during school hours, and while the playground was crowded with other students.

The principal filed a report with the local police, who conducted an investigation. The police could not locate anyone to corroborate the child's story, and consequently no charges were filed.

One week later the same child complained to her mother, who reported to the police that the child had been abused by the principal in his office. The police department conducted an investigation of this report, including a search of the principal's office for a "secret door" that the student claimed she had used to enter the office. Since the office was cinderblock and brick, and had only one door, in front of which a receptionist sat, the detective concluded that the student could not have entered the office except through the main door.

The kindergarten child also indicated that two classmates had witnessed the child entering the office, so the detective questioned these two children at their homes, in front of their parents. The other children could not confirm the first child's accusations. At the conclusion of the investigation, no formal charges were made against the principal.

Because there was no way to keep the investigation confidential once the other children were interviewed, the fact that the principal was under investigation for alleged abuse became known to the parents throughout the community.

In a final example, where the matter went to trial and the teacher was exonerated, a Minnesota physical education teacher was charged with sexual misconduct in the manner in which she spotted children during gymnastics class. The teacher was exonerated of criminal charges. However, the school district reprimanded her and returned her to the classroom.

Typically, if the teacher is exonerated, he or she usually will return to the classroom, but may continue to be involved in legal struggles with individual parents or children who subsequently file civil negligence actions. Even if the educator is not involved in any subsequent legal battles over the alleged incident, his or her reputation may be permanently tarnished or the school district may bring termination proceedings. At a minimum, the financial burden of defending the criminal charges may overwhelm the teacher. As noted earlier, NEA's liability insurance pays up to $25,000 if the teacher is exonerated. It is not unusual for charges to be in excess of $25,000, which on a teacher's salary means assuming substantial debt.

CONCLUSION

In summary, it is not suggested that all criminal charges against educators are unfounded. Nor is it suggested that there is not a real need for effective monitoring of professional behavior. In fact, as noted in other works on this topic, it is suspected that incidence of abuse in schools and other childcare or teaching institutions may be more common than previously thought.

The work of the NEA to support the reporting statutes and to educate teachers and other educational personnel regarding identifying and reporting abuse is, in part, in response to this new realization.

Nevertheless, it may also be true that the newfound awareness of child abuse may generate more false reports for a variety of reasons. From the perspective of the NEA as a professional organization, one must be concerned that, in the rush to report abuse, educators are not used as scapegoats or targets for the fears of worried parents or other school personnel.

The tension between protecting the child from harm and ensuring the rights of the accused is real. It has been with us for some time, and will not be easily resolved.

15

Sexual Abuse in Childcare: A Special Case in Regulation and Legislation

Abby J. Cohen

THE NEGATIVE CONSEQUENCES OF "DISCOVERING" SEXUAL ABUSE IN CHILD CARE SETTINGS

In 1984, the childcare community, parents, indeed the entire country, were shaken by allegations of widespread child sexual abuse at the McMartin childcare center in southern California. Like an earthquake, the repercussions and aftershocks of this event are still being felt in the childcare community. The McMartin case, and similar allegations of sexual abuse in other parts of the country, have had profound consequences for the provision of childcare in this country, many of them negative. These include a growing suspicion of vocational motives, particularly among men in the field, as well as increased self-consciousness about essential physical contact with children, damage to providers wrongly accused of abuse, distrust between providers and parents, ill-considered regulatory responses, and a diversion of attention from the critical role that childcare plays in the prevention and remedy of far more prevalent and complex forms of child abuse.

The Vocational Choice Is Becoming Suspect

Acknowledgment that pedophiles seek work that gives them easy access to children has led many people to assume that all persons who desire to work with children are child molesters. Such a notion has depressed the morale of persons already working in childcare and has discouraged those considering

The author gratefully acknowledges the assistance of Child Care Law Center attorneys, Carol Stevenson and Heidi Strassburger, in formulating some of the ideas reflected in this chapter. However, any opinions expressed are the author's own.

the field, at the very time when the need for more providers is burgeoning. Marcy Whitebook, director of the Child Care Employee Project, noted:

For child care workers, these new stories produce a different problem. We empathize with parent fears (many of us are parents), yet we don't know how to respond. We feel defensive, sensing that our every move is being scrutinized. We fear that all child care workers are seen as child abusers. We find ourselves tripping over words and monitoring our affectionate responses to children. (Whitebook, 1984, p. 6)

Growing Suspicion of Male Childcare Workers

A growing suspicion of men in the field is setting back the hard work of many who have sought (a) to encourage men in nurturing roles; (b) to provide new role models to young children; and (c) to upgrade the status of the profession.

In a thoughtful essay entitled "Day Care: Men Need Not Apply," a male child care worker wrote:

Given the low status of the work and the near impossibility of making a decent living, why would any man choose child care as a career? That has always been a question, and for many people outside the field the answer has often been "Well, he must be a little weird," which usually carried the implications of homosexuality. Now—in the light of proliferating revelations of sexual abuse in day care homes and centers and in the shadow of hysteria fueled by the media—the implication is much more sinister. It is—although few would state it so baldly—that any man who would want to work with younger children is a potential pedophile. (Richardson, 1985, p. 60)

These allegations, unwittingly perhaps, have fueled homophobia and have limited the career options of men, whatever their sexual orientation. At the same time, because of this society's deeply ingrained sexual role stereotyping, the absence of men in the field serves to reinforce the lesser status and depressed wages that childcare providers (overwhelmingly female) experience.

Discouraging Providers from Engaging in the Essential Elements of Care

Cleaning and diapering of infants and the touching and hugging of all children have become suspect. Concern that physical contact is now being discouraged and even eliminated has prompted a number of professionals in the field of child development and mental health to reemphasize the necessity and value of physical nurturance (Mazur and Pekor, 1984). The negative impact is also felt by childcare providers, since "[m]ost painfully, there is irony in the fact that what makes [their] jobs most worthwhile—intimate moments with children—is now an issue tinged with awkwardness and potential misunderstanding" (Whitebook, 1984, p. 6). This sorry state of affairs was epitomized by the title of a recent workshop at the 1985 National Association for the Education of Young Children Conference: "Whatever Happened to Laptime?"

Damage to Reputation and Livelihood of Those Wrongly Accused

In a number of instances, the rights of suspects have been ignored and highly damaging accusations have been made on the flimsiest of circumstantial evidence ("The Rights of Suspects," 1984). These allegations may be even more damaging to childcare providers than to the other professionals—doctors, lawyers, nurses—because even if the work of these other professionals brings them into contact with children, they usually have opportunities in their field that do not require contact with children. An adolescent practitioner, for example, could go on to target his or her practice to older persons. However, virtually no positions exist in childcare that do not involve contact with children. Consequently, the mere allegation of child abuse may effectively prevent childcare workers from making a living in their chosen field, no matter what the outcome of an investigation.

The Creation/Compounding of Mistrust/Distrust

An already fragile relationship, in need of strengthening, has been weakened by the surfacing of such complaints (Whitebook, 1984; Richardson, 1985). This author had the unfortunate experience of seeing the development of such mistrust firsthand. The nature of the work the Child Care Law Center engages in involves contact with both parents and providers. In 1985, a parent and provider called on the same day and related a course of events. The unique details of the story made it clear that the same event was being described from the different perspectives of parent and provider, a circumstance that is particularly distressing to a lawyer! As sometimes happens, the perceived "abuse" was actually the result of an accident. But because the parent and the provider were frightened and mistrustful, rather than open and communicative, they had already accused each other before they had fully investigated the situation. So, despite the fact that the child had been hurt accidentally, and the complaints were unfounded as defined by the child abuse reporting law ("unfounded report" means a report that is determined by a child protective agency investigator to be false, to be inherently improbable, to involve accidental injury, or not to constitute child abuse as defined in the law), neither parent nor provider can be certain they are not in the child abuse registry. California law does not require persons to be notified that their names have been placed in the registry.

Lack of Acknowledgment of the Role of Childcare in Preventing and Remediating Child Abuse

This critical and multifaceted role, for the most part, has gone unnoticed.[1] By assuring parents that in their temporary absence their children will be protected and well cared for, childcare providers help to minimize parental stress. They may also give respite to parents with particular needs. These needs may be related to illness in the family, a "difficult child," unemployment, or myriad other stresses that push parents toward, or even over, the edge. As a California editor noted, "What all parents need, but only some get, is the luxury of some time by themselves, out of the house and away from family stress, as well as information about who they can turn to when domestic life threatens to get out of hand" (Kirp, 1984). Child care providers also frequently serve as role models for parents, teaching them both about "normal" child behavior and development, and ways of accepting a child who may be "different" or "difficult." Finally, "quality child care, with a warm accepting supportive adult or adults in a developmentally appropriate stimulating environment with good feelings generated by other children can be an excellent therapeutic setting for a child who has been abused" (Weinstein, 1984, p. 9).

Diversion of Attention from Intrafamily Abuse

The vast majority of child abuse continues to occur within the family. According to 1982 national statistics collected by the American Humane Association and reported in 1984, 68 percent of child sexual abusers were parents, 1.5 percent were baby-sitters/childcare providers, and .08 percent were teachers. Intrafamilial abuse is not only more prevalent, it is significantly more intractable because of the discomfort involved in intruding into what is perceived as the private sphere of family functioning. While it is important to recognize that abuse can occur outside the family, it appears that society has chosen to overemphasize out-of-home abuse because of its inability to deal adequately with the more discomforting issue of intrafamilial abuse.

Ill-considered Legislative and Regulatory Responses

Legislative and regulatory responses are designed to assure parent constituents that something is being done, but the "something" is often of dubious value, leading to a false sense of security and bureaucratic nightmares:

> The [California] legislature responded [to child abuse] with no fewer than 50 bills on the topic, as if this seeming epidemic of mistreatment could be halted by the sheer weight of official paper. . . . But in general, panic is not conducive to good legislation. The lawmakers wound up passing measures that may undermine family life and privacy rights without actually confronting the child abuse problem. (Kirp, 1985, p. 80)

On the local level, the child abuse hard-line hysteria has been carried to an absurd extreme, with uniformed police entering a childcare center to interrogate a three-year-old—the alleged perpetrator—and advising the childcare center director that if she went ahead and notified his parents before they spoke to him, the police would remove him from care and interrogate him alone at the police station.

POSITIVE CONSEQUENCES OF "DISCOVERING" CHILD ABUSE

Notwithstanding these seriously negative effects, McMartin and its progeny have had some positive impact on the field of childcare and broader society. Obviously, these positive effects include a growing recognition that child abuse is occurring and that it is occurring in places other than those which have been traditionally identified: child abuse may occur in childcare as well as at home and in residential institutions. The result has been increasing interest in legislative reform, systemic reform in the interest of coordinated investigations, regulatory revisions in the interest of improved minimum health and safety standards, together with an increased appreciation of the complexity of the abuse problem and the system that responds to it.

The Need to Amend Legislation

Since abuse *can* occur in a childcare setting, it is imperative to review existing legislation in light of this new understanding. This may necessitate amending definitions, redefining the jurisdictions of the various agencies involved, and developing an understanding of all the different players who are involved when there are allegations of child abuse in a childcare setting.

For example, in California, it was learned that the Child Protective Services (CPS) had no statutory authority to conduct investigations in childcare settings and that neither CPS nor law enforcement had the responsibility to notify the Department of Social Services (which licenses childcare facilities), the State Department of Education (which purchases childcare services for low-income children), or resource and referral agencies (which refer parents of all incomes to available licensed care) of serious complaints of abuse in childcare settings. This was a particularly serious oversight because the remedy of revoking a license or enjoining the operation of an unlicensed facility requires a lower level of proof than criminal prosecution. Similarly, involvement by licensing rather than CPS could serve to ensure that all the children in the childcare setting were protected (by revoking the license) rather than protecting only the one child who might have been the subject of the complaint (by withdrawing that child from the particular childcare setting without informing other parents).

In other states, the mandatory child abuse reporting law did not clearly define whether childcare workers were mandated reporters or, for that matter, whether child abuse reports could be made about persons other than parents or legal guardians. If workers or licensees were included, terminology often did not parallel the terminology found in state licensing statutes. It was clear that many states' statutes, whether concerned with child abuse reporting or the powers of various agencies, did not contemplate the possibility of allegations of child abuse in a childcare setting. The laws were outmoded and in need of extensive revision.

The Need for Investigative Coordination

Coordination of activities by the various interested agencies is essential so that each may accomplish necessary objectives without unnecessary revictimization of children, harm to parents and providers, and wasting of precious social services and legal resources. In a variety of locales in California, all interested agencies have participated in investigations without any coordination whatsoever, with all players tripping over each other and revictimizing the child with interviews ad nauseum. This lack of coordination has hurt not only the children and their parents but also providers. Providers are frequently hurt because the investigations by the various agencies have taken so long. Consequently reputations are damaged, irrespective of the final outcome of the investigations.

The Need for a Regulatory Framework Establishing Minimum Health and Safety Standards

Notwithstanding a countercurrent of deregulatory fever, the conviction of a need for a regulatory framework is growing not only among parents but also among lawmakers and providers themselves. In 1983 Governor Deukmejian of California pushed hard for family daycare deregulation but was overwhelmingly defeated. In many states there is an ongoing fight to see that church-sponsored childcare programs are not exempted from regulation (Sanger, 1985).

Regulation Alone Cannot Eliminate Abuse

There are limits to the ability to protect children, given the less than optimal understanding of the causes of abuse and the limited ability to screen out those who are abusers or potential abusers. Furthermore, encouraging parents to believe that regulation alone can protect their children may be even more harmful than not strengthening the regulations if it convinces them that their active involvement in judging the quality of care their children are receiving is not necessary. Yet, the need for childcare grows, and so does the need for continued fine-tuning of the regulatory system. Licensing only provides a floor below which programs may not go, but it should be a continuously rising floor as new levels of consensus about appropriate minimum standards are obtained.

The Emerging Childcare System Is not Monolithic

There is now a developing understanding that what works for childcare centers may not be the appropriate response for family daycare, just as what is appropriate for less-than-24-hour childcare may be inappropriate for residential care, and vice versa.

CHILDCARE: AN EMERGING PROFESSION

Childcare, unlike many of the professions addressed in this book, is a "profession" that is still emerging, one not so well established as medicine, law, teaching, nursing, or psychology. Following in the footsteps of professions like nursing and social work, childcare providers are currently engaged in a struggle to raise their status and wages (Lubove, 1969). This struggle is made more difficult both because the work is frequently viewed as not requiring any special expertise and because it historically was provided "free"—in the sense that it took place outside the conventional market economy: "The problem for child care workers is that the care of normal preschoolers is very 'familiar to everyone,' and especially to their parent clients. Thus for . . . early childhood education, the main struggle with clients is . . . to be acknowledged as 'professional' . . . to make the status leap from 'babysitter' to educator" (Joffee, 1985, p. 22).

The struggle is nowhere more apparent than in the variety and "slant" of the terms used to describe the field by those inside and outside of it. We constantly see persons trying to pigeonhole child care as either "custodial" or "educational." Some say it is a business, others say it is a social service. Their professional perspectives color their views, and whatever the view, it tends to be quite rigid. The reality, quite removed from all these labels, is that child care is unique, a hybrid of *all* of these factors (see Cobb, 1983; Ohio AEYC, 1982; Pettygrove et al., 1984).

The struggle also is played out in the names actually given to the field, such as early childhood education, child development, childcare, daycare, educare, childcare industry, family daycare home, and family daycare business—all competing to name similar, if not identical, activities.

Consequently, many of the problems related to the reluctance of the criminal/civil system to prosecute professionals, or of professional regulatory boards unwilling to discipline their own, are in fact associated only with well-established professions and are inapplicable to the childcare field. It would be a rare childcare professional with the authority, power, and status in a community to secure a "quict" investigation of child abuse allegations, let alone quash such an investigation. Childcare workers have not secured special treatment in any positive sense; on the contrary, they seem to be treated more harshly even when engaged in behavior identical to that of other professionals. A good example of this would be the contrast between the virtually universal loss of license experienced by childcare providers upon substantiation of child abuse and the milder forms of discipline, such as temporary suspension and private reprovals, more commonly meted out to doctors and lawyers upon substantiation of the very same activity. This is not to approve of how these other professionals are treated, but simply to indicate the *different* treatment. Another example is the recent passage of a California law that allows two years to be added to the criminal penalty for child abuse *if the abuser is a childcare provider*, but provides no similar penalty for any other profession (Cal. Statutes, 1985).

At the same time, childcare's position as an "emerging" profession has had some hidden benefits, both for society and for providers. For one thing, it appears that childcare professionals have been less guilty of the typical professional response known as the "conspiracy of silence." Instead, because of the virulence of the attacks against the *entire* profession (not only abusers), childcare professionals recognized early on that they needed to take the high ground and, mixing metaphors, that they needed to publicly acknowledge the existence of "bad apples" while urging the public not to throw out the baby with the bathwater. Bettye Caldwell, former president of the National Association for the Education of Young Children, declared:

> As parents and citizens, we have to be concerned if even one case of sexual abuse occurs in child care. As professionals we have to be even more concerned. But we also have to help calm the hysteria that all too quickly results from such a situation, reminding people that a few isolated instances of malfeasance do not warrant a

condemnation of the entire field. Malpractice takes place in every field: physicians and attorneys are discharged for incompetence; pharmacists are fined for cheating on Medicaid. But we do not hear a public outcry for a cessation of the use of services of other representatives of those professions because of the inadequacies of a few (Caldwell, 1984, pp. 48–49).

CHILD CARE REGULATION

In order to better understand how we might adequately respond to child abuse allegations in childcare settings, it is imperative that there be an understanding of the childcare regulatory system. It is complex and varies greatly from state to state (for an extensive discussion of childcare regulation, see Grubb, 1986).

In each state there is some variation as to the types of programs that come within the scope of the regulatory scheme. Within the regulated programs there is generally a basic distinction in the nature of the regulations applied, depending on whether the program is within a "family daycare home" or a "childcare center." Family daycare homes generally serve fewer children and the care takes place in the provider's own home. In California, for example, family daycare *must* take place in the provider's home and the license may be for a small home (caring for 1–6 children) or a large home (7–12). These maximum numbers vary state by state, as does the minimum number that triggers regulation. Some states "register" rather than license family daycare. Childcare centers usually serve greater numbers of children and need not be located in the provider's home. More staff and more stringent regulations are generally applied to childcare centers.

Moreover, each state has developed its own list of programs that are exempted from the regulatory system. These programs may be school-operated, city-operated, church-operated, drop-in, and the like. Such exemptions raise serious questions as to the basis for such differential treatment as well as how well children are protected when they are enrolled in exempted programs.

Another important aspect of childcare licensing is the variation by state as to which agency or agencies are involved in the regulation of these settings. An example is California, where licensing is done by the State Department of Social Services. The State Department of Education, Child Development Division (which purchases childcare services for eligible low-income children), has additional, more stringent regulations that also must be met if a program and its providers are to be eligible to contract with the state to provide childcare services.

In almost all states where Title XX (now the Social Services Block Grant) monies are used for childcare (money is no longer specifically earmaked for childcare under block grants), there will be more stringent requirements, and these may be enforced by an agency other than the one that issues licenses. Thus, when substantiation of abuse occurs in a subsidized setting, the most efficient remedy is to terminate the purchase of care. In states where subsidized programs are licensed, the remedy is to terminate purchase of care and revoke the license.

Complexity within the childcare licensing system is compounded by its interrelationship with other licensing systems. An example of this complexity, with its resulting confusion and disastrous consequences, was a case that involved foster care parents who lived in southern California. A number of allegations were brought against them, particularly the husband, who had been involved in child pornography.

In face of the complaints, the foster care parents surrendered their foster care license. No prosecution followed; consequently, there was no record of the fact that there had been any allegations or any complaints. They moved to northern California, where they applied for a childcare license. In the state of California, family daycare providers and all adults residing in that home are fingerprinted. This check did not reveal anything because these individuals had no convictions. But no check was made between licensing systems. Foster care is different from other forms of care, so there was no check made on whether these people had ever had any other kind of license.

As a consequence of this particular episode, California now checks to see if *any* type of license has been issued previously. Moreover, if a provider surrenders a license, that does not preclude the licensing agency from being able to proceed with the case so that a final determination is made on the status of the licensee and some information is entered on the licensee's permanent record.

The interesting aspect of this episode is that it would never have been discovered through the licensing system. The licensing evaluators made numerous inspections of this facility and never found anything wrong. This case was uncovered through the mails. The FBI was following the mail that was being received by this particular provider's husband because it included a large volume of child pornography.

This case also provides another example of how insensitive the whole legal system can be in child sexual abuse cases. It is our understanding that the district attorney in this case, wanting the parents to identify the pictures taken from the child pornographer, asked the parents to come to his office with no notification of what his request was about. The very first indication that these people had that something was wrong was when they were shown pictures of their children in child pornographic materials and asked to identify whether those, in fact, were their children!

The parents of the children abused by the provider's husband brought a civil damage lawsuit not only against the provider and her husband but also against the state of California for negligence. The complaint alleged negligence in the manner in which licenses were granted and in the ongoing monitoring of programs.

This case has been settled not only because of the victimization of those children but also because out of the approximately 12 to 15 sets of parents that brought the suit, a large percentage are now divorced. This gives one some genuine regard for the kind of wrenching that such abuse and its aftermath bring to a family.

Despite the wide variations in certain aspects of childcare regulation, other aspects are virtually universal. Unlike other professions, the childcare license bears upon the adequacy of both the applicant *and* the facility where the care takes place. Licensing looks not only at the applicant's educational and experiential qualifications but also at the health and safety standards of a particular environment. Thus, a new license is required if the licensee moves or if a new provider purchases a program.

Childcare regulations typically address the following issue areas:

1. Definitions/exemptions (the scope and reach of the regulatory framework)
2. Staff qualifications (age, character, education, experience, and, of late, a background check)
3. Child-staff ratios and group size
4. Indoor/outdoor space requirements
5. Nutritional requirements
6. Fire safety requirements
7. Napping/toileting procedures and facilities
8. Health and emergency procedures—admissions policies, medical treatment authorization, disaster plans, and so on
9. Timing and frequency of inspections
10. Application, denial, revocation, suspension, nonrenewal, and hearing procedures; fines, civil/criminal penalties, and so on.

Typically, there are also provisions related to corporal punishment and other forms of abuse such that activities usually reportable as child abuse are also bound to be licensing violations. In effect, the licensing laws frequently incorporate the child abuse prohibitions of the penal code or child abuse reporting law by reference. Sometimes, the regulations are more stringent. For example, in California, while corporal punishment by parents is generally not reportable as child abuse, childcare licensing regulations prohibit corporal punishment in childcare.

An interesting case on this issue arose where parents claimed that since corporal punishment was a parental right, they ought to be able to delegate that right to a childcare provider. The California Court of Appeals, in

Johnson v. *California Department of Social Services* (1984), ruled otherwise:

When parents delegate to third parties those decisions regarding child rearing, care, discipline and education, such delegation does not carry with it the constitutional protections inherent in the rights of the parents. Moreover, this parental duty and right is tempered by and subject to limitations. When parental decisions may jeopardize the health or safety of a child, the state may assert important interests in safeguarding that health and safety.

Because child abuse prohibitions are incorporated into the licensing law, substantiation of child abuse will automatically trigger adverse administrative action in the form of temporary suspension, injunction, fines, revocation, and/or criminal prosecution for violating the licensing law. In addition, any other civil and/or criminal remedies available, were such activities done by someone other than a licensed child care provider, will also come into play.

When the licensing agency fails to follow its own regulations and does not ensure that its regulations are met, it too may be subject to a civil action by the parents of an injured child. This chapter already has noted cases where parents have sued the provider *and* the state agency when their child was injured in licensed care.

THE "SYSTEM" OR LACK THEREOF

In examining the "system," or lack thereof, that attempts to respond to allegations of abuse in a childcare setting, it is important first to recognize that the traditional legal model for viewing such matters—the child-family-state triangle—does not fit this situation. (See Table 1 for a more detailed explanation of the major players and their respective roles.) Instead, there are four, and usually more, points of reference; specifically, there is the child, the family, the childcare provider, and the state. Depending on the type of out-of-home care, there also may be multiple providers, and almost always there will be multiple children and parents. There are also multiple agencies that may receive such complaints; they may include children's protective services, law enforcement, childcare licensing (in whatever state agency it is placed), a state attorney general's office, a district attorney, purchase-of-service agencies, resource-and-referral agencies, hospitals, health departments, criminal courts, juvenile courts, and others. In reviewing the system one must determine the following:

1. Who is mandated to receive the complaint? Does this location make sense? Is there a lead or central agency to follow up? Which agency takes responsibility

Table 1
Investigating Abuse Complaints in Childcare Settings: Major Players and Their Respective Roles

Agency/Player	Mission	Powers
Law Enforcement	Determination of whether crime has been committed	(1) immediate protection through arrest of perpetrator 2) referral to DA for prosecution (3) testify in criminal/civil and or administrative proceeding
Child Protective Services	protecting individual child from harm; if possible, help to change situation so harm does not re-occur. Locus of concern is child	(1) remove child from home; (2) provide in-home supportive services; (3) provide therapeutic resources (4) testify in criminal/civil case and or administrative proceeding
Licensing	ensure minimum standards are met by child care license and facility. Locus of concern is standards non-compliance	(1) screening (2) inspections (3) cease and desist orders (temporary suspension (4) injunctions (5) fines (6) revocations/ denials (7) referrals of licensees for criminal prosecution (8) testify in criminal/civil case and/or administrative proceeding
Purchase of service agencies	pay for child care services for low-income families	(1) terminate funding
Resource and Referral Agencies	Assistance to parents in their child care search, promoting maximum parental choice, support service to present and future providers	(1) receive complaints; forward to licensing; encouraging complaints to be made directly to licensing (2) suspend referrals (3) remove providers from files

Agency/Player	Mission	Powers
Parents	obtaining supplemental quality child care for those hours they are unable to care for the child themselves	(1) make complaints to licensing, CPS, law enforcement (2) withdraw child from care (3) inform other parents, public media (4) bring civil liability action against provider and against state licensing agency (5) testify in criminal case and/or administrative proceeding
Children	obtain safe and nurturing care in the absence of parents	(1) learn, to the extent feasible, some self-protection (2)establish & maintain relationships with trusted adults enabling children, when possible, to communicate incidents of abuse when they occur (3) testify in criminal case and/or administrative proceeding

Note: Not all players are listed. The purpose here is to emphasize those players significant in childcare who are frequently left out of similar charts laying out agencies involved in investigating child abuse complaints of an intrafamilial or residential nature.

when the allegation involves abuse in an unlicensed or exempted childcare setting?

2. Is this information cross-reported to other relevant agencies? Is licensing the last to know? Is confidentiality or information sharing between agencies a problem?
3. Is there an understanding of the respective mission (statutorily defined) that each agency has and how its work relates to the others' missions? Separate or supplemental investigations? Statutorily required cooperation?
4. How, when, and by whom are parents to be informed?

The various agencies that have responsibilities in the area of responding to allegations of abuse need to know which other agencies are involved, and what each agency's respective roles and limitations are. In California, there is a lawsuit pending against a local law enforcement agency. The complaint alleges that the police closed down a family daycare home without statutory authorization and that the proper agency to shut a childcare facility is the Department of Social Services. One positive response in California has been a new requirement that the Department of Social Services (which is responsible for childcare licensing) hold regional seminars to educate law enforcement agencies about licensing's role and powers (Cal. Health and Safety Code). Once the agencies are familiar with each other's roles and personal contacts are established between agencies, the attitudes displayed by each professional group toward the others and the responsiveness of the system in general have shown marked improvement.

In the area of investigations, there has been a general movement away from multiple investigations and toward joint investigations, but this is being rethought in light of certain limitations of the joint investigation, including impediments to information sharing, the need for differing types of information to perform each agency's respective mission, problems of reliance by one agency on information gathered by another, and possible constitutional (Fourth Amendment) limitations. Much work remains to be done on which aspects of investigations can be coordinated and which cannot, along with suggestions on how such investigations ought to be conducted. Protocols that minimize trauma to child victims should be developed, and investigatory roles must be clarified so that responsibilities are not duplicated, impeded, or left unperformed. Finally, mechanisms for sharing information with parents and other agencies must be specified.

A major difficulty in developing such protocols is the seemingly endless permutations encountered in childcare situations (Class et al., 1985). For example, one problem that has cropped up repeatedly is when and how to notify parents, which may be particularly difficult in situations where it is equally likely that the parent *or* the provider is the perpetrator. The difficulties inherent in developing a standard protocol become apparent where the director rather than a worker is the target of the investigation, or where the target is another adult in a family daycare home rather than the childcare licensee, or where the abuse is between an older and a younger child.

In addition, it is imperative that investigations take place as speedily as possible after a complaint is made and that resolution follow speedily thereafter. This is important to ensure fresh evidence, protection of children, and apprehension of criminals, and to allay the fears of parents and the public. It is also important to ensure that no childcare provider is left to languish in the devastating state of limbo we now see so commonly, when investigations linger without resolution long after the initial allegation is made.

If there is sufficient evidence to proceed, revocations should occur quickly. Increased resources are needed in the legal departments of licensing agencies to ensure immediate action. This is money well spent—far better, in this author's view, than wasting dollars on screening schemes of questionable effectiveness.

ONE RESPONSE: SCREENING

Prior to the passage of P.L. 98-473, which conditioned the provision of child abuse prevention training monies on states having in place a system for national criminal record and background checks, states varied tremendously in *if and/or how* they screened prospective and current licensees, workers in childcare facilities and/or family members of family daycare providers. Since the passage of the law, the variation has become even more marked, because the law gives virtually no guidance to the states as to how to develop laws that comply with the new federal requirements. (For detailed information on the concerns in drafting measures that comply with P.L. 98-473 and screening practices generally, see "Vigilant in the Protection of Our Children or Vigilantes? Legal Considerations in Drafting Screening Laws and Recommendations for Safeguarding Children in Child Care Settings," "Use of Statewide Central Child Abuse Registries for Screening Child Care Workers: False Promises and Troubling Concerns," and "Do's and Don't's About Hiring and Supervision: Information for Individuals Hiring and Supervising Child Care Workers," all published by the Child Care Law Center.)

Before P.L. 98-473, some states had general laws that enabled certain employers who hired persons for jobs designated as sensitive by state legislatures to learn about an applicant's sex crime convictions (for instance, Cal. Penal Code) or other types of relevant convictions. In addition, some states' licensing regulations required applicants to make statements under penalty of perjury that they had no convictions of a certain type and, further, made clear that convictions of a certain type by the applicant or licensee would be grounds for denying or revoking the license. In a few states, criminal record checks were required.

P.L. 98-473 prompted many states to pass legislation allowing and/or requiring criminal record checks (National Legal Resource Center, 1985; Davidson, 1985), and many of these laws have been disastrously ill considered. In New York City, for example, the criminal R.A.P. sheet is not reviewed by the licensing agency but by the center director, raising serious concerns about disseminating arrest data (as opposed to convictions) and the ultimate confidentiality of this potentially damaging information. As if this were not enough, New York City provides virtually no guidance to directors as to how to consider the data offered in making employment decisions. Instead, the Human Resources Administration Agency for Child Development makes a feeble attempt to teach criminal law by telling directors: "A felony is a more serious crime than a misdemeanor. . . . You should also consider whether the crime was against a person or involved violence.

For example, robbery always involves the use or threat of force in taking something from a person as opposed to larceny which involves a taking of property, without force, such as shoplifting" (Flowers, 1984). Such lack of guidance and the lack of responsibility by the governmental agency leave open the possibility of wide variation in application, gaping holes in the wall of confidentiality, and, ultimately, expanded and potentially calamitous liability exposure for child care programs.

In many states, screening statutes have passed that lack waiver provisions. Waivers are frequently necessary to evaluate extenuating circumstances, and their absence may mean that persons will be denied employment automatically, and therefore unfairly.

As a reaction to the recognition that most child abusers will not be identified through a criminal records check (since few have been convicted), some states have turned to screening applicants against their child abuse registries. Depending on the implementing regulations and the original statute establishing the registry and its operational procedures, use of a registry for screening can raise deeply troubling concerns. For one thing, many of the registries lack any appropriate due process safeguards. They may have varying standards by which people are placed in them. There may be no way to contest being placed in the registry or to appeal a finding of abuse despite the absence of any judicial finding. Frequently, the names of individuals have been placed in the registry and intentionally mislabeled "abusive" by social workers, so the family or child could receive necessary support services that were not available by any other means (Rollins, 1985). Well-meaning social workers had no idea these registries might later be used for employee screening purposes.

In a time of limited resources, the cost of such screening seems a large price to pay for so little benefit, as most abusers in childcare settings have not had prior convictions and do not appear in any child abuse registry. In this light, it is important to review more appropriate and less costly responses to the problem.

OTHER RESPONSES: SOME IDEAS

The following list of responses is not all-inclusive. It focuses on prevention and enforcement, rather than prosecution, where significant changes also are needed and are occurring.

Licensing

1. Increase licensing's role in parent education about licensing requirements, provider communication, questions to ask, where complaints can be made, indicators of child abuse, community resources for learning about abuse and helping

victims of abuse. This should include use of the broadcast media, as well as other methods and materials.

2. Improve the complaint process by
   a. Instituting toll-free numbers
   b. Developing an ombudsman program
   c. Speeding response time and resolution.
3. Train licensing personnel about child development, investigation, gathering and preserving evidence, identifying child abuse, and knowledge of the roles of other related agencies.
4. Make reasonable parental access to a facility a licensing requirement.
5. Make availability of a parent roster to the licensing agency a licensing requirement. Parents should also have access to a roster, and should be able to request that their names be deleted from the list circulated to other parents.
6. Create a separate division or department to deal with childcare so its unique nature is understood; within the division, separate licensing and enforcement functions; beef up the enforcement division so response time is improved—which often means more resources for the legal department.
7. Require child abuse reports to be cross-reported to licensing and vice versa.
8. Require timely notification of parents and resource and referral when a license is suspended or revoked; develop policies for notification when administrative action is not as grave as suspension or revocation. Post the notice at the facility as well as directly contact parents.
9. Publicize revocations/denials and nonrenewals of licenses regularly and locally; publicize injunctions.
10. Add injunctive relief (to close down the facility) to standard revocation orders.
11. Develop a method for placing licensing revocations on criminal records.
12. Provide for provisional licensing status that cannot be renewed or extended indefinitely.
13. Develop formal methods of complaint information sharing between the following:
    a. Childcare, residential care, foster care, others (be certain to check if they have had a license that has been revoked, denied, or otherwise lost)
    b. Law enforcement, protective services, licensing
    c. State, county, local officials.

    Require all these sources of information to be checked before issuing licenses.
14. Keep records when a licensee *surrenders* a license.
15. Requirements for employees in centers: check at least three references thoroughly before hiring; require a probationary period for evaluation, during which time the new hire is adequately supervised and given increasing levels of responsibility; require statements under penalty of perjury regarding previous specified convictions.

16. Require protection through nonretaliatory provisions for childcare workers who report licensing violations.
17. Require licensing to document and study complaints for purposes of regulatory reform.
18. Develop interagency agreements among licensing, protective services, police, and district attorneys so investigatory responsibilities are not duplicated, impeded, or left unperformed. Possible joint investigation by CPS and licensing should be reviewed to see if this is desirable.
19. Develop and distribute to every licensee and childcare worker a booklet modeled on the Child Care Law Center's "Reporting Child Abuse: Rights and Responsibilities for Child Care Providers."
20. License terms in some states need to be shortened to provide for better review.

Child Protective Services/Law Enforcement

1. Staff of these agencies should be trained in identifying child abuse, and should understand the difference between investigations conducted in the home and those in a childcare setting. It is preferable to use a child protective worker rather than police, and if police are used, to employ plainclothes personnel in unmarked cars.
2. Notify licensing if CPS and law enforcement have complaints of child abuse in a childcare setting.
3. Develop procedures for investigation of child abuse in childcare—if parents are not targets of investigation, interviews with children should be conducted at home, or at the very least, parents should be notified before a child is interviewed.
4. Notify parents individually rather than at group meetings.

Government/Private Resources

More resources should be devoted to the following:

1. Provider training in the areas of emergency preparedness, child development, licensing requirements, child abuse identification and reporting.
2. Adequate subsidies for low-income parents so they have choices if they find their current childcare setting substandard.
3. Increase provider wages so that high-quality staff can be attracted and maintained.
4. Develop and maintain universally available resource and referral, which in turn can help promote better childcare and help parents in learning what to look for.

Resource and Referral

1. Establish complaint policies.
2. Develop publications on choosing child care programs.
3. Develop means of training parents to engage in ongoing monitoring of care.
4. Help in training providers regarding child abuse, and develop directories of community resources for their use.
5. Encourage parents to listen to children and to know what to expect—normal separation anxiety vs. symptoms of trouble.
6. Promote provider/parent communication on a regular basis.
7. Promote positive media coverage of childcare.

Parents

1. Learn about choosing childcare: "spotless isn't everything."
2. Learn about licensing requirements.
3. Learn about normal child development and indications of abuse.
4. Learn where complaints are to be made.
5. Obtain parent resources and support so they can feel more confident in their abilities and judgments as parents.
6. Obtain roster and talk to other parents of children in care on a regular basis.
7. Encourage children to talk, and act upon the things children say.
8. Advocate more resources for childcare, so parents have greater choices and need not leave their children in programs with which they are uncomfortable.
9. Visit programs without notice and see and judge for themselves.
10. Advise resource and referral and licensing if programs they have been referred to are rejected on the basis of substandard conditions.

Childcare Workers

1. Ensure adherence to wage and hour laws, and regulations on capacity, to minimize stress.
2. Learn licensing regulations and work with program to meet them; report licensing violations and child abuse.
3. Advocate in-service training opportunities, opportunities to learn about child abuse prevention, detection, and treatment, and provider rights and responsibilities under the child abuse reporting law.
4. Advocate program policies (if not licensing requirement) prohibiting corporal punishment.

5. Learn curriculum for teaching children about abuse, learn about community resources available to interested persons and victims.
6. Become familiar with the materials developed by the Child Care Employees Project and other groups to protect children and teachers (Protecting Children, 1985; Ginsberg and Whitebook, 1985; Child Abuse Accusations, 1985).

Children

1. Teach them about abuse.
2. Teach them how they can respond.
3. Use *trained* employees to teach them.
4. Encourage communication with their parents.

All of the Above

Develop task forces made up of representatives of all constituencies to identify gaps in the system or aspects that do not function properly (Lauten, 1985; Van de Kamp, 1985).

NOTE

1. This long-neglected role has received some recognition in California with the publication of a report summarizing results of a statewide survey of child development programs conducted to identify links between childcare and child abuse identification, prevention, and remediation. Copies of the report, "The Role of Child Care in Child Abuse Prevention," written by the State Child Development Program Advisory Committee, are available from CDPAC, 915 Capitol Mall, Rm. 250, Sacramento, CA 95814.

REFERENCES

American Humane Association. (1984). *Highlights of official child abuse and neglect reporting, 1982*. Denver: American Humane Association.

Caldwell, B. (1984, July). One step forward, two steps back, *Young Children*, 48–49.

California Health and Safety Code, sec. 1596.875(b).

California Penal Code, sec. 11105.3.

California Statutes, Ch. 1010 (1985). A.B. 762 signed by Governor Deukmejian.

Child abuse accusations: What to do? (1985, September/October). *Children's Advocates*.

Class, N., et al. (1985, October). *A casual inquiry into the problem of administrative coordination in the investigation of abuse complaints against licensed day care facilities*. Paper presented at the Virginia Commonwealth University Annual Institute on Human Services Facility Regulation, Richmond, Va.

Cobb, N. (1983, September 15). Day care workers: Are they the new American mothers? *San Francisco Examiner*.

Crissey, P. (1984). Concern vs. hysteria: Child abuse in day care. California Consortium of Child Care Abuse Councils, San Francisco, Ca.

Davidson, H. (1985, June). Protection of children through criminal history record screening: Well-meaning promises and legal pitfalls, *Dickinson Law Review*.

Flowers, D. (1984, December). Memorandum on policies and procedures for screening prospective and current day care personnel: Criminal record guidelines. Human Resources Administration, Agency for Child Development, New York, 4.

Ginsberg, G. and Whitebook M. (1985, Fall). Accusations of abuse: Confronting the unthinkable, *Beginnings*.

Grubb, E. (1986). Day care regulation: Legal and policy issues, *Santa Clara Law Review* 303.

Joffee, C. (1985). *Friendly intruders*. Berkeley: University of California Press (p. 22). Reprinted in J. Silin, Authority is knowledge, *Young Children* (1985), 41–45.

Kahn, A. (1984). Day care nightmares: Coping with child abuse anxiety, *East Bay Express* (Berkeley), p. 1.

Kirp, D. (1984, March 16). Commentary: Child abuse and its abuses, *Sacramento Bee*.

Kirp, D. (1985, January). The child abuse panic, *California Lawyer*, 80.

Lauten, N. (1985). Who's minding the cradle? Regulatory reform in the child care industry, 13 *Florida State University Law Review*, 633.

Lubove, R. (1969). *Professional altruist: The emergence of social work as a career 1880–1930*. New York: Atheneum.

Mazur, S. & Pekor, C. (1985, May). Can teachers touch children anymore? Physical contact and its value in child development, *Young Children*, 10–12.

National Legal Resource Center for Child Advocacy and Protection. (1985). Summary of legislation regarding criminal/child abuse history checks . . . as of October 1, 1985, Washington, D.C., Ohio Association for the Education of Young Children. (1982, November). Statement to the National Association for Young Children Conference, Washington, D.C.

Pettygrove, W., Whitebook, M., and Weir, M. (1984, July). Beyond babysitting: Changing the treatment and image of child care givers, *Young Children*, 14–21.

Protecting children, centers, teachers and parents from child abuse. (1985, Fall). *Beginnings*.

Richardson, D. (1985, July). Day care: Men need not apply, *Mother Jones*.

The Rights of Suspects. (1984, September 19). *New York Times*, 19.

Rollins, N. (1985). Screening the caretakers. In *The Compleat Lawyer*. Chicago: American Bar Association, pp. 32–33.

Sanger, C. (1985). *Day care center licensing and religious exemptions: An overview for providers*. San Francisco: Child Care Law Center.

Van de Kamp, J. (1985). Attorney General John Van de Kamp's Commission on the enforcement of child abuse laws, final report.

Weinstein, V. (1984, March). *Making the connection: Child care and child abuse prevention*. Keynote speech to the California Child Care Resource and Reference Network, Pasadena, Ca.

Whitebook, M. (1984, September 23). Child care, *San Francisco Sunday Examiner and Chronicle*.

Summary and Analysis

16

On the Decision to Report Suspected Abuse or Neglect

Susan J. Wells

While reporting suspected child abuse and neglect is, on its face, a socially desirable behavior, it is not always a foregone conclusion that professionals who are confronted with an abused or neglected child will be able to identify (or even acknowledge a suspicion) that abuse or neglect has occurred. Nor is it certain, once suspicion has been aroused, that a report will be made to the appropriate authorities. In this volume Herzberger, Garbarino, Conte, and Rindfleisch identify several factors that impinge on this process, including characteristics of the child and family, identity of the reporter, organizational climate, and concerns about the implications of reporting for the child and his or her family.

Herzberger notes that the decision to report is actually the culmination of a series of perceptions, judgments, and decisions. These may include the ability to recognize physical or emotional problems; determining the potential for a causal relationship between parental or caretaker behavior and the child's condition; assessing the seriousness of the problem; determining the threshold of possible abuse or neglect; and deciding to make a report to the appropriate authorities. At any point in this process there may be a breakdown in the observer's perceptual abilities, understanding of the situation, knowledge regarding the identification of abuse and neglect, or information-processing systems that lead to final decisions. In addition, the observer may make a cognitive decision not to report, even when maltreatment is suspected, due to a declaration of values that run counter to current reporting laws or because of a belief that the child and the family are better served if there is no report.

FACTORS INFLUENCING PROFESSIONAL JUDGMENTS

The first issue, that of formulating initial judgments about what is observed, has been addressed by Nisbett and Ross (1980) in a book that describes the "strategies and shortcomings of social judgment." They note that conclusions people make about their observations are influenced by the vividness of the observations made, availability of information, number of observations made, the biases that may result from inability to observe the entire picture, and the differential nature of recall or memory. That is, the more an event is available for observation and the more vivid it is to the observer, the more likely it is that conclusions will be biased by those factors.

Another source of bias is the extent to which observations are similar to events previously experienced by the observer. Because people come to situations with previous experience and seek to make sense out of current events in terms of that experience, they may alter what they see to fit into what they already know.

Even those who have the benefit of professional training are subject to misperceptions and mistaken judgments when they do not thoroughly investigate the basis of their beliefs. Those who are mandated to report suspected abuse and neglect may not recognize it for a variety of reasons, only one of which is insufficient evidence to suspect maltreatment. As noted by the authors, these perceptions may be influenced by previously held beliefs about minority groups, poor people, middle-class or affluent people, the ability of the child to protect himself or herself because he or she is an older child, or the severity of abuse or neglect that might be inflicted by a mother or father.

ORGANIZATIONAL INFLUENCES ON PROFESSIONAL BEHAVIOR

At the same time, factors operating in the professional environment appear to have a considerable effect on reporting behavior. Organizational issues may influence decision-making processes or behavior indirectly or directly.

Indirect Influence

Indirectly, the organizational environment may lead one to unwittingly adopt certain decision-making behaviors (Janis and Mann, 1977). These influences may result from the types of decisions required, such as their perceived consequences and whether they are made under conditions of stress. Additionally, environment may be influential in terms of the time available for making decisions, resources available for problem resolution, perceived suitability of alternative solutions, and risks of inaction. These factors may combine to create an environment that guides individual patterns of decision making or molds the behavior of the entire group, creating a "groupthink" situation.

Individual or group reactions to high-stress situations might include unconflicted inertia, unconflicted change, defensive avoidance, hypervigilance, or vigilance. The first coping behavior, unconflicted inertia, is thought to occur when the decision maker does not perceive any threat or risks in ignoring the situation. These perceptions may be based in reality or in a misunderstanding of the actual nature of the situation. The parallel in child protection would be the physician who either does not recognize signs of abuse in the course of examining a child or who recognizes abuse but believes the caretaker when he or she assures the physician that it will not happen again. In either case, no report to protective services or the police is made.

The second coping behavior, unconflicted change, occurs when risk of inaction is recognized and there is an immediately available alternative that has no observable negative consequences. For example, if a psychologist is confronted with an abusive family who is seeking assistance with the problem of abuse and recognizes the need to report the abuse to child protective services, the risk to the child is clear, the alternative is readily available, and the family's reaction will not be a source of negative consequences for the therapist.

Defensive avoidance results when risk is recognized and the readily available alternative is not perceived as a safe one. In fact, the decision maker believes that it is unrealistic to find a better means of dealing with the problem. In this case, the behavior of choice is to avoid the problem altogether by denying it, relying on others to make the decision, or selecting a less-than-desirable alternative and ignoring information about its negative consequences. The example given by Conte of less powerful members of interdisciplinary teams yielding to other members for the decision about whether to substantiate a case is a good example of defensive avoidance.

If, on the other hand, one can hope for a better solution, he or she will be more likely to choose a vigilant approach rather than defensive avoidance. If there is not sufficient time to make a careful search for, and evaluation of, information and advice with which to solve the problem, the decision maker is likely to become hypervigilant or panicked by the situation. In this state, the choices made are likely to be snap judgments based largely on observations of what others in the same circumstance are doing, regardless of observed effectiveness. One example of a hypervigilant response to a high-risk situation would be unnecessary or indiscriminate placement of a child when the worker is concerned for the child's safety but does not feel there is enough time to search out reasonable alternatives that would protect the child in the home.

Janis and Mann (1977) note that:

> When a decisionmaker faces a highly conflictful dilemma involving a threat of serious losses and a very short deadline for making a choice, the quality of his

thinking will be poorest of all on multivalued decisions (those that require evaluating the consequences of alternative courses of action in terms of a large set of values, not just in terms of one or two objectives). (p. 61)

When the time to make a decision is not foreshortened, the likely approach to decision making will be one of vigilance. This is the preferred mode of decision making in which there is risk in not acting, the first available alternative is not without risk, it is realistic to hope for a better solution, and there is sufficient time to consider alternatives and their consequences.

The foregoing model of decision making is not the only one that might be applied to the act of considering alternatives, making judgments, and selecting preferred approaches to problem solving. However, it is particularly applicable in situations dealing with child protection due to its relevance for decisions that have real consequences for the decision maker and are therefore associated with psychological stress. The issue that appears to determine the type of decision-making behavior involved in problem solving is the "consequentiality" of that decision, whether it has real consequence for the decision maker or for significant others.

In applying this model to group decision making in high-stress situations, one may often observe patterns of defensive avoidance. Janis and Mann (1977) describe "groupthink" as a pattern of avoidance in which the entire group participates. The group is insulated from outside information, and has high cohesiveness, directive leadership, and high stress with little hope of finding solutions outside those offered by the group. This leads to insufficient consideration of alternatives, rationalization, and generally maladaptive decision-making behaviors. In this situation, defensive avoidance is characterized by pressures to conform, striving for unanimity, and "reliance on shared rationalizations that bolster the least objectionable alternative" (Janis and Mann, 1977, p. 133).

These characteristics may be operative in multidisciplinary groups when the group is faced with a crisis, the available alternatives are all perceived as risky, and there is little hope of finding suitable alternatives. Depending on the structure and mission of the group, these pressures may influence decisions to report abuse or neglect, decisions to substantiate a case, and decisions regarding the type of intervention to be taken.

Direct Influence

Direct influence on decision-making behaviors may include an "unofficial" policy that the institution does not want to become involved in reporting abuse or neglect, particularly when the subject is an affluent or influential member of the community. This concern was expressed by respondents to Alfaro's study (1985) and is clearly the issue in a suit filed by a teacher in Orange County, California, against the local school district (Crewdson, 1985). In the suit she claimed that she was harassed for more than two years for cooperating with police in an investigation of alleged sexual abuse after being told by officials "to keep quiet."

In childcare institutions, organizational factors influencing reporting behavior are even more critical. Rindfleisch notes that in residential institutions, willingness to report may be closely connected to fear of retribution that may follow such a report. Only an overriding commitment to resident well-being, regardless of personal consequences or consequences for the agency, was a sufficient motivator to induce reporting when such threats were present. In addition, the professional staff, including child welfare workers, were more reluctant to report than were residents; of the professional group, thc administrators were the most reluctant of all.

However, organizational support for reporting was not necessarily a motivating factor in reporting behavior. In a demonstration project to examine the influence of different reporting mechanisms on reporting behavior, Rindfleisch found that the availability of a child advocate outside the organizational hierarchy was most influential in encouraging reporting.

As many have noted, legislation mandating reporting and professional regulation alone will not encourage reporting. Rindfleisch believes that, in addition to these means for protecting children in residential institutions, it is imperative to provide an independent child advocate to whom reports can be made and to assure that the investigatory response is independent of the traditional child welfare agency. This is especially critical due to the multiple roles of the child welfare agency with respect to childcare agencies. The licensing authority of the agency and its role as guardian or protector of the children in its care may contribute to an institutional "blindness" to maltreatment in order to protect previous decisions to license the facility or to place children there.

LEGAL AND ETHICAL CONFLICTS

The conscious decision not to report suspicion of abuse and neglect may come, as stated above, from organizational influences, or it may come from a personal/professional decision not to report due to the perceived iatrogenic nature of the protective services system, as noted by Garbarino. Further, such a decision is often linked in the mind with a professional obligation to a greater good, such as upholding professional ethical standards to guard the confidentiality of the client or to provide services that are healing as opposed to harmful.

At the same time, as Davidson notes, most state laws are unequivocal in mandating that certain professionals (or all persons) report *suspected* child abuse or neglect. In several states this includes lawyers and clergy as well as physicians. For these professionals the law may not always be consistent or clear-cut in defining how the abuse came to be known or defining in which relationships the mandate is effective. Nevertheless, the intent is clear: Protection of children is considered a priority over other professional or organizational commitments, and this protection can be ensured only through the notification of the state or county agency appointed to this task.

Yet there are professionals whose work depends on the principle of confidentiality, such as the priest-penitent privilege, and who are loath to comply with such laws. Clergy, in particular, feel that they are called to obey higher laws and that they must not yield to secular reporting laws. In the Catholic Church, for example, canon law expressly states that it is a crime for a confessor to betray a penitent in any way or for any reason. If this promise is broken, excommunication is automatic.

These obligations notwithstanding, some states have passed legislation requiring clergy to report suspected abuse and neglect. In Texas, the attorney general released an opinion pursuant to state legislation saying that if a clergyman came to know about a case of child abuse, he or she was required by law to report it (Associated Press, 1985). While not all states have taken such a definite stand on this issue, the problem is apparent, not only for those states that name clergy as mandated reporters but also for those requiring that "any person" should report.

To aid in dealing with this conflict, one could differentiate between the role of the clergy as confessor and as a counselor, suggesting that as a confessor all information is privileged, but that as counselor, the clergy have the same obligations as a mandated reporter. California's reporting law, for example, specifies that any nonmedical practitioner who diagnoses, examines, or treats children in a professional capacity is required to report. Any clergy or other religious personnel who act in capacities outside ordinary clerical duties, such as giving spiritual counsel, would presumably be included as mandated reporters (California State Penal Code, no. 11166). This solution is appealing in helping to provide guidance on this matter, but it is far from exact. The unresolved issue is that the priest-penitent privilege includes not only the confessional but also other circumstances in which the priest, minister, or rabbi may hear such information in the course of performing his or her clerical duties.

Certainly, identifying the roles that the clergy assume in these cases is a point at which to begin. For example, if as part of his or her work a cleric gives therapeutic counseling to individuals and family members, information gained through these sessions should be subject to the same laws and regulations that govern other professional counselors.

However, the expressed attitudes of other professionals in this area often sound much like those of the clergy instead of the other way around. In a study of perceptions of professional responsibility of licensed clinical social workers, with particular reference to the Tarasoff decision (*Tarasoff* v. *Regents of California*, 1976), requiring therapists to take protective action when a client threatens the welfare of another, Weil and Sanchez (1983) found that while two-thirds of the respondents felt a professional responsibility to potential victims of violent clients, their actions did not support their beliefs. Weil remarked that regardless of the statement in the NASW Code of Ethics acknowledging that "social workers might have to reveal client confidences for 'compelling professional reasons'" (p. 123), the social workers studied did not adopt the law (as represented by the *Tarasoff* decision) as a critical part of their understanding of their professional obligations. That is, even when giving reasons for believing that protection of potential victims was an important professional obligation, they cited personal and professional ethics as the basis for this belief, ignoring almost completely the legal mandate for such action.

This attitude is not peculiar to social workers. In an "accidental" sample of 39 psychologists, Muehleman and Kimmons (1981) found that for 41 percent of the respondents, considerations of law ranked behind confidentiality in determining professional behavior. These respondents reasoned that loyalty to one's own ethics was more important than the letter of the law, and that if one is protecting the child, there is no need to report. They "shrank neither from making a judgment about the dangerousness of the abuse nor from deciding what was going to work best for a particular family. The law did not interfere with this process" (p. 636). In the same vein, Hinkeldey and Spokane (1985) used Janis and Mann's conflict theory of decision making in a study of American Mental Health Counselor Association members. Using a random sample of 72 respondents, they found that decision making in conflicted situations, such as duty to warn (*Tarasoff*) and child abuse, follows the patterns suggested by Janis and Mann, such as defensive avoidance. Further, they found that legal guidelines were not used in making responses to ethical conflict dilemmas. Given these findings, one must wonder if, in fact, defensive avoidance is masquerading as adherence to one's own definition of personal or professional ethics.

These studies demonstrate an appalling lack of knowledge on the part of the respondents regarding their own professional codes of ethics and the interplay between legal mandates for professional behavior and their professional responsibility. In addition, there is a fundamental lack of understanding of the concept of confidentiality in the professional relationship. As many professions acknowledge, confidentiality exists for the protection of the client only when the safety of others is not in question. In considering the obligation of the professional to society as a whole, the good of society and the safety of others are paramount.

This, however, does not address the concerns of Garbarino and Conte. Their point is not necessarily that confidentiality should prevail, but that the harm done by the protective service system is a powerful deterrent to reporting. In this case, the ethical issue is one of protecting the client from further harm.

The American Academy of Child Psychiatry deals with the issue of protecting the client from harm in a way that might be responsive to these concerns. Principal II of its Code of Ethics states:

> The child psychiatrist shall avoid all actions which may have a detrimental effect on the optimum development of the child. Further, by utilizing means appropriate to the context of the clinical contact with the child or adolescent patient or the population being served, the child psychiatrist will strive to reduce any deleterious effects of the behaviors of others. (American Academy of Child Psychiatry, 1980)

While this paragraph might be interpreted to suggest that involvement of protective services is not in the child's best interests, the clarifying notes suggest just the opposite:

> This paragraph addresses the historical commitment of medicine to "do no harm" and extends that commitment to attempting to reduce the potentially harmful interactions of others. It is acknowledged that there are situations in which "ultimate good" may involve temporary discomfort or the choice between alternatives none of which are without negative consequences. The principle of "all things considered" is appropriate. When there are difficult choices, the decision should rest with those which have the potential for greatest "ultimate good," all things considered. (American Academy of Child Psychiatry, 1980)

The recognition that temporary discomfort may follow an action taken for the child's benefit and that all alternatives in a situation may have some undesirable consequences directs one to consider not only the consequences of less-than-desirable state intervention, but also the consequences of no protective intervention. For while professionals may believe that they are able to protect a child in the context of their own practice, the reality is that no one person is competent to take on such a responsibility.

INTERORGANIZATIONAL RELATIONSHIPS

Response of CPS Agencies to Reports

Other organizational factors identified by the authors as influential in reporting behavior include interorganizational relationships between mandated reporting agencies and the investigating agency (usually child protective services [CPS] and the ability of CPS to respond in a helpful way. The discussion focuses on concern about the competence of CPS staff; the use of a punitive approach by investigative and law enforcement agencies; the absence of support services for the family; and the availability of sufficient resources to respond to the increasing numbers of reports. These are very real concerns and are being expressed in the community by CPS staff and allied professionals alike.

Some of the factors that impinge on the ability of CPS to respond to reports are much the same as those which affect mandated reporters. For example, while the mission of CPS workers is to define and recognize abuse and neglect, the absence of a societal consensus as to what constitutes abuse and neglect has many repercussions for those who must operationalize the concept. Laws vary from state to state regarding definitions of abuse, and the interpretations of laws vary even more between local agencies, particularly when those agencies are administered at the local level. While ideal practice may dictate that all workers agree on one definition of what constitutes abuse or neglect, the reality is that even the most learned experts in the field do not agree on the definition or on the appropriate threshold for intervention.

At the same time, as Herzberger points out, there are notable and systematic differences between professions in their assessments of severity of maltreatment. It appears that the role of the professional in the protective service system has a marked influence on these assessments. Giovannoni and Becerra (1979) hypothesized that lawyers saw some types of maltreatment as less severe than did other professionals because they were relying on clear evidence that a form of maltreatment was harmful to the child. Given the same case vignettes, police and CPS workers were more closely aligned to each other in their judgments of severity than they were to the lawyers or physicians. Such alignments may be due to role definition in the protective service system. In fact, in the study state police and CPS workers served much the same function in the system: that of making the initial response to reports. It would be instructive to see replications of this study in situations where professionals have taken on different roles as a response to local conditions, laws, or regulations.

Another condition influencing protective service response is that the ability to predict violent or neglectful behavior has always been limited by the current state of knowledge. In the field of probation and parole, experts with many years of clinical experience commonly have a failure rate of 66 percent when trying to predict future arrests of parolees (Monahan, 1981). With new technologies, however, and the use of scoring systems developed by empirical analysis of recidivism rates, predictive abilities have improved significantly (State of Michigan, 1978). These technologies are now being examined for use in protective services.

Additional factors that affect the decision-making behavior of CPS workers include the role of protective services in protecting children, as determined by state and federal legislation, the organizational and community environment, the state of the art in intervening effectively to control or change human behavior, and the resources available for problem resolution.

Interorganizational Coordination

The context in which organizations operate is critical in understanding the relationship between organizations and professionals with regard to reporting. Interorganizational coordination (or lack thereof) has been the subject of many studies and publications.

Historically, cooperation between agencies has been stymied by lack of goal congruence, professional territorialism, political constraints, limited technology, and difficulties in coordinating the private and public sectors (Rice, 1977). These habits of relating are obvious in the descriptions of relationships between protective services and the community. One need only refer to Garbarino's concerns about the influence of the nature of system response on reporting behavior to understand that the above factors are alive and well in the community's response to child protection.

In child protection some sources of interorganizational tension are noted by Conte and Garbarino. The system limitations noted by them include effects of legal requirements on reporting behavior and system response, and the varied role of orientations of different professional groups. While multidisciplinary groups and interagency community child abuse councils have been employed to try to cope with these difficulties, Cohen notes that too much homogenization of roles could also be counterproductive. By blurring roles in investigation procedures, professionals have sometimes succeeded in creating as much confusion as if there were no cooperation.

Finally, there appears to be, in many places, a sort of institutionalized reactiveness between different professions. This tendency to blame others for the failure of the system might be understood in the context of Janis and Mann's (1977) conflict theory of decision making. Because the risk to the child (and one's professional reputation) is great when one is confronted with the decision to report, the alternatives appear to be equally unattractive to the reporter, and there is no perceived hope of a satisfactory solution, defensive avoidance activities such as garbled information processing or blaming of other actors in the protective system may become the preferred method of coping. This style of reacting to high-stress, low-option situations is possible not only in the community but also in the protective service system itself. While these are normal reactions to such situations, it is possible to deal with dysfunctional habits through increased awareness of decision-making processes and recognition of the realistic constraints of each professional group.

Reid (1969) has suggested that in order for true coordination to occur between agencies, the agencies must perceive themselves as interdependent. Only when the agencies involved perceive a need to exchange resources such as information, money, clients, or services in order to achieve common goals (Taylor, 1979), will there be a real unity of effort on behalf of children. While the barriers to coordination are real, such as the laws of confidentiality surrounding reporting of abuse that prohibit the sharing of information, a conscious and well-conceived attack on these barriers could be undertaken. This would include a systematic recognition of factors that influence identification of abuse and neglect, barriers to reporting, and problems inherent in system response when children are recognized to be at risk.

It appears that the problem (and the solution to the problem) of child abuse and neglect is one of community ownership. In the 1960s there was little recognition in the community of child maltreatment as a pervasive problem. With the recognition of the battered child syndrome and rising community awareness, many programs were undertaken to respond to the problem and to provide more adequate protection for children. Some of these included the development of child abuse hot lines, the provision of 24-hour response to reports, the creation of community child abuse councils and advocacy organizations to identify and ameliorate service gaps, and training programs for allied professionals in recognizing and responding to abuse and neglect.

These programs and services had the effects not only of enhancing system response for some communities and increasing the feeling of community ownership of the problem but also of raising public expectations about the ability of CPS to respond. The message to the community was to report any problems to CPS and that the agency would be able to help the child and family (Barry, 1986). This approach, coupled with the existing practice of referring all hopeless cases to protective services, began to show that CPS was not able to cure these damaged families on a wide scale—indeed, it had some organizational problems of its own.

Yet, in spite of some early disappointments, the solution would appear to be continued emphasis on community ownership. Not only are multidisciplinary groups important to effective CPS functioning, but it is critical, as pointed out by Conte, that professionals act as advocates not only for children but also for the system assigned to protect them. Some beginning reforms are proposed in this volume by Conte, Davidson, Leaner, and Cohen to build further on the integration of services through legislation, regulation, and clearly defined cooperative working relationships.

REFERENCES

Alfaro, J. (1985). *Impediments to mandated reporting of suspected child abuse and neglect in New York City*. Paper presented to the Seventh National Conference on Child Abuse and Neglect, Chicago.

American Academy of Child Psychiatry. (1980). Code of Ethics and Explanatory Notes.

Associated Press. (1985, August 15). Divulging child abuse opposed by clergy. *Washington Post*.

Barry, F. (1986). Personal communication.

California Penal Code, sec. 11166.

Crewdson, J. (1985, November 12). Laws no guarantee of child abuse reports. *Chicago Tribune*, p. 6.

Giovannoni, J., & Becerra, R. (1979). *Defining child abuse*. New York: Free Press.

Hinkeldey, N. S., & Spokane, A. (1985). Effects of pressure and legal guideline clarity on counselor decisionmaking in legal and ethical conflict situations. *Journal of Counseling and Development, 64*, 240–45.

Janis, I. L., & Mann, L. (1977). *Decisionmaking: A psychological analysis of conflict, choice and commitment*. New York: Free Press.

Monahan, J. (1981). *Predicting violent behavior, an assessment of clinical techniques*. Beverly Hills, CA: Sage.

Muehleman, T., & Kimmons, C. (1981). Psychologists' views on child abuse reporting, confidentiality, life and the law: An exploratory study. *Professional Psychology, 12*, 631–38.

Nisbett, R., & Ross, L. (1980). *Human inference: Strategies and shortcomings of social judgment*. Englewood Cliffs, N.J.: Prentice-Hall.

Reid, W. J. (1969). Interorganizational coordination in social welfare: A theoretical approach to analysis and intervention. In R. M. Kramer and H. Specht (eds.), *Readings in community organization practice* (pp. 176–87). Englewood Cliffs, N.J.: Prentice-Hall.

Rice, R. M. (1977). A cautionary view of allied services delivery. *Social Casework, 58*, 229–35.

State of Michigan. (1978). Summary of parollee risk study. Department of Corrections. Unpublished manuscript.

Tarasoff v. *Regents of the University of California*, 17 Cal. 3rd 425, 551, P.2d 334, 131, Cal. Rptr. 4 (1976).

Taylor, S. (1979). *Lecture on community organization*. Los Angeles: University of Southern California.

Weil, M., & Sanchez, E. (1983). The impact of the Tarasoff decision on clinical social work practice. *Social Service Review, 57*, 112–24.

17

Professional Misconduct: Mechanisms of Control

Susan J. Wells

The discussion on professional obligations to report abuse and neglect focused on the right of children to be protected from maltreatment and the role of the professional in ensuring this protection. Central to the issue were questions of judgment, interpretation of ethical obligations, and the role of the law and the courts in shaping the definition of professional obligations.

The next step in examining professional responsibility to children is to look at mechanisms that guide professional conduct and the ways in which misconduct is handled. Nowhere is this issue more critical than when a professional abuses children who are entrusted to his or her care. Through the example of child sexual abuse, it is possible to focus the discussion on this compelling problem and, at the same time, examine the more general issues rising from circumstances of professional misconduct with children.

SEXUAL ABUSE OF CHILDREN BY PROFESSIONALS

Child sexual abuse is increasingly recognized as a problem that can cause a great deal of trauma for the child and is much more common than originally suspected. As public awareness of the problem of sexual abuse has grown over the past several years, reporting statistics have increased (Russell and Trainor, 1984). With this increasing knowledge has come the recognition that professionals who work with, or take care of, children are not immune to the conditions that lead one to take sexual advantage of a child. Professionals, by virtue of their calling or status, are no less likely to be perpetrators of sexual abuse than any other group of people; sexual abuse crosses all class and cultural lines. In fact, as the Newbergers note in Chapter 6, pedophiles actively seek work in which there will be ready access to children.

In recent years there have been many local and national newspaper accounts of childcare workers, doctors, psychologists, and teachers who have sexually abused children in their care. At the same time, as Bulkley and Eatman recount in Chapter 11, there have been actions by professional licensing boards dealing with professionals who have taken advantage of children in the context of their work or of their family life. Yet, licensing boards and professional organizations on a national level have little or no systematic information on the number and types of complaints that have been made in this regard.

In an ABA telephone survey of national organizations of nurses, physicians, social workers, psychologists, and teachers, not one group kept records that would enable it to determine how many members, if any, had been accused of or disciplined for abuse of children or nonreporting of abuse (Wells, 1985). While data were kept at the national level by several organizations regarding disciplinary actions against members, the type of infraction was not coded in sufficient detail to allow the isolation of such a specific charge. At the state level, a similar inquiry yielded some case examples, but most states did not have any record of such board actions.

The results of this inquiry and the case examples presented by the Newbergers and by Burgess (in Chapter 7) lead one to question the preparation of professional organizations and licensing boards to respond to the growing number of recognized incidents and even, as Ohman noted (Chapter 14), the concomitant incidence of false complaints. Burgess' experience indicates that in many cases authorities are likely to brand a complaint as false, while Hebert's (Chapter 8) and the Newbergers' experiences show that even when the complaint is recognized as true, there may be little motivation to take strong enough measures to redress the grievance and to protect the children who are at continuing risk. In sum, a general reluctance to deal with the issue of professional misconduct becomes evident in our search for information on how the community is responding to such reports.

ETHICS AND REGULATION

There is a need, then, to examine the issue of professional ethics, to describe how they influence practice and the regulation of practice, and to determine how children might be better served.

While it is tempting to say that thinking about such a morally reprehensible behavior in the context of ethics is a gross understatement of the issue, it is instructive to think about professional misconduct in an ethical context in order to better understand the regulation of those who are in a position to take advantage of children and to evaluate professional responsibilities in responding to such reports.

Clouser (1975), in discussing the uses, abuses, and limitations of medical ethics, outlined two major functions of professional ethics: (1) sensitizing people to issues that have ethical implications by applying moral rules that are commonly recognized in everyday life and (2) structuring the issues to be considered, determining the consequences of each action, and the risks and benefits to those involved. Structuring includes delineating and questioning the conflicting ethical principles involved in any dilemma, and isolating "the pivotal concepts that need clarification, definition or defense" (p. 385).

While the limitations of ethical interpretation of practical dilemmas are acknowledged—for instance, that in many cases there is seldom one right answer—the use of ethics to structure decision making can be very helpful. Misunderstanding of the application of ethics, however, can be its biggest limitation. Clouser emphasizes that ethics are not just a matter of "his values against mine . . . anyone's opinion is just as good as anyone else's" (p. 387). He believes that this response often leads one to "quit the discussion" long before each perspective is thoroughly explored. He further states that the exercise of ethics is the examination of rules and principles that will bring people together in a just and harmonious society, not just a matter of one opinion being as good as another.

The use of ethics as a way of developing and interpreting ordinary rules and principles for the realization of the common good emphasizes the obligation of the professional not only to self and profession but also, even more important, to society as a whole. Moore (1978) applies Clouser's framework to understanding the development of regulation as a function of enforcing ethical standards.

Professional ethics, and legislation that supports their enforcement, have evolved from early medical prayers and the Hippocratic Oath, dating from the fourth century BC. The latter oath, and those that followed, were characterized by pledges of secrecy, compassion, proper care of patients, and upholding the dignity of the profession (Moore, 1978). In 1847, the American Medical Association adopted a similar code of ethics but also included a protectionist perspective that defined appropriate behavior for physicians. While these provisions were seen as necessary to protect the public from charlatans, they have also served to isolate the professional from the public he or she serves. These issues were vigorously debated in the 1960s and early 1970s, and a demystification of professions was pursued. This resulted in increased public monitoring of professional practice, a more contractual approach to the relationship between the patient or client and the professional, and the increased use of monitoring devices such as professional standards review organizations.

PROBLEMS IN REGULATION

Yet, an examination of these new approaches to the professional-client relationship continues to identify the same problems in successfully monitoring professional behavior that were decried in the 1960s and 1970s. These are inadequate identification of ethical misconduct, inadequate recording of and response to complaints, lack of communication of complaints to national organizations that tabulate the data and act as a central information system about such complaints, and a general lack of responsiveness to the concerns of those victimized by professionals.

Moore outlines several problems in enforcement of ethical standards by professional organizations and proposes mechanisms for solution. Regarding investigations of complaints, he recognizes that members of ethics committees are not skilled investigators and that often the only evidence before the committee may be that assembled by the complainant and the complainee. Second, he notes that those serving on review committees are often in the position of acting as investigator, prosecutor, judge, and jury. By engaging an investigative or complaint officer and a hearing officer, the committee can more properly assume the role of jury, which, in Moore's opinion, they are best qualified to do.

Additional problems are the inability of many potential complainants to access the system; inadequate case reporting from local branches; fear of liability on the part of the complainant; lack of enforcement of rules of fair procedures; and the confidential nature of the proceedings.

Moore believes that limited access to the system could be addressed through greater publicity of the ethical review process and the provision of assistance to those seeking to make a complaint. Inadequate case reporting must be addressed at the local level and motivation given for participating fully in the system. Fear of lawsuits is an often mentioned reason for not pursuing a complaint, but the relative unlikelihood of this action, given that a complaint is made in good faith, leads Moore to suggest that it is an excuse for not getting involved. The lack of formal hearings that would ensure fair procedure is a critical problem that could be more effectively addressed by changes in the attitudes of the committee regarding such hearings. Finally, the question of confidentiality arises. Moore defends the maintenance of confidentiality, even after a breach of ethics is discovered, by saying that publicizing the findings would drive the procedure further underground by further intimidating those who seek to make a complaint. (It should be noted here, however, that not all professional associations seek to protect all such hearings.)

Moore's discussion was concerned basically with the development of professional ethics and professional self-governance through the professional's own organizations. Ginsberg (Chapter 2) notes that for some professions, the only governing or monitoring body consists of these professional groups. For other professions, however, such as psychology, medicine, and (increasingly) social work, the monitoring of professional conduct and ethical behavior is a matter for the state. Bulkley and Eatman (Chapter 11) show that in protecting the public from unscrupulous or incompetent professionals, the state has wide powers for hearing complaints and barring professionals from practice.

Furthermore, increasing efforts to communicate between state licensing bodies will lend even more power to these bodies by blocking licensure and practice in other states after a license has been revoked. As yet, however, this type of communication is in its infancy. This is due not only to absence of appropriate mechanisms for such communication but also to differing state laws regarding reasons for license revocation.

The ability of the state to control selected professionals lies in the obligation of the state to protect the public from harm. State licensure laws, while varying a great deal from state to state and profession to profession, are grounded in constitutional guarantees of due process. That is, as long as they proceed in a manner that adheres to principles of specificity, rationality, and fairness in determining matters of licensure (and the public believes that such oversight is effective in protecting consumers), statutory regulation is likely to remain the preferred method of monitoring professional conduct (Herbsleb, Sales, and Overcast, 1985).

Regardless of these wider powers, however, effective statutory regulation of professionals has suffered from many of the impediments described by Moore. Some of the most critical problems in terms of consequences for current and future clients, consumers, or patients include the use of secrecy (even when not mandated by law) to protect the accused professional, inadequate coordination of law enforcement investigations when complaints of illegal behavior are brought, confusion regarding the appropriate timing of board proceedings with regard to legal proceedings, inconsistency between states regarding grounds for revocation of a license, inconsistent response to complaints on a local level, and insufficient monitoring of board activities to assure responsible action.

Issues of Role and Setting

There are two issues in the regulation of professionals who work with children that are not sufficiently covered in a discussion of statutory and organizational disciplinary actions. The first is that the nature of the profession and its organization can vary widely with the type of work performed. The second is that regulation of professional behavior is accomplished not only through examination of individual work but also through the regulation of the institutions that offer professional services. Cohen (Chapter 15) notes that many of the problems of reluctance of professionals to discipline their own are associated only with well-established professions or those with high status. For childcare workers, however, and for early education teachers, these issues may not be pertinent. Instead, workers may be more concerned about being publicly tried and convicted even before the evidence is gathered. There is no ethics board, as such, that would have the status or power to withhold such information from legal authorities or the public at large.

As a response to this rather different set of circumstances, the nature of professional organizations in these fields may take on quite a different role. Ohman (Chapter 14) describes this very well in her discussion of the National Education Association (NEA) as an advocate for teachers. Rather than acting only as a professional association, the NEA is actually a union that exists to protect the rights of teachers until it can be shown through legally acceptable channels that the teacher's conduct is indeed illegal, immoral, or unethical.

By jealously guarding the teacher's right to due process, the organization also protects the child. This is accomplished by ensuring that all requirements of law are met when accusations are made and ensuring an immediate hearing. It thereby aids in maintaining evidence, obtaining immediate statements from victims and/or witnesses, and generally ensuring that a complete and thorough investigation is conducted. This approach leaves the organization free to pursue, with honor, its basic charge—that of protecting the teacher.

In some cases, organizational licensing may provide an extra layer of protection for the consumer. Not only are the professionals licensed, but the organization must "pass muster" or lose the sanction needed to provide services. Ginsberg (Chapter 2) notes that the Joint Commission on Accreditation of Hospitals (JCAH) is a powerful force holding hospitals to some minimum standards of care, including regular in-house reviews of quality assurance.

In addition, there may be special means of enforcing organizational standards of practice and service, such as withholding funds used to support services to clients or rescinding a license to receive or serve clients. Nevertheless, there may also be some difficulties in monitoring professional behavior in organizations due to the size of the operation, an overriding culture that hides or protects misconduct in order to protect organizational licensure, and the difficulty of quantifying exactly what constitutes misconduct and what level of evidence is necessary to proceed against an organization or one of its members.

Beyond Regulation

When licensing actions fail or when it is desirable to obtain compensation for the injured party, civil court actions may be desired in addition to, or in place of, the above-described actions. Eatman (Chapter 10) and Hebert (Chapter 8) discuss circumstances in which pursuit of civil liability may aid in bringing the matter to the attention of the authorities and may aid the victims in dealing with their grievance against the professional. In the case of Father Gauthe, for example, the organization had a vested interest in protecting itself over and above that of protecting the children at risk. In such cases, where damages are clearly warranted and the organization is clearly culpable, such a suit may be an additional (or preferred) means for dealing with professional misconduct.

Justice vs. Care and the "Impaired Professional"

One response to professional misconduct that was not addressed in the discussion of regulation is the concept of the impaired professional. Recent advances in dealing with drug use or alcohol abuse among professionals have resulted in dealing with many of these professionals by treating their illnesses instead of using punishment and retribution to address their problems.

Dr. Sharon Satterfield has initiated just such a program in Minnesota for professionals who have sexually abused children. While she did not start out to develop a program specific to this group of offenders, she found that she had enough such people to justify such a group. She also found that although the dynamics that led to the abuse were not different from those with nonprofessionals, the extent of denial by the professionals suggested that they might be able to help one another confront their problems.

This treatment program has undertaken a follow-up of previous patients and has found that of 55 people, not one "has been caught reoffending." In addition, Satterfield notes that in many states, the time served for such an offense is minimal, certainly not sufficient to protect children from future exposure to the offender. In Minnesota, for example, there are mandatory sentencing guidelines that would result in an offender actually serving 29 months to 4 years.

As a consequence of the requirement of a rather brief sentence and knowledge that many offenders will soon be returning to society, many are often sentenced to serve their time in treatment programs or facilities. Some are sentenced directly to the workhouse and released during the day in order to go to their regular jobs.

Dr. Satterfield presents these facts as support for using the concept of the impaired professional with some sexual offenders. By using sentencing modified to allow for treatment or arranging for a diversion program, she believes that many offenders can be enabled to live in the community and that their abusive behavior can be controlled.

One issue to be addressed in the adaptation of the concept of the "impaired professional" to professionals who sexually victimize children is the idea that the professional may be allowed or even encouraged to remain in his or her professional practice after treatment for the impairment has been completed. The implications of such a suggestion are far-reaching, particularly in light of very limited knowledge about recidivism in such cases, and should not be dealt with lightly.

While this approach would appear to care for the professional and the child (if the professional is removed from contact with children), there is some question whether the state of the art is such that one can ever pronounce such offenders cured, particularly those who take advantage of their young patients, clients, or students. For example, there is still some question whether pedophiles can be successfully enlisted in voluntary treatment, whether they will stay in treatment, and whether actual changes in behavior will occur. For those who stay in treatment, there may be some success observed—yet these results are far from universally applicable (Abel, 1985). Further, the argument has not yet been settled as to the preferability of using the criminal justice system to ensure cooperation from the perpetrator. There are many who believe such measures are absolutely essential to the protection of the child (Blick, 1985).

It appears that even if the system is working optimally, there are many ethical questions to be raised, both in the treatment of a child who reports an incident of abuse and in the system response to the perpetrator.

CONCLUSION

In this book on the role of professional ethics and responsibilities in protecting children, many issues have been brought forward as being critical to the functioning of an effective child protection system. Yet in the search for solutions, the authors have raised many more questions than can be answered immediately. These areas of concern bridge all facets of the professional community and all levels of system response. Some of the more immediate issues and recommendations are discussed below.

Regulation of professions serving children. In some cases, those who serve children on a daily basis are not governed by any statute-based program. Without such oversight, there is no systematic way to govern who practices or to eliminate from practice those who have been found unfit or guilty of serious misconduct.

Coordination between professional licensing and institutional licensing. Professional licensing bodies, and agencies that license the institutions in which professionals practice, should formulate a unified response to professional misconduct and a mechanism for information sharing.

Gaps between law enforcement efforts and licensing board activities. The legal framework within which one may organize a response to abuse and neglect is multifaceted, yet offenders may manipulate the system to continue in the practice of their profession unimpeded. Difficulties in coordinating investigation of reported cases between law enforcement and professional licensing boards must be identified and resolved. This would include standardized mechanisms of notification between agencies about such reports.

Coordination of information systems and agency response. The actual possibilities and potential sources of funding for coordination of system response to professionals who abuse children should be examined and concrete recommendations made for the legal, medical, education, childcare, and mental health professions. Some of the most critical needs for professional associations include improved record-keeping abilities at local, state, and national levels, with information on offenders being made available pursuant to reference checks.

Prevention of psychological trauma for the victim. The multiplication of investigation efforts that results from the involvement of licensing, law enforcement, and child protection agencies, as well as the courts, will require even more attention to the plight of the victim, so that the protection of the child alleviates, not increases, the child's psychological trauma.

Reported treatment success rates for pedophiles. Reported research on nonincestuous pedophiles does not reflect the same success rate as that with incestuous pedophiles. Developmental research must be done in an effort to translate results to date into operating programs for screening and treating pedophiles.

Need for professional training. The hesitance to deal with issues of professional misconduct must be recognized by the professionals themselves, clearing the way to develop a more comprehensive and systematic response to aberrant behavior. One means for addressing the issue of professional awareness is through mandatory training programs dealing with the recognition of abuse and neglect and the professional's responsibilities for taking action. This training should deal not only with parental abuse but also with possible abuse by others outside the home and in the professional community.

Legislation mandating reporting of abuse and neglect. While the difficulties of identifying and reporting abuse and neglect are recognized, the often recommended solution to these difficulties—that of modifying the reporting laws to include only cases of serious harm—has not been systematically researched. The implications of confining system response to those with serious injuries are unknown at this time, but they may be very great. It is possible that such an approach would result in increased injuries to children who would not come to the attention of the system until much later than they now do. In addition, such an approach would seriously alter the mental set with which we now approach the recognition and treatment of child abuse and neglect. Instead of being proactive, the system would become reactive, serving only those children who have already been severely injured.

Creation of professional task forces. Finally, each professional group should form a task force to look at legislative and regulatory issues that aid or hinder the carrying out of professional responsibilities to protect children not only from harm within their families but also from abuse committed by professionals, including noncompliance with reporting requirements. Representatives of these groups might then come together to make recommendations to look at these issues from an interorganizational perspective.

REFERENCES

Abel, G. (1985). *The treatment of child molesters.* Report # ROI MH 36347. Rockville, Md.: National Institute of Mental Health.

Blick, L. C. (1985). Presentation made to U.S. Army committee considering revision of regulations guiding response to reports of abuse and neglect. Alexandria, Virginia.

Clouser, K. D. (1975). Medical ethics: Some uses, abuses, and limitations. *New England Journal of Medicine, 298*, 384–87.

Herbsleb, J. D., Sales, B. D., & Overcast, T. D. (1985). Challenging licensure and certification. *American Psychologist, 40*, 1165–78.

Moore, R. A. (1978). Ethics in the practice of psychiatry: Origins, functions, models, and enforcement. *American Journal of Psychiatry, 135*, 157–62.

Russell, A. B., & Trainor, C. M. (1984). *Trends in child abuse and neglect: A national perspective.* Denver: American Humane Association.

Satterfield, S. (1985, November). Discussion at Symposium on Professional Ethics and Child Abuse. Washington, D.C.

Wells, S. (1985). Telephone survey conducted in preparation for Symposium on Professional Ethics and Child Abuse.

Index

About the Editors and Contributors

ELAINE A. ANDERSON, Ph.D. is an assistant professor in the Department of Family and Community Development, University of Maryland, College Park, Md.

JOSEPHINE BULKLEY, J.D. is director of the Abuse Allegations-Domestic Relations Project for the National Legal Resource Center for Child Advocacy & Protection for the American Bar Association.

ANN W. BURGESS, R.N., D.N.Sc. is the van Ameringen Professor of Psychiatric Mental Health Nursing at the University of Pennsylvania School of Nursing, Philadelphia, Pa. 19104 and associate director of Nursing Research, Boston City Hospital, Boston, Ma. 02118.

ABBY J. COHEN, J.D. is managing attorney of the Child Care Law Center in San Francisco, Ca.

JON R. CONTE, Ph.D. is an associate professor at the School of Social Service Administration, the University of Chicago, Chicago, Il.

HOWARD DAVIDSON, J.D. is director of the National Legal Resource Center for Child Advocacy and Protection, American Bar Association.

ROSS EATMAN, J.D. was formerly an assistant staff director of the Child Sexual Abuse Law Reform Project for the National Legal Resource Center for Child Advocacy & Protection for the American Bar Association. He is now practicing law in Philadelphia, Pa.

JAMES GARBARINO, Ph.D. is president of the Erikson Institute for Advanced Study in Child Development, Chicago, Il.

MARK R. GINSBERG, Ph.D. is the executive director of the American Association for Marriage and Family Therapy.

CAROL R. HARTMAN, R.N., D.N.Sc. is Professor and Coordinator, Graduate Program in Psychiatric Mental Health Nursing, Boston College School of Nursing, Chestnut Hill, Ma. 02167.

PAUL J. HEBERT, J.D. is a partner in the law firm of Sonnier and Hebert, Two South Magdalen Square, Abbeville, La., 70510.

SHARON D. HERZBERGER, Ph.D. is chair of the Department of Psychology, Trinity College, Hartford, Ct.

SUSAN J. KELLEY, R.N., M.S.N. is an assistant professor, Boston College School of Nursing, Chestnut Hill, Ma. 02167.

MARIE LEANER is associate deputy director of the Division of Child Protection, State of Illinois, Department of Children and Family Services.

ANN MANEY, Ph.D. is currently on the staff of the National Institute of Mental Health, Office of Prevention and Special Projects.

CAROLYN MOORE NEWBERGER, Ed.D. is research director of the Family Development Study at Children's Hospital in Boston, Ma.

ELI H. NEWBERGER, M.D. is the director of the Family Development Study at Children's Hospital in Boston, Ma.

LYNN OHMAN, M.P.A. is manager of the Legal Services Programs, National Education Association.

NOLAN RINDFLEISCH, Ph.D. is an associate professor at the College of Social Work, the Ohio State University, Columbus, Oh.

SUSAN J. WELLS, Ph.D. is director of the project on Screening and Prioritization in Child Protective Services, National Legal Resource Center for Child Advocacy and Protection, American Bar Association, Washington, D.C.